Brandjack

How your reputation is at risk from brand pirates and what to do about it

Brandjack

Quentin Langley

palgrave
macmillan

First published 2014 by
PALGRAVE MACMILLAN

Palgrave Macmillan in the UK is an imprint of Macmillan Publishers Limited, registered in England, company number 785998, of Houndmills, Basingstoke, Hampshire RG21 6XS.

Palgrave Macmillan in the US is a division of St Martin's Press LLC, 175 Fifth Avenue, New York, NY 10010.

Palgrave Macmillan is the global academic imprint of the above companies and has companies and representatives throughout the world.

Palgrave® and Macmillan® are registered trademarks in the United States, the United Kingdom, Europe and other countries.

ISBN: 978–1–137–37535–3

This book is printed on paper suitable for recycling and made from fully managed and sustained forest sources. Logging, pulping and manufacturing processes are expected to conform to the environmental regulations of the country of origin.

A catalogue record for this book is available from the British Library.

A catalog record for this book is available from the Library of Congress.

Typeset by Aardvark Editorial Limited, Metfield, Suffolk.

Contents

Foreword

Brands have never embodied more power than they do today. It is widely acknowledged that a brand is an essential asset, and often the market value of a company's brand is greater than the book value of a company's tangible assets.

Brands have even *greater* significance in the non-profit world. NGOs, governments, Hollywood celebrities, and social and fraternal organizations all recognize that brand and reputation may be their primary – or only – real asset. Even individual professionals are urged to create and manage "personal brands" to support the success of their careers.

As the importance of brands has grown, the task of protecting a company's brand has grown more complex. Now everyone in an organization has the ability to protect – or detract from – an organization's brand. There is no longer a news cycle; news that can impact a brand now moves constantly. And no longer are there discrete communications channels: today, we are all interconnected through networks that can instantly spread comments on brands through new and unexpected communities.

For those charged specifically with protecting an organization's brand – especially communications professionals – these complexities have created opportunities. There are new leadership opportunities within organizations, and new tools, strategies, and techniques available to manage, monitor, and harness digital communications.

But these are also perilous times for brands and those who protect brands. Technology has created a world in which a single misstep by an organization can result in a tidal wave of complaint. More ominously, technology has empowered those who intentionally want to attack a brand for malicious, political or adversarial reasons: those who engage in brandjacking.

If we can vicariously learn from the trials of others, *Brandjack* distills a lifetime of experience into one instructive volume. Whether the threat to a brand is self-inflicted or originates externally, a quick, confident, and clear response is necessary to respond successfully. Readers of *Brandjack* will learn from the experience of others, without suffering firsthand the trauma of the experiences that led to the learnings.

Of course, there will be more examples of brandjacking in the months and years to come. Three years hence there will certainly be enough new material for a sequel to *Brandjack,* but with a little luck and careful attention to the case studies in this book, the readers of *Brandjack* should be sufficiently forewarned so as to avoid being featured as future case studies. That alone should make *Brandjack* a required read by anyone charged with protecting a treasured brand.

WILLIAM MURRAY
CEO, Public Relations Society of America (2007–14)

Acknowledgments

I would like to thank all those people who encouraged me and believed in this project. That would include my good friend Jim Holtje, Bill Murray at PRSA, and the whole team at Palgrave Macmillan, including Tamsine and Josie. I would like to thank all those people from whom I learned about PR and especially crisis management, including Terence Fane-Saunders and the late (and much missed) Mike Hogan.

Most especially, I want to thank the one person without whose encouragement and support this book would not have happened, my wife, Julia Gleich.

Introduction

Brandjacking is the hot new craze that is turning business upside down. Anyone can do it. Jeff Jarvis, a journalist and blogger, did it when he was sold a "lemon" of a Dell laptop and became dissatisfied with Dell's customer service. He wrote about his experience on his blog and was deluged with emails and comments from people who had had similar experiences. "Dell Hell" became the aggregator of dissatisfied customers who had previously been isolated and may have thought their experiences unrepresentative (CS 4).

Dave Carroll did it. When United Airlines baggage handlers broke his Taylor guitar, and customer service gave him the runaround because he did not submit his claim within 24 hours, he wrote a song about his experience that became a viral YouTube sensation. United Airlines lost 10 percent of its value on the New York Stock Exchange in just four days (CS 32).

Greenpeace did it. It made a spoof Kit Kat advert that was disturbing in the extreme. The Kit Kat finger turned out to be an orangutan's finger, which dripped blood down the customer's chin. Nestlé had the video removed from YouTube on the grounds of copyright violation, but other users kept posting new copies and debating Nestlé's "censorship" of YouTube. Nestlé caved in to Greenpeace's demands in a matter of weeks (CS 38).

Leroy Stick (Josh Simpson) did it. He set up a fake Twitter account called @bpglobalpr, which provided a satirical commentary on BP's woes in the Gulf of Mexico. Pretty soon he had twelve times as many followers as the real BP Twitter feed (CS 40).

Greenpeace (again) did it to BP (again). The group held a competition inviting people to submit redesigned BP logos. Initially targeted at BP's plans for exploiting Canadian tar sands, the campaign had been months in planning, but was recalibrated to take account of the oil spill in the Gulf of Mexico (CS 40).

Anyone can do it. If Bill Clinton, Pope Francis, or Rudy Giuliani was your dissatisfied customer, you would handle them very carefully, right? Those people have contacts. They have access. They could damage your business. Each has been *Time* magazine's person of the year. Well, so have I; 2006 was the year I won the award. I was not alone, you understand. *Time* did not have my name and photo on the front cover. It had the word "you" and a mirror. The award went to the Internet content creator: to people like Jeff Jarvis, Dave Carroll, and Leroy Stick. They have contacts. They have access. They could damage your business. And they could be any one of the people sitting on your airplane or ordering your laptop right now.

The Internet content creator (ICC) does not (always) travel first class, or arrive at your business in a chauffeur-driven car with police outriders. There is no red carpet. You won't see the ICC coming. If you want to treat this powerful person like a VIP, you are going to have to treat *all* your customers that way. Scary, isn't it?

This is the age of the brandjacker. They can lead and even dominate the social media conversation around your reputation. This book was written to help guide you out of this mess.

The chapters of the book progressively set out the issues:

- Chapter 1 explores matters of *brand* and *reputation*
- Chapter 2 explains about *issues* and *crisis management*
- Chapter 3 explains how *digital technologies* have turned organizations upside down
- Chapter 4 sets out *140 case studies of brandjacking*
- Chapter 5 discusses *engagement* and *transparency* – how to turn your organization inside out
- Finally, we conclude with *eleven rules* for dealing with brandjacking

Good luck!

chapter *1*

Brand and reputation

The etymology of the word "brandjack" is obvious – it merges "brand" with "hijack." But it is worth considering, for a moment, the meaning of the word "brand."

World English Dictionary offers as its primary definition: "a particular product or a characteristic that serves to identify a product."[1] Its second definition is that it can be a trade name or trademark. Naomi Klein, author of *No Logo*,[2] might prefer the sixth definition: "a mark of disgrace or infamy; stigma: *he bore the brand of a coward.*" In marketing, branding is much more than this. Wikipedia notes that: "The word brand has continued to evolve to encompass identity – it affects the personality of a product, company or service." In practice, the word "brand" is interchangeable with the word "reputation." The former is preferred by marketeers and the latter by those in public relations (PR). I prefer the word "reputation" because I find it clearer. People not actually engaged in PR or marketing often equate "brand" with the logo or trademark without seeing the deeper meaning. This book has the word "brand" in its title simply because "brandjack" sounds better than "reputationjack." You may assume, however, that unless I have stated otherwise, any time I use the word "brand," I mean it as being synonymous with "reputation."

The choice of wording has an impact on the subject matter. Take this quote from Leroy Stick, the expert brandjacker behind the satirical Twitter feed @bpglobalpr:

> FORGET YOUR BRAND. You don't own it because it is literally nothing. You can spend all sorts of time and money trying to manufacture public opinion, but ultimately, that's up to the public, now isn't it?

It sounds both scary and insightful. But what if he had said "reputation" instead of brand? Then his remarks seem less radical and rather more obvious. Your reputation has always existed in the minds of other people. Marketeers tell people that they can decide on their brand. To PR practitioners this is always a negotiation: a two-way process of communication. The Chartered Institute of Public Relations (CIPR) says that your reputation is "the result of what you do, what you say and what others say about you."[3] It should be obvious that within that troika, what you say is the least important. We know and practice that in our own lives. The person who says he loves you, but keeps beating you and stealing from you deserves to be judged by his actions and not his words. More positively, Cordelia's actions ultimately impress King Lear, not her modest but honest words.

So if your brand is your reputation, you don't get to decide what it is, and you never did. This reality is merely rather starker in today's world of social media.

That organizations have critics is also, of course, nothing new. One of my early posts on Brandjack News was titled "Back to the seventies." It was about a planned industrial dispute in the UK. Unions are among the many big battalions with which organizations have long had to contend. Competitors also fall into this category. But when coalition forces entered Iraq, it was not Saddam's much hyped army that was to cause them trouble. Iraq's conscript army was one of the largest in the world, but it did not stand and fight. It ran away. What coalition forces had to learn to contend with was asymmetric warfare. Large armies being attacked by small, highly mobile units, or even individuals. There were no battles, just improvised explosive devices. The battle in reputation management is similar. Asymmetric warfare pits your corporate PR department against bloggers in pajamas. The rules have changed dramatically, and just like the mighty US Army, you cannot assume that size makes you invincible. Far from it. Size makes you an easy target, and leads others to sympathize with your opponent.

This is why Greenpeace likes to portray every battle in which it engages as David versus Goliath – and Greenpeace sees itself as plucky David taking on the mighty Goliath. No matter that Greenpeace is actually one of the most sophisticated and professional campaigning organizations in the world. No matter that campaigning is its core business, with the bulk of its multimillion dollar resources devoted specifically to PR. (In passing, when I joined the Global Media Relations Office of Shell International, there were already two people in the team.) Most nongovernmental organizations (NGOs) deny that they engage in PR at all, although to professional outside observers it seems as though that is most, or even all, of what they do. They talk about having media teams, campaigning teams, advocacy teams, and the rest, but think that "PR" is something the big bad corporates do.

For all these reasons, brandjacking is not new. People have always had their own thoughts and opinions about you. But now they have new platforms to broadcast these opinions, to make contact with others who share them, and to draw themselves to the world's attention and to yours. This brings risks to every business and every organization. But it brings opportunities too. Twitter is a platform through which people can broadcast their hatred of you. But what if those people have always hated you, and you just didn't know about it before? Well, now you do. And now you know *why* they hate you. Perhaps you can do something about it now.

For PR practitioners, this is not new territory. Excellent PR has always been about two-way communication. The Public Relations Society of America (PRSA) said in 1982 that: "Public relations helps an organization and its publics adapt mutually to each other."[4] Inherent in that definition is the idea that the organization cannot simply persuade the rest of the world to adopt its products, it needs to adapt its products to what the rest of the world wants. This is the world of make what you can sell, not sell what you can make.

For years, PR academics have been obsessed by a long slow-motion argument about something called excellence theory. In the way of academic debates, years can pass with neither side responding. The debate began in 1984 and, at the time of writing, the last major contribution was in 2001. In the meantime, the real world has changed.

The University of Maryland's James Grunig and Todd Hunt devised excellence theory,[5] in which they argued that PR progressed through four stages:

1 *Publicity model:* the organization seeks to gain coverage under the theory that all publicity is good publicity.
2 *Public information model:* the organization seeks to inform the publics; truthfulness becomes important.
3 *Two-way asymmetric model:* the organization listens and learns, but still seeks to persuade the publics to its point of view.
4 *Two-way symmetric model:* the organization and the publics seek to learn from each other and adapt to each other.

Excellence theory has been controversial. It was criticized by L'Etang and Pieczka in 1996[6] with the suggestion that the fourth and final stage is unrealistic. Grunig himself accepted in 2001[7] that the two-way symmetric model is idealistic. But we need to consider that the entire media environment has changed since Grunig and Hunt first advanced their theory. In 1984, the Internet was unknown outside the military and academia. In 1994, it was still the pastime of a limited number of geeks. By 2001, the Internet was established, but the era of Web 2.0, involving two-way communication and mass user-generated content, was barely beginning. From the vantage point of 2014, the two-way symmetric model no longer looks unrealistic, and may even be starting to look dated. With lone individuals such as Leroy Stick and Dave Carroll already exercising considerable power in the marketplace, we are faced with a new five-stage model. Like stage three, it is a two-way asymmetric model, but with the asymmetry tipped decisively in favor of the publics.

L'Etang and Pieczka's argument may have been valid when they made it, but it has been swept aside by history.

Notes

1   Via dictionary.com, accessed 01/20/2014.

2   Klein, N. (1999) *No Logo: Taking Aim at the Brand Bullies.* Toronto: Knopf Canada.

3   CIPR: www.cipr.co.uk/content/careers-cpd/careers-pr/what-pr, accessed 01/20/2014.

4   PRSA: www.prsa.org/AboutPRSA/PublicRelationsDefined/Old%20Definition, accessed 01/20/2014.

5   Grunig, J.E. and Hunt, T. (1984) *Managing Public Relations.* New York: Holt, Rinehart & Winston.

6   L'Etang, J. (1996) "Corporate responsibility and public relations ethics" in L'Etang, J. and Pieczka, M. (eds) *Critical Perspectives in Public Relations.* London: International Thompson Business Press.

7   Grunig, J.E. (2001) "Two way symmetrical public relations: past, present and future" in Heath, R.L. (ed.) *Handbook of Public Relations.* Thousand Oaks, CA: Sage.

2

chapter

Issues and crisis management

Issues

One way to avoid brandjacking is to identify in advance the issues that might cause a problem for you. Sometimes this will be easy, but don't stop with the easy choices. When I joined Shell International in the 1990s, crisis preparedness was heavily focused on exercises around an oil tanker going down. It makes a lot of sense, when you ship more oil around the world than anyone else, to consider what will happen if – or rather when – a tanker goes down. But this is far from the only risk facing a global oil giant. What about a chemical plant exploding? Or some of the real crises Shell has faced concerning a reformulated petroleum that was damaging car engines, the disposal of a North Sea oil storage platform, or the company's relationship with a brutal dictatorship in Nigeria?

But it is important to think outside the confines of the core business altogether. A friend of mine brought in to revamp the crisis management procedures at Shell developed a scenario around the website being hijacked by a disgruntled ex-employee. An employee of a major multinational – involved in highly controversial science and loathed by environmental groups – recently told another friend and colleague that its biggest worry was not green protestors but bribery. How would it handle the situation if a member of staff was implicated in giving or taking bribes? How to do business in environments where the law and cultural norms differ greatly from the home country is a major issue for all transnational corporations. This was at the heart of Shell's problems in Nigeria. Producing oil in countries such as Nigeria often involves dealing with governments that the liberal-minded British and Dutch people who run the company would never want to live under.

Maybe the issue is directly linked to your core business. But how fundamental is it for you? Take two issues that dogged Nestlé in 2010: one has been dragging on for decades, the other is now resolved. The first is the sale of infant formula in developing countries. Since 1973, campaigners have been calling on Nestlé to dramatically alter its practices in developing countries, which, they claim, actively promote formula milk over breast milk. For a variety of reasons – most critically, the lack of access to clean water – formula milk has risks far greater than in Western countries. Since 1977, groups have been calling for a global boycott of Nestlé and its products. Nestlé claims it is in full compliance with the international code governing the marketing of breast milk substitutes. Campaigners disagree. At root, campaigners want Nestlé to walk away from a large and profitable market. Whoever you believe about the code, that is the fundamental issue. Whether or not Nestlé's current practices are in compliance with the code, campaigners plainly want it to go much further and doing so would have a substantial effect on Nestlé's business. We can rule out the idea that minor changes that did not have much effect on sales would satisfy campaigners, or the controversy would not have continued this long.

Nestlé's other controversy was the use of palm oil. Greenpeace claimed that Nestlé was sourcing palm oil from suppliers that damaged the rainforest and threatened the habitat of the orangutan. Nestlé folded on this issue in a matter of weeks following the viral success of Greenpeace's "Give the orangutan a break" ad. This has been presented – and I am one of the offenders here – as an example of the power of social media and the sheer quality and professionalism of Greenpeace's campaigners. Both points are entirely valid, but we also need to bear in mind that palm oil is but one ingredient in Nestlé products. Greenpeace was not asking the company to stop making some of its popular brands altogether, just to source one of the ingredients in a different way. Nestlé could comply with this at a relatively low cost. This issue was tied to Nestlé's core business, but was not fundamental to the product.

Mike Regester and Judy Larkin identified five stages to an issue: potential, emerging, current, crisis, and dormant.[1] This should not be taken as an indication that all issues will go through all stages. Crisis can sometimes be averted. Some issues will go on for years, never reaching a critical point. In other cases, crisis is more or less inevitable. In the case of oil companies, some form of oil spill is going to happen at some point. The questions that will then emerge are fundamental: Where does it happen? How developed are your plans to deal with it? Was it bad luck, or could it have been avoided? Are you able to communicate your message clearly? These were all the issues faced by BP after the explosion on the Deepwater Horizon rig in April 2010.

But let us take another issue that has been bubbling away in the background for years – allegations that cell phones can cause brain tumors. This goes to the heart of a cell phone company's business. And yet, phone manufacturers and service providers continue to achieve enviable growth in their business. Certainly, the science is complicated, and no matter the level of evidence, some people will continue to dispute it. But the real reason campaigners have not gained traction with this one is that cell phone *users* don't want them to be right. People will complain about some of the practices of oil companies and confectioners, but there is no clamor for oil and chocolate to be banned altogether. Do not take this as a prediction that the cell phone/brain tumor issue will never blow up into a crisis. The science could change. Someone could develop a cheap redesign to phones that clears up the area of dispute. But phone users will want compelling evidence before they stop using their phones. This is one issue that could remain in the potential stage indefinitely.

Some issues, however, reach a tipping point. From being small, they tip over into being very big in a short space of time. This is not new, and does not depend on social media. However, it is reasonable to suppose that social media may have brought two changes to this process. For one thing, tipping points may now be achieved even more rapidly. For another, it may be easier to spot rising trends.

The question as to whether the mainstream media lead or follow social trends has been much debated in media studies for many years, and will no doubt continue to be so. I was struck, however, by the light shed on this debate by some MA research into the advocacy around the Make Poverty History campaign. The student had graphed the growth of donations to the campaign and the media coverage. Both followed a similar trajectory: they rose, slowly at first, then sharply, just before the launch. Then, just as sharply, they both declined. But the growth (and decline) in donations was two to three weeks *ahead* of the growth (and decline) in media coverage. How can we account for this anomaly? The media coverage can't have caused the growth in donations, since it came later. Instead, we must assume that either the donations caused the media coverage or, more likely, they were both caused by the same thing – the campaign itself.

This particular campaign tapped into a number of existing social networks, such as established development charities, and the largest and oldest voluntary social networks in the world, churches. As the campaign approached its launch, the participating groups would have alerted their members to the upcoming activity. The members would have responded by making donations.

This buzz of activity, as much as the formal media relations prior to the launch, would have alerted the media to the fact that something big was going on. Social networks were crucial to the campaign's launch. By making use of such established networks as churches, the campaign did not need the extensive online social networks that were to become available within a few years. But this example does demonstrate the effectiveness of social networks, which is likely to have been greatly magnified by online social networks.

In any campaign, it is essential to know who your allies are and who is against you. A great deal can be won by picking your enemies carefully, as anyone who has followed Hollywood scripts can tell you. Take the 2003 movie *Bulletproof Monk*, which pits Tibetan monks against Nazi invaders. Anyone in any doubt as to who you are supposed to cheer for?

The mistake is to wait until the crisis has arisen and then seek to build relationships with your natural allies. One of the key themes of this book is that internal communications – once the overlooked Cinderella of PR strategies – has blossomed into a princess. Investing in your relationships with your staff is the only way to make them ambassadors for you in a difficult situation. Social media have turned the power structures of business upside down. Your response has to be to turn your business inside out, but I will come on to what I mean by that in later chapters.

Preparation for crisis management involves identifying all the publics that may influence the issues you face and establishing an ongoing relationship with all of them. This may seem obvious – we are talking about PR, after all – but, sadly, it seems that it isn't. Far too many organizations, in identifying their publics, start and end with the most obvious, usually (in the private sector) customers. This misanalysis of PR is damaging. Marketeers have always claimed that PR is nothing other than media relations, and sits as part of the "marketing mix" inside the marketing function. This is problematic because there are a great many people other than customers on whom your organization will depend. The best starting point for any analysis is probably that by Roger Haywood, even though it dates from 1984.[2] He divides publics into six main groups:

- customers
- investors
- staff
- neighbors
- politicians and regulators
- business partners.

Not all organizations have all these groups, and the list was designed primarily for a publicly traded company. A charity, for example, has no shareholders. For a government-sponsored enterprise, shareholders and politicians/regulators are the same. Equally, in a partnership, shareholders are identical with, or a subset of, staff. Amazon.com doesn't really have neighbors, and some public sector or voluntary organizations don't really have customers. Take the Royal Society for the Protection of Birds. Are the RSPB's members and donors its customers? Or are they investors and birds the customers?

To what extent do people in these groups form communities of interest around your organization? This will vary tremendously. You cease to be a customer of a confectionery company moments after you have purchased and consumed the product. But as a customer of an automotive manufacturer, you continue to use the product and purchase parts and supplies for some years. Some products are aspirational. Others generate considerable loyalty. Maybe you buy the same chocolate bar again and again.

Such factors will determine the extent to which you can rely on these publics to take an interest in your issues. If, like Toyota, you are an automotive manufacturer facing a recall issue, then customers are likely to have a keen interest in the safety of your product. They may also feel a considerable loyalty to your product if it is under threat. Detroit's big three – GM, Ford, and Chrysler – were able to stir up a scare story that if they sought Chapter 11 bankruptcy, it would become difficult for past customers to buy parts.

Your neighbors may be interested in you. Some organizations are both the largest employer and the largest polluter in the town. Everyone in the town will then be affected – positively and negatively – by that organization.

Those publics with a long-term interest in your organization need to be engaged on a long-term basis. You can even take this to another level, as Shell did with its post-Brent Spar, post-Nigeria "burden-sharing strategy." This involved identifying "special publics" – academics, NGOs, and the media – and engaging with them in round-table discussions about the problems facing oil companies. The Brent Spar crisis – when a Greenpeace campaign had forced Shell UK to back down on plans to dispose of an oil storage platform by deep sea disposal, almost certainly the safest way, and adopt a risky and expensive strategy of onshore dismantling – had taught Shell important lessons. Greenpeace was free to be *against* deep sea disposal without having to be *for* anything. This is the nature of being a campaign group. You can ask awkward questions, but you don't have to provide answers in anything but the vaguest terms. Shell's solution was to involve campaigners in the hard decisions that go into running a complex multinational.

Burden sharing was Shell's solution to the soft power of environmentalists and public opinion. Like most large organizations, Shell had developed a relatively cozy relationship with governments, and thought that securing the necessary licenses was all it had to do before proceeding with its disposal strategy. But there is a power in public opinion, too, and Shell neglected that. It was shocking for the company to discover that people were hostile to the organization. A reputation that had always been golden was suddenly damaged. Shell's people had always been proud to work there. And why not? My own experience can hardly have been unusual. When I joined Shell in 1996, I was just getting into Internet chat. Suddenly I was talking to people all over the world, and whenever I told them I worked for Shell, they were impressed. The company had long been regarded as an exemplary employer and was well known on every continent. It was the type of organization every parent wants their children to work for. Even at the height of the Nigeria controversy, this was still the normal reaction of most people I spoke to. But, after a documentary linking Shell to the Nigerian government's judicial murder of Ken Saro-Wiwa (Nigerian writer and environmental activist) in 1995, I still had to take a call from an angry member of the public demanding "why did you have that bloke killed?"

Crisis

Both Brent Spar and Shell's operations in Nigeria were issues that spilled over into crises. Why was one of the most successful companies in the world caught out so badly? The consensus of most commentators looking back is that on the Brent Spar issue, Shell was in the right. The Nigeria case is much messier and more complicated. Many issues came together in Nigeria, and Shell's critics were not simply wrong, as Greenpeace was about the Brent Spar. The real villain in the Nigerian case was the Nigerian government, and Shell's critics felt that the company could have done more to restrain the government from its more offensive actions.

One reason Shell was caught out may be because it is an organization that plans its business in terms of decades. Dealing with tight media deadlines is alien territory for such an organization, but not for Greenpeace, whose core business is campaigning. To take one example, when Shell had Greenpeace protestors forcibly removed from the Brent Spar, the company took video cameras to ensure that the confrontation could not be misrepresented afterwards. But by the time Shell got to the shore with its film, the Greenpeace film of the same events was already being broadcast. Greenpeace had thrown its waterproof camera into the sea, where it was retrieved by a helicopter. As a result of this clever maneuver, Shell was caught on the wrong side of one of the key rules of crisis management. As Terence Fane-Saunders of Chelgate puts it, "you need to be the source of your own news."[3] Shell wasn't. Greenpeace moved faster and was telling Shell's story. You can't let someone else decide the pace of your narrative.

In 1992, in Bill Clinton's election war room, there stood a big sign saying "Speed Kills Bush." Speed still kills, but the speed is much greater today. When I started in PR, most trade magazines were weekly or monthly. A typical deadline was Tuesday for Friday publication. Things have changed. By 2000, weekly magazines were typically updating their websites three times a week. Within a few years, they were updating them in real time. These days, news publications rarely, if ever, hold a story for the print edition. An editor would have to be very confident that no one else had the story even to contemplate such a thing. We are going to have to stop thinking in terms of print publications altogether. All news outlets are moving towards tri-media presentation. Every story has to be prepared in three, or possibly four, formats: text, audio, and video. Sometimes, there will be two text versions, one for the space-limited print edition and one for the unlimited space of the online version.

According to the Institute for Crisis Management, some three-quarters of crises start internally – half with management and a quarter with other employees.[4] Enhancing your employee engagement may help to reduce these instances, but they will continue, through error, incompetence, and malice. Inevitably, such internal crises are the hardest to manage. The organization is always, to some degree, in the wrong. This is where the lawyers get involved, and try to insist on silence. Silence was not a sustainable strategy even before the development of social media. It is incredibly damaging today. Organizations need to learn to express concern without conceding liability.

Even when the crisis is clearly not the fault of the organization at its center, mishandling the situation can still be disastrous. Take the example of Pan Am. When Pan Am flight 103 exploded over Lockerbie in Scotland on December 21, 1988, some 270 people were killed – 259 of them were on board the aircraft (243 passengers and 16 crew) and 11 were in the town of Lockerbie. The explosion was caused by a terrorist attack. Pan Am was a victim. The corporation lost 16 of its staff and its aircraft. No one thinks the explosion was its fault. But the airline was not very good at expressing concern or taking account of the needs of families. Later investigations revealed holes in security procedures. There had been warnings, of which the airline was aware, of possible terrorist attacks on US airlines. Rumors spread that Pan Am had tipped off diplomatic officials and warned them not to fly at that time. It is recorded that Pik Botha, South African foreign minister, and his party, who were due to take the flight, did not actually do so. On the other hand, Brent Carlsson, UN commissioner for Namibia, who was flying to New York for the same meeting, was one of the victims. It is also known that there were at least four US intelligence officers on the flight, so it seems unlikely that either the intelligence community or Pan Am had anything but the vaguest suspicions about the flight. Nonetheless, Pan Am's reputation was hit very badly, and the company folded a couple of years later.

Facts aren't everything. Indeed, in the early stages of the crisis, facts may have nothing to do with the way the crisis unfolds at all. You simply won't know all the facts. This is crucial, and people will understand this, if you put it in the right way. When Tony Hayward of BP told the US Congress that he didn't know the facts, he put it the wrong way. When Lawrence Rawl, Exxon CEO, said the same on American TV regarding the 1989 Exxon Valdez oil spill, he even went so far as to correct the journalist for her misunderstanding of what a CEO's role is. There is, however, an established way of answering those exact questions, whether it is on TV, in front of Congress, or on Twitter. Take the example of another air crash, that of British Midland flight 092 in 1989. Sir Michael Bishop, chairman of the airline, phoned the media from his car as he raced to the scene of the crash. He told them that his first priority was to ensure that everyone who was injured was taken care of and that families of those killed would be able to visit the area, at the airline's expense, if they so wished. As to the causes of the crash, he assured the media that he was investigating and would report back.

It is acceptable, even expected, that you don't immediately have the answers, provided you make it clear that you are trying to find them out. But you do need to go further, and express your commitment to transparency. Once you have found out, you will publish the answers. While Tony Hayward mishandled a great deal of the PR surrounding the 2010 Gulf of Mexico disaster, his apparent lack of interest in the questions that Congress put to him was his single biggest failing. It is possible that if he had followed Sir Michael Bishop's example, his controversial leadership of BP would have survived the Deepwater Horizon incident.

Engagement with your staff is critical to your handling of the crisis. Your staff have their own social and professional networks. Even before the huge range of weak social links we have developed since social media came into being, everyone had friends and relatives. Your staff are sure to be asked by their contacts what is going on. What do you want them to say? Do you really think "I don't know! Nobody tells me anything" is going to impress anyone? Your staff need to be aware of the organization's key messages. Later on, I will explore why it is no longer practical nor acceptable for you to simply demand that your staff repeat these to everyone. But they *do* need to be aware of what the corporate line is.

It is worth bearing in mind a distinction between two types of crisis, described by Seymour and Moore as the cobra and the python.[5] The cobra strikes suddenly out of nowhere. The python takes you in its grip and slowly squeezes you to death. Of course, this distinction is often more apparent than real. Take one of the first instances of social media brandjacking – the Kryptonite/Bic pen debacle.

In 2004, a video posted online showed how easy it was to compromise a Kryptonite bike lock using a Bic pen. It was the work of seconds. Until this time Kryptonite had had a good reputation. The locks are strong and light. Prior to the invention of the Kryptonite lock, the safest method of securing a bike was using a heavy chain. The ability to easily forward links to the video makes use of weak social links. You can send a link to a contact you see only rarely, but happen to know enjoys cycling. You would be much less likely to phone such a person to tell them of something you had read in a newspaper or seen on TV. The online revelations hit Kryptonite very hard. The company offered to exchange all the affected locks, redesigned the product, and ultimately had to settle a class action lawsuit. This was a cobra. It struck in a sudden and deadly way.

But in another sense, it was a python. There had been a 1992 article on a trade website, bikebiz.com, covering the same issue, although using other makes of lock. In the UK, a BBC consumer program had also addressed the Bic method of picking bike locks. So the issue had been burning slowly for more than a decade. Indeed, the fact that Kryptonite either knew, or should have known, about the vulnerability of its locks was a key issue in the lawsuit.

Equally, the explosion on the Deepwater Horizon rig was as sudden as any crisis gets. But the weaknesses exposed in BP's crisis preparedness were very much of the python variety. BP had lodged an environmental plan with the US federal government that was riddled with absurd weaknesses, including its plans for the potential harm to sea lions and walruses, native to the Pacific and the Arctic respectively and both unknown in the Gulf of Mexico.

Terence Fane-Saunders of Chelgate estimates that 75 percent of good crisis management takes place before the crisis begins.[6] And that is where BP fell embarrassingly flat.

All this mention of BP naturally leads on to the key question: Should a CEO be speaking for the company in the event of a crisis? It is tempting to say "not if your CEO is Tony Hayward or Lawrence Rawl" and move on. After all, Sir Michael Bishop did a great job for British Midland, and, in the similar circumstances of a rail crash, so did Sir Richard Branson of Virgin. In all honesty, this has to be part of the answer: Does your CEO have the requisite talent for the job? And if not, should that person be CEO in the first place? But there are some general factors to consider. Putting a very senior person up to speak for the organization gives the message that the organization is taking the crisis seriously – provided they don't take time off to go sailing in clean waters thousands of miles from the seas their company has polluted. On the other hand, if you put your CEO forward, you face a more serious challenge if they mess things up. If another senior person – the COO, for example – is your initial spokesperson, and something goes wrong, you have a fall-back position. And there are many things that can go wrong in a crisis. Maybe the operation – the environmental cleanup, the investigation, the recall, whatever it is – will go awry. Maybe your spokesperson will say something stupid, or even say something sensible while coming over as arrogant or offhand about it. If this spokesperson is a COO or a vice-president or similar, you can always have the CEO step forward at this point and say "right, now I am taking charge." One compromise is to have someone below the level of CEO acting as spokesperson, with the CEO taking charge of operational decisions. This still leaves you with the question of how to handle things if the operation is seen to go wrong.

Before the crisis erupts, you need to be clear in your planning what channels of communication you have available to you. The old way of organizing, say, a product recall was to place advertisements in newspapers with details of which products were affected by the recall. That's still appropriate in some cases. But, increasingly, purchasers of many products – especially consumer electronics – are encouraged to register their warranties online with the manufacturer. This means that the manufacturer has a direct line of communication to the customer. In part, this is so the manufacturer can use this channel to sell upgrades and consumables associated with the product, but it is also critical in a recall situation. You can contact the customers affected by the recall and, just as importantly, contact your other customers to reassure them.

Issues and crisis management have been at the heart of PR for decades. The principal purpose of this book is to explore how they have been changed by the existence of social media and, in particular, how malicious critics can take control of the conversation around your reputation.

Notes

1   Regester, M. and Larkin, J. (1997) *Risk Issues and Crisis Management.* London: Kogan Page.

2   Haywood, R. (1984) *All About Public Relations.* London: McGraw-Hill.

3   In conversation with the author.

4   Cited in Sapriel, C. (2003) "Effective crisis management: tools and best practice for the new millennium" *Journal of Communication Management,* 7(4): 348–55.

5   Seymour, M. and Moore, S. (2000) *Effective Crisis Management: Worldwide Principles and Practice.* London: Cassell.

6   In conversation with the author.

3

Rise of the machines

It is hardly surprising the Internet is having revolutionary consequences. This is the purpose for which it was designed.

The Internet was a revolutionary idea from the unlikely source of the US Pentagon. Defense planners were considering the question of how the US would react to occupation by a hostile power. What if the occupier controlled all the normal channels of communication? How would resistance forces communicate with each other using channels no government could disrupt?

The idea that came out of this was called ARPANET – Advanced Research Projects Agency Network. Instead of using traditional circuit switching systems – in which a dedicated circuit is used to communicate from one machine to another – ARPANET uses packet switching, in which packets of information are sent via different routes and reassembled at their destination. It is as though you sent a letter to a friend by posting all the Es in one mailbox, the Ts in another, and so on for each letter of the alphabet, relying on your friend to reconstruct the letters into an intelligible form at the other end. Since all the packets of information are replicated, it doesn't matter if some fail to get through. The process seems complicated and inefficient, but with the processing speeds of modern computers, this doesn't matter. What matters is that no central authority can disrupt the messages.

This is not to say that governments do not try to disrupt the Internet, or that they will not continue to do so. China has its "Great Firewall" (formally known as the Golden Shield Project) and, in alliance with other bastions of human rights such as Libya, Saudi Arabia, Zimbabwe, and Iran, it pressed for the United

Nations (UN) to be given control of ICANN, the US-registered company that registers domain names. Critically, ICANN does not exercise any control over the content of websites, it merely maintains a central register of domains. Given the record on censorship of the governments that initiated this plan, it is fortunate that the UN has no authority to take control of a US-registered company.

Governments are sometimes able to bully private operators into adopting policies that restrict people's access to the Internet. Some of these policies are more successful than others. A Chinese student once told me of a popular social networking site in China, where certain characters simply cannot be typed. If you input on your keyboard "Tibet independence," "Taiwan independence" or "Tiananmen Square," the characters simply do not appear on the screen. But computers are very literal. They do what you tell them to do, not what you want them to do. So if you deliberately insert a minor spelling error, along the lines of "Tiibet independence," the phrase will appear on screen, and everyone knows what you mean. People – perhaps especially young people – are almost infinitely resourceful. Censorship of the Internet can usually be evaded or outwitted.

ARPANET was developed in the 1960s and ARPANET mail, the first email, followed in the early 1970s. At this point, we had not reached the Internet, as we know it. The term "Internet" was coined in the 1970s, but is taken to refer only to the fully interoperable network of networks that came about after a standard system of protocols (known as TCP/IP) was developed in 1983. It was the fact that a wide variety of networks – government, academic, and commercial – could all link to each other that created an interlinking network that no person or organization could control.

The next big step in the development of the Internet was the invention of the World Wide Web. The first website was created for the CERN particle physics laboratory in Geneva, Switzerland by Sir Tim Berners-Lee in 1991. Soon the HyperText Markup Language (HTML) developed by Berners-Lee was adopted by other organizations and the web began to grow. For a couple of years, it remained of interest mostly to scientists and other academics. Within a few years, private and commercial users began to dominate, in what might be called the "porn phase" of the Internet's development. Although the web was a small fraction of its current size, search was inefficient and heavily spammed. According to John Battelle, most searches for "car" on Lycos in the late 1990s actually led you to porn sites.[1]

What some people have called Web 2.0, or the social web, really began in 2000. The first of the genuinely important collaborative websites was

Wikipedia. Now, I am a geek. I was a huge fan of the Internet from the day I discovered it, some five years before Wikipedia launched. Like Jimmy Wales, Wikipedia's founder, I am also a great admirer of the libertarian/objectivist philosopher, Ayn Rand. But if Jimmy had pitched me the idea of Wikipedia before it launched, I would have laughed in his face. Fortunately, Wikipedia was already a success before I ever heard of it, so I never got the chance to talk Jimmy out of his crackpot idea.

Wikipedia's collaborative writing is based on the idea that if enough people contribute, you will probably end up with something that is more or less right. It is the wisdom of crowds, so elegantly explored by Surowiecki, in his book of that name.[2] It won't be 100 percent accurate, but nor is any other source of information. Any source needs to be read intelligently. Where Wikipedia definitely scores, even if it is slightly less accurate than, say, the *Encyclopedia Britannica*, is in its speed and its coverage. It has many, many times more articles than any other encyclopedia. These facts about Wikipedia – its speed, its size, and its accuracy – are all easy to measure. And yet they are the very things that I would never have believed in 2000. I would have denied outright that anything more than a handful of people would ever contribute their time for free. Even if they did (and they wouldn't), I would have denied that the popularity of a proposition is in any way related to its truth. And given that only a few dozen retired people would ever contribute, it would, obviously, never be fast or ever grow very big. My theory still seems sound to me, although the facts contradict it.

The second of the major social media sites was LinkedIn, founded in 2003. It is tempting to describe it as a business or professional version of Facebook, except that it predates Facebook, so it is a business version of Myspace or Friendster. (Intriguingly, as I type this sentence, I notice that Word 2007 recognizes "Myspace" and "Friendster" but not "Facebook." Things change fast online.)

LinkedIn does not replace face-to-face networking, any more than Facebook does. But it is a good way of maintaining and renewing a network of weak contacts. People you see or speak to regularly remain contacts without the benefit of social networking sites. But the search facility of LinkedIn enables you to find people with whom you fell out of touch some years ago. It means that you are less likely to lose people's contact details when they move house or job. It provides a simple-to-use platform to keep cold contacts fairly warm. It is also a research tool: you can search through the contacts of your contacts for someone who has expertise in a subject you are researching or who is in a place you are visiting. It is a platform where people with similar interests – both professional and social – can come together to discuss their common interests. It is a powerful tool, which you can make work for you. It is also a platform that others can use against you. As with all social media, the person driving the agenda could be a large, well-resourced organization – a union or an environmental group – or it could be a lone disgruntled customer.

At this point, it is worth discussing how people use LinkedIn groups to drive their agenda. I use the group Brandjack to drive traffic to my website, BrandjackNews.com, and also to encourage professionals to talk about brandjacking as a concept. It is a way of leading the conversation. With more than 1,500 connections, the large majority of whom are actively engaged in PR or marketing activities, I sit at the center of a network that is well placed to promote understanding of brandjacking.

I am a member of 50 LinkedIn groups. (This is not an approximation. This is the maximum number, at least at my grade of membership, so every time I discover a new one I wish to join, I have to cull one of my current crop.) I display the badges of my groups on my LinkedIn profile, so anyone reviewing my profile can get a picture of the sort of person I am. Some of my groups – such as Adam Smith Admirers or Economist Readers – I have joined principally for that purpose. Others reflect organizations in which I am involved offline – the Chartered Institute of Public Relations, the Public Relations Society of America, or the Higher Education Academy. Others reflect the different businesses in which I am engaged – PR, media, recruitment, education – or quirkier, semi-professional interests such as children's books or Sherlock Holmes. At least one is the support group for an organization of which I am not a member offline, but which I professionally observe – Greenpeace. Some groups are more active than others, but all extend the range of people you can contact directly on LinkedIn, without need of an introduction.

Most commercial organizations have a LinkedIn page and many have a group that discusses their products or services. The group may, or may not, have been established by the organization itself, and it may, or may not, be of people who *support* your brand. Well-run organizations that wish to engage with their publics will be aware of what is being said about them on LinkedIn, and will seek to engage positively there. It is wise, however, to avoid being heavy-handed. If the corporate PR department immediately jumps in to every critical discussion, it may drive people away to a different forum, where the organization is not so embedded. Participate with some humility and try to be helpful. Users should be able to regard the group as *their* space in which you participate, not *your* space into which they intrude on sufferance. Always,

always, declare that you are speaking on behalf of the organization. If you do not, it is likely to emerge anyway, and your credibility and trust will have been eroded. If your organization is a publicly quoted company, you could even face criminal charges or a US Securities and Exchange Commission (SEC) investigation. Ask Rahodeb if the SEC looking into your affairs is fun (CS 15).

Imagine, for a moment, that America's big three TV networks (ABC, CBS, and NBC) had been broadcasting 24 hours a day, 365 days a year since 1948, when ABC was founded. Imagine the sheer quantity of broadcast material. This is the quantity of video that was uploaded to YouTube over the past few weeks. Much of it is repetitive and the technical and editorial standards are variable. The same can be said of the big three networks. The scale of YouTube should not be underestimated. It is the second largest search engine in the world, and fully integrated with Google, the largest search engine. YouTube is now available in 61 countries and across 61 languages. Today, three-quarters of YouTube uploads come from outside the US. As the site expands its geographical reach, it is sure to grow even faster. It is a reasonable supposition that YouTube will also expand its demographic reach. Over half of YouTube users are teenagers or younger. As this generation gets older, it is possible they will use YouTube less, but as each cohort is replaced by younger people, the total number of YouTube users is going to carry on growing enormously.

YouTube is younger than LinkedIn and Wikipedia, dating only to 2005. Like most other social media sites, it is essentially simple. It offers a user-friendly platform to upload videos and search through videos uploaded by others. It also provides an "embed code" so anyone can display a video from YouTube directly on their site. It is a cheap and simple platform through which users can upload any video – from the most obviously amateur drunken antics to sophisticated satire or art. Millions of users sift through the dross – and there is a lot of it – and the material of interest to no one but the poster and their immediate circle. The jewels stand out. The sheer quality of the material in some classic brandjacks – the brilliantly funny "United Breaks Guitars," for example, or the Greenpeace spoof "Give the orangutan a break" – is a large part of the success of these campaigns. But Greenpeace also relies on meticulous PR planning for all its stunts, demonstrating a professionalism, as well as a mass of resources, that few corporates can match.

Greenpeace, like Wikipedia, depends on volunteers, which inevitably keeps its costs down. The hundreds of millions of euros it spends on campaigning is, therefore, a massive underestimate of its actual resources. Before it ever opened its YouTube channel, Greenpeace had a worldwide network of supporters. While some do little more than pay an annual subscription, others are extremely active. All these people have networks. Little wonder that any video Greenpeace posts has an immediate audience, many of whom will actively promote it to their friends, relatives, and colleagues. Even the soft supporters, who in previous years would have done little more than paid a subscription and received mailings, now have easy ways to become involved – simply forwarding messages, URLs, news stories, and the like to their network of contacts, strong and weak.

Facebook is colossal, and its influence is astounding. Just 10 years ago, most older people had email because it was the only way of communicating with their grandchildren. Today, most college students only bother with email as a way of communicating with their grandparents. Their friends, they message by Facebook. Obviously, the site is controversial. As the film says, you can't make 500 million friends without making a few enemies. Leftwing writers have been known to use phrases like "global conspiracy" and "money grub-bing" when writing about the founders of Facebook. Journalists who would be careful not to stereotype African Americans don't seem to mind using phrases like that about entrepreneurs with names such as "Zuckerberg." And the usual crowd of stuffy colonels will intone with horror about pedophiles "on the Internet" as though it is the Internet, and not the pedophilia, that is the problem. But Facebook has opened doors and knocked down barriers. Young people are practicing the skills they will later apply on LinkedIn to expand their social and professional capital.

The problem is that most commercial organizations don't know how to use Facebook. Having a great Facebook fan page, even one with lots of fans, is not the point, or at least it is only part of it. Lots of people are prepared to hit a button saying they like Coke or Kit Kat. But how passionate are people about this affiliation? Will Kit Kat supporters dive into battle on behalf of their brand in the way that NGOs will? How are you engaging with your fans on Facebook? Do they feel that they are part of your community, with early access to new products, and even the opportunity to influence product development? Tens of billions of pieces of Internet content – news stories, videos, songs, blogs, pictures, the list is endless – are shared on Facebook every month. But integrating your website with Facebook is not enough to give you an army of activist supporters to match Amnesty International, Greenpeace, or PETA (People for the Ethical Treatment of Animals). Those people care, in a way that most of your customers probably don't, and probably never will. Greenpeace International has 1.5 million fans for its Facebook page, which is a fraction of the 29 million for Pepsi, but which organization has the most *motivated* fans?

The newest of the main social media platforms is also one of the more international ones. Under half of YouTube use is within the US. More than 40 percent of Twitter access is via phone or tablet rather than computer (if there is still a meaningful distinction between the two). Perhaps this is not surprising. Twitter was originally a cell phone text messaging platform, and the 140-character limit is based on the SMS (text) definition of a page. Inevitably, the mass of short messages makes it a great way of mapping trends in conversation in real time.

Twitter first came to the attention of the wider public in 2009. The mainstream media (MSM) seemed to take the declared results of the Iranian presidential election at face value. On Twitter, people objected that these results simply could not be true. Believing them involved accepting truly astonishing swings against opposition candidates in their home regions. Iran was suddenly facing something that had already become familiar in the West. New technology provides excellent platforms for organizing anti-government demonstrations. Anti-globalization demonstrations at G8 summits and World Bank/IMF meetings have long made use of modern technology to summon flash crowds. No single organization is responsible for the demonstrations, thus no organization can be sued for any damages that result. Crowds can be summoned by a cascade of text messages and emails. Iran does not have the same level of development as the G8 countries, but does have one of the youngest demographics in the world, with a higher proportion of its population under the age of 20 than almost any other country. The result is a population relatively attuned to Twitter, and demographically suited to mobilizing for demonstrations.

The hashtag (subject line) #iranelections electrified Twitter. CNN – a broadcaster with a strong tradition of reporting from Middle Eastern dictatorships – came in for particular criticism for ignoring the protests against Iran's stolen election. Soon, CNN and the rest of the MSM began to follow the story.

Twitter's role in brandjacking was firmly established by Leroy Stick and his spoof Twitter feed, @bpglobalpr. At the height of the Deepwater Horizon crisis in the Gulf of Mexico, Stick was producing a steady stream of satirical commentary about BP and the Gulf. He had 12 times as many followers as the official BP feed, @bpamerica. Stick stayed within his chosen paradigm, always speaking as though he was a BP official. He was just much, much funnier. BP objected to Twitter that Stick's home page implied he was an official spokesperson for the company, which led to his amending the description but, on the whole, the company ignored him. It could have asked Twitter to close the account down, but it would only have been a breach of Twitter's terms if people were genuinely being misled by the account; that is, if significant numbers genuinely believed that Stick was speaking on behalf of BP. Given the content he was producing – "safety is our first priority; well, profits, then safety; well, profits then image then safety, but it's right up there" – it would be embarrassing for BP to argue that people believed this was its official line.

To try to act against Stick's account would have been an error, and BP was wise to avoid falling into that trap. This was possibly the single best decision the company made among a catalog of poor judgments. Legal actions against social media outlets tend to promote a backlash among consumers, who often equate this with censorship (see CS 38). The only way to counter social media brandjacking is honest and transparent engagement. Getting heavy-handed nearly always makes things worse.

As a means of communication, then, the Internet in general and social media in particular bring key changes to organizations. The key features of the digital age can be summarized as: speed, globalization, merging technologies, disintermediation, lack of regulation, data democratization, and interactivity. Each of these is worth a chapter in itself, but this is a brief introduction prior to exploring specific examples of brandjacking:

- *Speed:* social media put gossip onto steroids. In 1885, Charles Spurgeon said (in a quote often attributed to Mark Twain): "a lie will go round the world while truth is pulling its boots on." If that was true a century and a quarter ago, it is much more so in the world of "business at the speed of light."
- *Globalization:* social media are inherently global, and MSM are globalized too. There is no such thing as a local story any more, and trying to maintain one reputation in one market and a different one elsewhere is increasingly a losing strategy.
- *Merging technologies:* what is the difference between CNN, the *South China Morning Post*, and BBC Radio 4? Clearly, each was founded in a different market – the US, Hong Kong, and the UK respectively – but also in different media – a cable TV channel, a print newspaper, and a speech-based radio station. Increasingly, they compete head to head, both internationally and in the online medium. CNN's website still has more of a TV look and feel than either of the others. Radio 4 still gives primacy to audio communication. But these differences are blurring at the edges. Increasingly, all news is tri-media: video, text, and audio. In the case of media that maintain a print presence, there will often be two text versions, one for the space-limited print version and another online.
- *Disintermediation:* social media create direct channels of communication that would previously have been mediated. Instead of using newspapers,

say, to communicate to your customers or stockholders, you can now communicate directly. For many organizations, this was previously impossible. It was especially difficult in markets where the consumer relationship was itself mediated: for example, Mars sells to Walmart and Walmart sells to the consumer. Mars had no direct link with the people who eat its product.

• *Lack of regulation:* the Internet is inherently unregulated, and governments that have attempted to exercise control over it have hit problems. This does not mean that existing laws do not continue to apply. Laws governing defamation, copyright, privacy, national security, and other things certainly do apply. Indeed, something published online might well be subject to laws in multiple jurisdictions, after all, the material is published worldwide. Enforcing the law might, however, be difficult. The Internet also finds itself outside the gentlemanly self-regulation of the media. For example, the story of Bill Clinton's affair with Monica Lewinsky was well known to MSM some time before it was broken by the Drudge Report (a US news aggregation website). Equally, the US media have a tradition that they do not publish election exit polls until the polls have shut. Websites do not share this assumption.

• *Data democratization:* information previously reserved for the elite or the in-crowd is now much more widely available. Think about the implications for investor relations and financial PR. It was once possible for businesses to reveal information to institutional investors first, with retail stockholders finding out the information by post a few days later. As information is released electronically, the data gap between institutional investors and your grandma has greatly diminished.

• *Interactivity:* this refers to the rise of the social web. Gone (thankfully) are the days when the CEO would say "put this brochure on the web." Interactivity is your opportunity to make your website "sticky" – so people will not just arrive, but stay. (Facebook is one of the stickiest websites in existence.) It is your opportunity to gather data from your publics, so you can communicate with them directly. Most of all, it is your opportunity to listen to what your publics are saying, so you can genuinely build a relationship with them, and adapt your organization as it grows.

Notes

1   Battelle, J. (2005) *The Search*. London: Nicholas Brealey.
2   Surowiecki, J. (2005) *The Wisdom of Crowds*. New York: Doubleday.

chapter 4

The brandjacks

To be classified as a brandjack, something needs to be both a *crisis* and, specifically, one that plays out significantly in *digital media*. Some begin in digital media, such as Twitter impersonations. Some, like the fake sign in a McDonald's window (see CS 70), are then circulated in social media and largely ignored in mainstream media. But the key combination is crisis and digital.

Brandjacks fall into a number of categories. The most common are those that focus on the ethics of the organization, those that start with a strategic error by the organization, and those that begin with the organization's staff. Any given brandjack can fall into more than one of these categories. Others, such as entirely fake stories or impersonations, are much rarer.

This book identifies nine categories of brandjack, and divides the 140 case studies below into those categories.

SELF BRANDJACK	The Institute of Crisis Management estimated that some three-quarters of crises begin internally, with two-thirds of those starting with management,[1] so it is unsurprising that the self brandjack, a policy failure within the organization, is the most common type of brandjack. There is a rare subcategory of self brandjack, best exemplified by Skittles, in which the organization voluntarily cedes control of its reputation. Far more frequently, the self brandjack involves an accident (BP), a poor advertising choice (Chapstick, American Apparel), or something that goes to the heart of the organization's business model (Hosni Mubarak and other Arab dictators).

See Whole Foods Market, Paperchase, NPR and the various errors made by Barack Obama and Mitt Romney.

Organizations have always been under fire for the morality or ethics of their decisions or even their business model. But boycotts have usually been hard to organize. Few people are sufficiently motivated to boycott a company that provides products or services they want at good prices. This is especially true in strongly differentiated markets. For an Apple fan, giving up Apple products is a big step. Digital channels already make markets more competitive and give people more choices between highly branded and more generic products. This is an excellent background for creative and professional organizations – and Greenpeace is the most effective – to use customers to press for policy changes.

See the progress in the Greenpeace campaigns from Apple through Kleenex and Nestlé to Mattel and Shell.

 This comes in two forms. It is either also an aggregation brand-jack, such as Dell Hell, or it is when a lone customer can present a complaint in such a creative form that it goes viral and puts clear pressure on the organization. By far the best example of this remains "United Breaks Guitars."

See Dell Hell, United Airlines.

 Many crises begin internally, and this still applies in the digital and social age. It can be foolish behavior that ends up being reported virally (Jet Blue and Steven Slater, Comcast), or something a member of staff does in social media (Vodafone, Virgin Atlantic).

See Comcast, Vodafone, Chrysler f-bomb, Virgin Atlantic.

IMPERSONATION BRANDJACK This rare category of brandjack arises when an impersonator purports to be speaking for an organization (or person) but isn't. Sometimes, they are fairly obvious hoaxes, such as Josh Simpson's @bpglobalpr, which was a parody, but stayed in character at all times. Sometimes, as with ExxonMobil, the impersonator is making a sincere – if not transparent – attempt to reflect the views of the organization. Janet, the Exxon impersonator, attracted favorable comment for the oil giant. Sometimes, the motivation is less apparent, such as impersonating comedian David Mitchell.

See ExxonMobil, BP, David Mitchell.

FAKE BRANDJACK These are rare, but consist of completely false memes spread deliberately. Some are designed to hurt an organization, such as the fabricated story that McDonald's was to start charging more to African American customers, or the TV program that showed footage of rats on a building site and billed it as rats in a restaurant. Another example is when a business puts out a fake blog designed to appeal to customers, such as the thinly disguised "alliwantforxmasisapsp."

See Taco Bell rats, alliwantforxmasisapsp, #SeriouslyMcDonalds.

AGGREGATION BRANDJACK This is one of the great innovations of the social age. Social media enable people who would otherwise be isolated critics to combine their voices. Sometimes, customer failings are sufficiently rare that people would simply never encounter others who have suffered from the same problem. Jeff Jarvis's problems with Dell probably fall into this category. Sometimes, the issue itself is so fleeting that, in the offline world, people would simply not have had time to organize on the scale required to make a difference. The Motrin Moms would be an example here. In all cases, the aggregation brings together people who may have little or nothing in common except a single – and possibly fleeting – grievance about one organization. They may be spread out and isolated from each other. Social media channels provide such people with ways of organizing comparable with local groups. People who share a grievance that is based on locality – a village threatened by a bypass, for example – have always had the means to combine and organize. Things have generally been more complicated for people who are more widespread and with a single uniting factor, such as an objection to a particular ad for Motrin.

See Dell Hell, Motrin Moms.

UNANTICIPATED RESPONSE BRANDJACK Sometimes, an organization seeks a response from its publics (usually customers) as a way of engaging them, and gets a response that it doesn't like. This may be people simply mocking the organization, or engaging in reasoned critique.

See GM: Chevy Apprentice, GMNext, Molson Coors, Bic pink pens, Chapstick.

CHEEKY BRANDJACK This is the deliberate attempt to tease another organization, mostly in a fairly harmless way.

See Barclays, Smirnoff Ice, Samsung.

Table 4.1 Summary of case studies and their categories

		Ethics	Customer revolt	Aggregation
	2001–07			
1	NIKEiD	x		
2	Kryptonite		x	
3	L'Oréal Vichy	x		
4	Dell Hell		x	x
5	GM: Chevy Apprentice	x		
6	Dell: laptop batteries			
7	Comcast			
8	Starbucks: fake ad	x		
9	Apple: Green my Apple	x	x	x
10	Walmart			
11	Sony PlayStation			
12	JetBlue: stranded passengers		x	
13	Taco Bell			
14	Kleenex	x		
15	Whole Foods Market			
16	Molson Coors			
	2008–10			
17	GM: GMnext	x		
18	Target			
19	Louis Vuitton	x		
20	Dove: "Dove Onslaught(er)"	x		
21	JCPenney			
22	ExxonMobil			
23	Motrin		x	x
24	Virgin Atlantic			
25	Tropicana		x	x
26	David Mitchell			
27	Skittles			
28	Domino's Pizza			
29	Habitat			
30	WMATA			
31	Maytag		x	
32	United Airlines		x	
33	PepsiCo			
34	Vodafone			
35	Southwest Airlines		x	
36	Paperchase			
37	Toyota			

Staff	Self	Fake	Unanticipated response	Impersonation	Cheeky
			x		
	x				
x					
	x				
	x	x			
		x			
	x				
	x		x		
	x		x		
	x				
	x				
	x				
				x	
x					
				x	
	x				
x					
	x				
	x				
	x				
x					
	x				
	x				

		Ethics	Customer revolt	Aggregation
38	Nestlé	x		
39	Facebook	x		
40	BP	x		
41	Boeing			
42	Pampers Cruisers		x	
43	Smirnoff Ice			
44	Barclays			
45	JetBlue: Steven Slater			
46	McDonald's: heart disease	x		
47	Burger King	x		
48	Ryanair: I Hate Ryanair			
49	BP: Banksy	x		
50	Maldives			
51	NPR: Juan Williams			
52	Amazon Kindle	x		
53	Alaska Airlines		x	
54	John Lewis	x		x
	2011			
55	Zine al-Abidine Ben Ali	x		x
56	The Red Cross			
57	Hosni Mubarak	x		
58	US Department of State			
59	Ali Abdullah Saleh			
60	John Galliano			
61	Muammar Gaddafi			
62	NPR: Tea Party			
63	Vogue: Asma al-Assad, rose in the desert			
64	Chrysler 'f-bomb'			
65	Mark Zuckerberg: "kill what you eat"			
66	Dove accused of racist ad			
67	David H. Koch	x		
68	FIFA corruption scandal	x		
69	TSA #diapergate			
70	McDonald's: #SeriouslyMcDonalds			
71	Mattel: Ken and Barbie	x		
72	U pay tax 2?	x		
73	Starbucks: homophobic rant	x		
74	Chesapeake Energy	x		
75	BART scripted writers			

Staff	Self	Fake	Unanticipated response	Impersonation	Cheeky
	x			x	
	x				
				x	
					x
				x	x
x					
	x				
x					
	x				
	x				
	x				
x					
	x				
x	x				
	x				
	x				
	x				
	x				
	x				
x					
	x				
	x				
	x				
	x				
		x			
x					
	x				

		Ethics	Customer revolt	Aggregation
76	Gmail Man	x		
77	Airbnb #ransackgate		x	
78	Wenzhou train crash			
79	IE users less intelligent			
80	"Facebook riots"			
81	Nivea "recivilize" ad			
82	Indiana University Health			
83	Lacoste, Anders Breivik			
84	Bank of America		x	x
85	Celebrities support Chechen dictator	x		
86	Chapstick			x
87	Chris Huhne			
88	Beyoncé			
89	Herman Cain	x		
90	Johnson & Johnson	x		
91	Sam Brownback and Emma Sullivan			
92	SapientNitro			
93	Skyrim for PS3		x	
94	FedEx deliverer			
2012				
95	Apple gets 'Samsunged'			
96	Mattel: bald Barbie		x	x
97	Costa Concordia			
98	McDonald's: #McDStories			x
99	"Mad Men" poster			
100	LA Fitness			
101	Susan G. Komen, Planned Parenthood			
102	Oprah: Nielsen box appeal			
103	Claire's plagiarism			
104	"Kony 2012", Invisible Children	x		
105	Goldman Sachs/Darth Vader resignation			
106	SXSW: Homeless Hotspots	x		
107	"Pink slime"			
108	Heineken: dog-fighting	x		
109	Dole Food Co.			
110	Aviva: accidental firing			
111	Spirit Airlines Secret Service			
112	Obama: "Polish death camps"			

Staff	Self	Fake	Unanticipated response	Impersonation	Cheeky
					x
	x				
		x			
		x			
	x				
	x				
	x				
	x				
	x				
			x		
	x				
	x				
	x				
x					
	x				
				x	
x					
					x
x					
	x				
	x				
	x				
	x				
	x				
	x				
x					
	x				
		x			
	x				
x					
	x				
	x				

	Ethics	Customer revolt	Aggregation
113 Best Buy			
114 Yahoo! CEO			
115 Fiat/VW			
116 Starbucks Ireland			
117 Oreo: Gay Pride	x		
118 @Sweden			
119 Veet flashmob			x
120 Argyll & Bute: NeverSeconds		x	
121 Lance Armstrong			
122 Chick-fil-A	x		
123 "Deserve to die"			
124 Shell "Arctic Ready"	x		
125 BMW Olympics			
126 Progressive insurance	x		x
127 Bic pink pens			x
128 Obama: pirate day			
129 Romney: 47%			
130 Berman and Sherman			
131 BlackBerry		x	
132 Mitt Romney			
133 Jack Welch			
134 BBC: Lord McAlpine			
135 Oprah: Microsoft Surface			
136 Cheerios memories	x		
137 American Apparel			
138 CB2: mocking the homeless	x		
139 NASA: end of the world			
140 NRA: Newtown shootings			

Note

1   Cited in Sapriel, C. (2003) "Effective crisis management: tools and best practice for the new millennium" *Journal of Communication Management*, 7(4): 348–55.

Staff	Self	Fake	Unanticipated response	Impersonation	Cheeky
	x				
x					
					x
	x				
	x				
	x				
					x
	x				
	x				
	x				
	x				
				x	
		x			
	x				
	x		x		
	x				
	x				
	x				
	x				
	x				
	x				
	x				
	x				
	x				
	x				
	x				

The case studies: 2001–07

1 Personalize your sneakers, but only if you're nice
January 2001

In January 2001, a story came to light that might be thought of as the proto-brandjack, when Jonah Perretti made public his email exchange with NIKEiD about its personalize service. This was before the days of social media or Web 2.0, but Nike had come up with a product promotion idea that was very much in the style of social media, and Perretti rather neatly brandjacked its idea.

The scenario was simple. You could order an expensive pair of Nike sneakers online, and personalize them. You could add your own wording, right next to the famous Nike swoosh. It was a great way to make a statement. This was all so dot-com. The problem – at least for Nike – is that the statement Perretti wanted to make was about Nike's employment practices in the developing world. He asked Nike to print the word "sweatshop" on his sneakers.

Nike promptly canceled his order and sent him a form email to explain that it had done so for "one or more of the following reasons," citing mostly things to do with trademarks or intellectual property. The only light touch in the email was when it offered the possible explanation: "contains profanity or inappropriate slang, and besides, your mother would slap us."

Perretti responded, forensically dissecting the explanations and pointing out that none really applied to the word "sweatshop." Sweatshop is the name of a chain of sporting goods stores, and although that doesn't make the word itself a trademark, Nike could possibly have stood its ground on this. Nike tried to dig its heels in on the idea that the word was slang, only for Perretti to point out that, according to Webster's, it is Standard English, and has been for more than a century. Oops.

Finally, Nike fell back on the point it probably should have gone for in the first place, that the rules allowed it to turn down any requested personalized iD for any reason. Perretti responded that he would choose another iD, if Nike would agree to supply a photograph "of the 10-year-old Vietnamese girl who makes my shoes." Nike didn't respond. Perretti forwarded the full correspondence to others, who forwarded it on in a cascade and the whole thing went viral.

Many of the key characteristics of later brandjacks were there back in 2001. It pitted a lone customer against the might of a multinational. He was battling principally by using humor and the company responded with pomposity and evasion. The email exchange went viral and became a major talking point among the wired generation before it hit the mainstream media (MSM), although it was reported in *Village Voice* within a few weeks.

Learnings

The hints were all there that a whole new way of digitally brandjacking corporations was in the making. Perretti was consistently casual and humorous in his style, while Nike fell back on an initial form letter and corporate speak. Incidentally, Perretti may have been casual with the facts as well as his language. Nike's policy is not to use factories that employ under-18s.

The principal lesson Nike should have taken from this is simple. You had a great idea, but when you were had, you should have realized it. Nike should either have made Perretti's shoes, or told him upfront that it was refusing to do so because it simply didn't choose to. It could have sent him its policy on suppliers in the developing world, which might have gone some way to satisfying him that conditions there were not as bad as he was assuming. It could have thanked him for raising the issue and promised to keep it under review. It could even have admitted that he caught them out. Nike's actual response just allowed him to milk the issue for more humor.

✓ What Nike did right

- It set up the rules in a way that allowed cancelation of his order for any reason, perhaps anticipating that something awkward would arise.

☒ What Nike did wrong

- It failed to recognize that a brandjack was in progress. Management replied with a form letter, offering a number of possible reasons, none of which precisely applied in this case. Someone should have spotted that this was a difficult customer who required an individual response from the beginning.

ETHICS BRANDJACK An outsider co-opts the agenda to talk about ethical issues and places the company on the defensive.

2 How a video revealed that Kryptonite locks don't secure your bike
September 2004

From its invention in 1972 until its brandjacking in 2004, the Kryptonite lock had a tremendous reputation. It was strong and light. Its U shape was emulated by numerous competitors, and it was widely considered almost impregnable. Prior to the Kryptonite U-lock, upgrading to a more expensive bike with a lighter frame almost inevitably meant sacrificing the weight gain to a thicker and heavier chain.

In 1973, *New York* magazine reported that a bike secured with a Kryptonite lock had been left in Christopher Street, Greenwich Village for four weeks; at the end of which time, the lock showed 23 marks or abrasions from bolt cutters, but remained intact.

In 2004, a viral video circulated online – not on YouTube, which did not launch until the following year – showing that the tumbler lock on a Kryptonite U-lock could be compromised using a cheap ballpoint pen in a matter of seconds. The revelations were not actually new. But the online format offered a convenient way to demonstrate how easy it was to compromise the lock, and then tap into people's social networks to spread the word. The video was extremely powerful, and went to the heart of Kryptonite's business. The lock simply didn't do what it was supposed to do.

Kryptonite was forced to change the locking mechanism of its product, replace locks already sold, and even settle (out of court) a class action lawsuit. Intriguingly, as explained in Chapter 2, the story had actually been around for 12 years when the video went viral – indeed, this was a key part of the lawsuit against Kryptonite. It was the combination of the visual representation and social networking that raised the profile of the issue to crisis level.

Learnings

While Kryptonite did the right thing in the end, its crisis came about because it had failed to engage with customers. In its defense during the lawsuit, Kryptonite pointed out that none of the compromised locks discussed in the original 1992 BikeBiz article had been Kryptonites and the company simply did not know that its locks were so vulnerable. Possibly, but Kryptonite should have known, and if it had been as engaged with its publics as we now expect businesses to be, it would have done. Granted, we had no such expectations in 1992.

☒ What Kryptonite did wrong

- It failed to follow its own market effectively, and therefore didn't know the weakness of its product.

☑ What Kryptonite did right

- When the problem came to its attention, it responded quickly, fixing the problem and recalling the product.
- It made a point of shipping replacement locks to customers ahead of dealers.[1]

CUSTOMER REVOLT BRANDJACK	Consumers rebel at a problem with the product and force the company to settle.

3 L'Oréal uses a blogger to promote its product, but the blogger turns out to be a fake
June 2005

In June 2005, L'Oréal launched a blog to promote its Vichy line of skincare products. The "blog" had none of the features we associate with blogging. There were no trackbacks, and only moderated comments. The supposed author of the blog was a fake character called Claire, who struggled with the everyday problem of being invited to far too many parties and thus not getting enough sleep. In fairness, the picture associated with this "Claire" was of someone who looked like a professional model, and maybe people who look like that really do get invited to more parties than they can manage to fit in. Anyway, the upshot of Claire's nocturnal lifestyle was that she was terribly worried about lines around her eyes, and needed first-class skincare products like, er, L'Oréal's Vichy.

Claire was very interested in her skin. According to *Business Week*, she once blogged: "My skin is definitely smoother ... although it's not so radiant that you need to wear sunglasses to look at it." The problem was, of course, that "Claire" did not exist. The "blog" was just a website that presented advertising copy in the format of a blog.

L'Oréal's defense for this faux pas was pure ignorance. It simply hadn't occurred to the company that this was either unethical or a breach of blogging conventions. Indeed, the company had press released its innovative approach to marketing its products, and the story had already been written up in advertising publications before the seemingly inadvertent deception was "exposed" in the blogosphere and subsequently the general media. The "deception" can't have been very effective, as bloggers were complaining about the fictitious character within an hour of the blog going live.

The result was an "oops" rather than a "caught in the act." L'Oréal rapidly apologized once it realized that its tactic had caused offense.

Learnings

Having made a genuine mistake, L'Oréal rectified the matter quickly and effectively. The company relaunched the blog on Movable Type, a real blogging platform. The Vichy team blogged there using their own names and real photographs rather than a picture of a model. All the features of an interactive blog – including comments from real customers – were enabled. An external blogger, Sophie Kune, was brought in to blog authentically on Vichy and its products. What started as a simple advertising platform became a genuine conversation, which leading French business publications praised as an innovative marketing strategy. "Strategy" might be the wrong word, as it was a recovery program, but this is one of the best measures of a strong organization. After a disastrous misstep, L'Oréal was able to recover and gain the confidence of its key publics.

By 2008, L'Oréal was being praised by *Business Week* for its innovative and successful social media strategies, such as sponsorship of online business games as a way of recruiting the best graduates.

As Carol Matlack put it in her January 2008 report:[2]

While other multinationals (PG) sponsor business games, none draws as many participants as does L'Oréal. The games have attracted a flood of players from Asia and Latin America, two regions where the $22.6 billion company needs managers. Only 4 of the 10 best teams in e-Strat and Brandstorm were from Europe last year, while the rest came from places such as Brazil, Indonesia, and Turkey.

☒ What L'Oréal did wrong

- It didn't research the platform before diving in. It should have realized that blogging is based on authenticity.

☑ **What L'Oréal did right**

- It apologized immediately.
- It launched a genuine conversation.
- It learned from its experience, and used it to bolster recruitment as well as marketing.

 A serious misjudgment provokes a backlash from bloggers.

4 How one blogger took on Dell and won: the first aggregation brandjack
August 2005

In 2005, blogger Jeff Jarvis purchased a Dell laptop that he was later to brand a "lemon." But far worse than the fact that the product underperformed was the treatment he received from the customer service team. He had paid for the at-home service agreement and therefore felt that Dell should, er, provide some actual at-home service. Eventually, he wrote about his experience on his BuzzMachine blog:[3]

> I just got a new Dell laptop and paid a fortune for the four-year, in-home service. The machine is a lemon and the service is a lie. I'm having all kinds of trouble with the hardware: overheats, network doesn't work, maxes out on CPU usage. It's a lemon.

Under the new heading "Dell Hell," the blog became a refuge and rallying point for other customers with similar experiences. It seems that problems with Dells were common enough to attract other dissatisfied customers to BuzzMachine, while not so common that any such mutual support groups had already arisen in the offline world. This is an interesting cutoff point. If your product or service is consistently awful, your customers will spontaneously form protest groups. But Dell's situation was different. If the majority of your customers are happy, it is possible for the minority to imagine that their own experiences are unrepresentative or even unique. But can you really afford to have a significant minority of your customers grossly dissatisfied?

This is an example of the aggregation brandjack: previously isolated critics of an organization are able to come together and organize through social media when they would previously have had no way of doing so, or could not have invested the necessary time in doing so.

For Dell, the Dell Hell blog came as a shock. The company was founded on Michael Dell's belief that by getting close to its customers, a company could serve them better. A Dell computer can be assembled to the customer's own specification. To be attacked precisely for failing to understand and meet the needs of its customers was a significant psychological blow. And it came at a time when the company was already psychologically vulnerable. Michael Dell had stepped down as CEO in 2004. It was as though the company's vision had gone with him.

Learnings

Dell decided to learn from its crisis. Jeff Jarvis was invited inside the company to critique its entire customer service procedures. In 2007, Michael Dell himself returned to the helm. In the same year, he appointed the company's first in-house blogger, Lionel Menchaca. As Jarvis commented, Menchaca engaged customers in a "human voice." He admitted that the company had problems, and involved customers in the process of putting them right. By respecting the customers, he earned respect from them.

Jeff Jarvis was able to leverage an entirely new career from this. Already a journalist and popular blogger, he became an in-demand speaker on customer service, a published author, and an academic teaching at City University of New York.

Dell fully committed itself to the process of transparency and engagement. It became an open organization, with customers as its partners in the process of improvement, not a nuisance to be swatted away. This is why Dell is still in business and still prospering.

The Dell Hell experience was not the only factor that initiated Michael Dell's return from retirement. Dell's financial performance had been lackluster. But this brandjack played a role in triggering a radical transformation of the company.

For Jarvis, too, the Dell Hell experience has been seminal. He has gained a reputation internationally as an expert on customer service, and developed an entirely new strand to his career, speaking and training on these issues.

☑ What Dell did right

Once the issue arose, Dell handled everything in a pitch-perfect way:
- It recognized that the problems were systemic, and set about solving them.

- It involved Jeff Jarvis from the beginning and he gradually became an ambassador for the brand.
- It launched an entire process of engagement with its publics through blogging.

CUSTOMER REVOLT BRANDJACK	Customer rebels against both faulty product and flawed service.
AGGREGATION BRANDJACK	Blog becomes a focus for numerous, previously isolated, consumers.

5 Crowdsourcing backfires: how GM opened its doors to fans, and let in the activists as well
April 2006

When your campaign links a well-known brand with a huge advertising spend and a popular TV program, you have to expect a great deal of interest, so the Chevy Apprentice campaign started with a number of advantages.

Promoted on the popular TV program *The Apprentice*, the special website gave people the opportunity to make their own TV ads for the Chevy Tahoe. The winning ad was to be shown on primetime TV. The TV series, hosted by Donald Trump, has a cult following, and, by its nature, something of a pro-business outlook. Nonetheless, a controversial company like General Motors (GM) should have been aware of the risks.

The Chevy Apprentice website gave contestants the opportunity to cut and paste together footage of the Tahoe driving through a range of environments – urban, desert, and tundra among them – and intersperse it with shots of the engine, the car's interior, and so on. The contestants could add their own captions to deliver the key messages they associate with the Tahoe.

At one level, this was a great experiment in crowdsourcing. GM was able to tap into the enthusiasms of its customer base to arrive at a shared brand image. It was an outreach to the goal of two-way symmetric reputation management: the co-created brand. But an invitation to brand co-creation is equally an invitation to brandjacking.

Naturally, along with the Tahoe enthusiasts, activists descended on the site. GM cannot have hoped for – although it probably expected – the environmental campaigners talking about the staggeringly high carbon footprint of a short journey in a Chevy Tahoe. The comments about drivers of the Tahoe suffering from penis envy were also unlikely to have been the messages to which GM aspired.

Overall, GM considered the campaign a success. There were 20,000 entries, and only 400 of them were critical. But a search on YouTube four and a half years later puts the negative ads right at the top. Media coverage also focused heavily on the critical ads. GM was also criticized for not promptly removing the negative ads – taken as a sign that the company was not on the ball – although it is not clear whether this was indolence or a policy of transparency. Removing the negative ads would undoubtedly have provoked hostility from activists, who would have called it censorship, and provoked them to post their entries elsewhere, including YouTube.

Learnings

There is no doubt that the campaign had positive as well as negative effects. Third-party coverage – both online and in the MSM – was critical, but the level of engagement with brand supporters was high. GM was not seeking popularity – journalists and bloggers, many of whom are frustrated politicians, often fail to understand this. Ultimately, GM was seeking sales, and a product with a cult following among a minority, even if it is loathed by another group and ignored by a third, can be profitable. People who submitted positive ads for the contest were the target audience for GM, and may well have felt drawn in and engaged. Green activists did not represent lost sales, since these people were never potential customers in the first place.

Overall, GM probably underestimated the downside to the campaign, and I doubt it will be doing it again, but it was far from a total failure. The main lesson is this: you don't control social media, and that is exactly why it presents both opportunities and risks.

☑ What GM did right

- It trusted its customers, and thus recruited enthusiasts as brand ambassadors.
- It bravely experimented with crowdsourcing.
- It refrained from "censoring" the critical ads.
- It refused to be diverted, recognizing that customers are essential to the company and critics are much less important.

☒ What GM did wrong

- It may have underestimated the opportunity it was giving to brandjackers.

- It failed to realize that its critics have a high-value social network: they are connected to other activists and can promote their versions of the ads within this network.
- It failed to anticipate the extent to which the media would focus on the critical ads.

| **ETHICS** BRANDJACK | Activists raise the profile of environmental issues to put pressure on GM. |
| **UNANTICIPATED RESPONSE** BRANDJACK | Multinational seeks the views of public; public responds with hostile views. |

6 With a safety crisis blowing online, one manufacturer manages an exemplary recall
June 2006

In June 2006, the Inquirer website published a photograph of a Dell laptop in flames at a conference in Japan. The photograph immediately went viral. This was inevitable, as laptop users and people engaged in social media are groups that significantly intersect on the Venn diagram. The problem turned out to be with the battery, and led to the largest ever consumer electronics recall.

Recalls can often proceed smoothly without any poor reflection on the organization concerned. There is, however, always a clear reputational risk when there are safety implications to the problem that occasioned the recall. Laptops suddenly bursting into flames fall into this category. As one blogger put it, "it's only a matter of time before this happens on a plane." A burning or exploding laptop is also highly photogenic. That particular picture is worth a lot more than a thousand words.

Dell managed the recall in an exemplary way. Four years on, a Google search for "dell battery recall" produced Dell websites with information on the recall as the first four matches. Dell was proactive in putting out its messages and, importantly, addressing the actual problem. The PR campaign was awarded a Public Relations Society of America Silver Anvil for its competence and professionalism.

Interestingly, Dell didn't manufacture the batteries concerned: they were a Sony product. Dell avoided the tempting – but ultimately fruitless – blame game. Dell sold the batteries as an integral part of a Dell-badged product. Dell put those batteries into its laptops and, quite rightly, accepted full responsibility for the disaster.

Learnings

Dell got this one pretty much spot-on. Communicate as openly and transparently as you can. Accept the blame – even if there is a basis on which you might pass the buck. Communicate directly with your customers. (As a company that manufactures to order, Dell was in a good position to do this, as it had direct contact details for a great many customers.) Address the issue and replace the faulty product. Apologize, profusely, for the inconvenience.

☑ What Dell did right

- It owned up and fixed the problem.
- It put the information out there in an easily accessible way.

SELF BRANDJACK A product problem puts the reputation of the company at risk of going up in flames.

7 How one sleepy tech highlighted Comcast's failings
June 2006

In June 2006, Brian Finkelstein's customer service problems with Comcast left him with no choice but to call out a technician. Brian had already encountered serious problems with the technical support *help*line. The technician came to Brian's home, but could not immediately fix the problem, so he too had to call the *help*line, and was kept waiting just as long. Finally, the technician dozed off, phone in hand, on Brian's couch.

This was too good an opportunity for Brian, a law student at Georgetown University, to miss. He filmed the sleeping technician and created a YouTube video. The video, titled "A Comcast technician asleep on my couch," was brief, but carried all the messages that Comcast dreaded. Set to "I need some sleep" by the Eels, it showed the technician sleeping peacefully. Shots of the technician were interspersed with slides, in the style of black-and-white silent movies, which bore comments "thanking" Comcast for such things as its unreliable service and the four-hour appointment windows. The video was amusing enough to instantly go viral on YouTube, with 300,000 hits in a few days. Comcast became the object of much (frankly deserved) ridicule. The employee was promptly fired.

In many ways, none of this is very new. Comcast and other utility companies have often had problems with customer service. It may be particularly embarrassing that a technician fell asleep on the job, but he would never have fallen asleep if the call center had only kept him waiting for a minute and a half. And if he had not fallen asleep, but still been kept waiting for an hour or so, the customer experience would not have been any better. But this is the power of social media. A few neatly edited moments of footage can create a video entertaining enough to go viral. If it had just been an isolated incident, Comcast could have laughed it off. But it was illustrative of wider customer service failings, and that meant it was extremely serious for the company. One embarrassing incident could never have been fatal to the company, but as a focal point for widespread customer dissatisfaction, it possibly could.

Learnings

Comcast treated the video as a "serious wakeup call," according to Jenni Moyer, senior director, corporate communications – network & operations.[4] The company decided it was necessary to reconnect with its customers. Senior management initiated a national listening tour, consulting with customers about their experience of Comcast, and also asking customer-facing staff what they needed to do their job better.

The result of the listening tour was "significant operational changes in the way we interact with customers," according to Moyer. There are now 11 operational centers conducting interactive network diagnostics. When a customer calls, the operator can identify which services the customer subscribes to, how old the equipment and connections are, and often diagnose any problems with the infrastructure. There has also been significant investment in diagnostic tools for the fiber network. Four-hour appointment windows have been reduced to two–three hours, with the hope of reducing them further. There is a $20 credit to the customer if the appointment time is missed. Technicians are equipped with handheld devices and laptops that directly interrogate the system and provide guidance on how to deal with the problem.

But these changes do not mean that the conversation with customers is over. The strategy now is to engage directly and transparently in social media. Comcast monitors the whole range of social media for indications of customer dissatisfaction. Previously, the strategy was to contact the customer individually and offer to help. But now Comcast engages publicly, with customer service personnel identifying themselves as being from Comcast, and offering to help.

Comcast faced a classic brandjacking crisis. For customers, the best possible interaction with a customer helpline is none at all. The best situation is if the customer experience never goes wrong in the first place. So, the starting point of the helpline needs to be that things have already gone wrong. All the days that the Internet worked perfectly are as nothing compared to your experience of the day it went wrong. To put it bluntly, no one even notices the service going right, and the Comcast brand will always be judged on the customer experience on the worst day. The challenge is to make sure that even the worst day goes as smoothly as possible. To do that means engaging openly with the customer, which seems to be Comcast's approach.

Another question worth asking is this: Was Comcast right to sack the technician? Was he made a scapegoat for wider customer service failings? Most of the media coverage of the issue mentioned that the technician was fired, but there was little sympathy for him in any of the coverage. Speaking to the author in 2010, the company, without defending the technician, recognized that it got things wrong, corporately. That is why it moved to address these issues. That said, the technician was most certainly at fault, even if his fault was a symptom of something much wider.

When Jeff Jarvis became the face of dissatisfied Dell customers, the company brought him inside to help reengineer its customer services and subsequently used him as the face of the new Dell. Could Comcast have used its sleepy technician or its dissatisfied customer in the same way, expressly linking its changes to the embarrassing incident? It is difficult to judge, without knowing anything about the personal capabilities of the individuals, whether this could ever have been a viable strategy. But one point worth noting is that in researching this case study, I had to approach Comcast directly to find out what its response to this brandjacking was. There are not many case studies already in existence. It seems that Comcast did not trumpet its response to the wake-up call, but instead got on with fixing the problem. This was probably the right call. Loudly announcing a new initiative, which required considerable investment in technical and human infrastructure to implement, would have raised expectations much faster than it would have raised customer service standards. It would have been an invitation to journalists and bloggers to write endless "same old Comcast" stories.

☒ What Comcast did wrong

- Getting into a situation where this incident could be seen as emblematic of a wider problem was the disaster. Its response to the problem once it had arisen seems to have been spot-on.

☑ What Comcast did right

- It quickly recognized that this was not an isolated incident, but part of a wider problem, and turned its attention to fixing that.
- It has proved tempting for companies facing a similar crisis to loudly proclaim what they are doing about it, before the problem is fixed. This is to get things backwards, and Comcast recognized that the right thing was to address the issues first, then talk about what had been done.

STAFF BRANDJACK Staff misconduct highlights wider customer failings.

8 The ad that Starbucks didn't make, but couldn't counter

August 2006

A spoof advert for a Starbucks Frappuccino caused a bit of a stir. It was simply one girl talking to camera about how good the product was, but also contrasting the cost with the price of sustaining the life of a child living in a refugee camp in Africa. She said nothing bad about Starbucks – in fact, she lavishly praised the product as delicious – but there was a strong, implicit condemnation of the coffee chain's customers who spend more on luxuries than it costs to keep starving children alive.

There's a logical response. Why pick on Starbucks? People in the West spend more, daily, on many other luxuries, but this contrast seems especially sharp, and Starbucks was also under fire for its treatment of suppliers in Ethiopia at the time. And, let's face it, no one is ever going to win a PR campaign by saying "giving up coffee won't help as much as giving up cosmetics or perfume."

According to the company Social Media Influence, it was this experience that led Starbucks to take social media seriously – something it has certainly done over the past few years. Starbucks has always maintained that "it's all about you" and that it is "your Starbucks." This made it an especially suitable business model for the social media age. In March 2008, it opened a dedicated website, http://mystarbucksidea.force.com, which generated 70,000 customer suggestions for the product range or service proposition in its first 12 months. As a result of a customer suggestion, customers who vote on the website get a free coffee. Although run on a standalone website, My Starbucks Idea is regularly pressed as part of the corporate website, the Facebook page, the YouTube channel, and the Twitter feed. It is a fully integrated social media campaign promoting crowdsourcing.

By March 2010, Starbucks was claiming to have implemented over 50 ideas submitted through My Starbucks Idea or through the "partner," that is, employee, equivalent. John Moore at Brand Autopsy ripped shreds off this claim, pointing out that some of the employee ideas, however worthy, have no impact at all on the customer experience, for example electronic pay stubs.[5] Other ideas were clearly in the pipeline or had been introduced in other markets prior to being rolled out in the US home market. I am not sure this part of the criticism is wholly relevant. Nonetheless, it seems to be true that the ideas under discussion were popular with the Starbucks community. The ideas submitted by customers don't have to be wholly original to be part of a crowdsourcing experiment.

Learnings

This is a remarkable case study, because the inciting incident – the video contrasting the price of a Frappuccino with the cost of keeping a child in a refugee camp alive – and the response – huge engagement in social media and crowdsourcing – are unrelated to each other.

Starbucks could have responded with a strengthened corporate social responsibility (CSR) campaign, for example a sponsored goat for every store. But this would never have solved the issue in the critical video. Whatever Starbucks does, there will still be poverty in the developing world, and the contrast between the lifestyles of people in the West and in much of Africa will remain stark. This is particularly the case in failed states or war zones – the issue of refugee camps raised in the video. Starbucks can contribute to alleviating these problems, but will still be open to the criticism that it could do more.

The crowdsourcing experiment seems to be a successful one, and to set a standard for the industry.

☑ What Starbucks did right

- It ignored the issue in the "ad," and changed the subject.

- It engaged heavily with social media, creating a community for what is, essentially, a transactional product.
- It has set a new industry standard for crowdsourcing products.

IIII➤ What it might have done differently

- It could have boosted its CSR activity, but this would not have affected the issues raised in the ad, and kept the focus in an uncomfortable area.

ETHICS BRANDJACK	The video highlights an ethical issue, not necessarily by Starbucks, but putting the company in a bad light.

9 Green my Apple
September 2006

This was, perhaps, the education of Greenpeace. The campaign that taught the NGO how to brandjack. It arose from the notorious secrecy surrounding the Apple Corporation.

Greenpeace launched its electronics campaign – to get consumer electronics companies to phase out the use of certain chemicals – in 2004. In 2006, it produced a rank order of how companies were faring. Dell and Lenovo reacted to the challenge. Greenpeace was surprised to discover that Apple had not. Perhaps it should not have been. Apple has always been hip and trendy. It has been popular with young, trendy people who see themselves as nonconformist or rebellious. This is much the same demographic as Greenpeace reaches, which may be why the NGO thought Apple would be responsive to its demands. But Apple has also always been very much a closed system. It has always been secretive and does not generally prioritize consumer research. Apple doesn't seek to find out what people think is trendy: it designs its products and *makes* them fashionable. In short, it is not a company that is very good at listening.

The result was that Greenpeace had to rethink its whole approach to the campaign. The group wanted to co-opt Apple customers – its fans – into the campaign. It wanted the fans to demand change.

As Greenpeace puts it:

> In considering how we might win improved policies from Apple, we knew one thing for certain: Apple might tune out Greenpeace, but they would

never tune out their customers. Apple's famously loyal fan base was the one force on the planet that was guaranteed to get the attention of Apple CEO Steve Jobs.

So we decided this was to be a very different Greenpeace campaign, one in which we would turn over the reigns [sic] to Apple's customers. We would stand in the shoes of Apple fans, we would speak as fellow believers in the wizards of Cupertino, and we'd try to channel waves of Apple Love at corporate headquarters.

The result was the launch of the "Green my Apple" website in September 2006, the first words of which were, "We love Apple."[6]

This approach of focusing on customers to demand change was to prove the basis of many future campaigns. In the case of Sinar Mas and APP, it means focusing not on the customers directly, but on *their* customers. Consumers demand change from Nestlé and, as a result, the corporation starts to boycott Sinar Mas (see CS 47).

The campaign was widely praised, including by the International Association of Business Communicators, which called it "virtuoso activism."[7] It developed many techniques that Greenpeace was later to hone, including aggregation websites and spoof videos on YouTube. And it was successful. In 2007, Steve Jobs announced that the company would begin phasing out the chemicals on the NGO's hit list.

Learnings

Apple certainly learned that it needs to listen to its customers. It remains a secretive company, and will not announce timetables for its future plans. In 2010, three years after Greenpeace was claiming victory, Apple still would not tell the group how its tests were proceeding.

The most important learnings here were by Greenpeace. This was the prototype for future campaigns targeting Unilever (CS 20), Nestlé (CS 38), Burger King (CS 47), and Mattel (CS 71), which would set new standards in the field of global communications.

CUSTOMER REVOLT BRANDJACK	NGO mobilizes consumers against multinational.
AGGREGATION BRANDJACK	Customers are brought together at a fan website.
ETHICS BRANDJACK	NGO injects environmental thinking into a highly secretive business.

10 **Walmarting across America**

September 2006

It was a beautiful story, and a tremendous PR scoop for Walmart. An ordinary young couple were traveling across America in a motorhome and parking overnight in Walmart parking lots. The title of the blog they were writing was especially powerful. "Walmarting" has been used as a term of abuse to describe the way large stores move in and drive smaller operations out of business. This sort of term rankles with corporations. Think of the way McDonald's petitioned for the word "McJobs" to be taken out of the dictionary. (The head of media at Rolls-Royce once told me that it is perfect branding when your brand name becomes a verb or an adjective. That's true, for Rolls-Royce, but I guess it depends what the adjective is taken to mean.)

As Jim and Laura continued their journey, they met numerous happy Walmart employees, and told heartwarming tales, such as that of Cragg Thompson, whose $300,000 bill for treating his son's cardiomyopathy was met through his Walmart employee medical insurance. All great stuff. But some people started to nasally detect the presence of a rodent from the superfamily Muroidea.

Jonathan Rees, a labor historian and associate professor at Colorado State, asserted flatly: "Walmart has hired fake people."[8] Investigations by *Business Week* revealed that the academic's charge was simply untrue. Jim and Laura were not "fake" in the way that "Claire" of the Vichy blog was. "Claire" was a composite of several people blogging from L'Oréal's headquarters and a photograph of a model (see CS 3). Jim and Laura were real people, who really were traveling across America using Walmart parking lots. As far as we can tell, all their accounts of meeting Walmart employees were also true. What Jim and Laura did wrong was to fail to declare their financial relationship with Walmart.

This is a gross breach of journalistic ethics. Such ethics should apply in social media, but it is not clear that any such conventions exist. Incidentally, taking vox pops from employees who are unrepresentative of employees as a whole and writing them up without declaring that a whole bunch of other employees told you something different is *not* considered a breach of journalistic ethics, and the MSM, print and broadcast, do this all the time. It is failing to declare a financial interest that puts this one into the unethical category.

Business Week was able to reveal the full story behind "Walmarting across America." According to Laura St Clair, the idea for the journey and the blog came from her and her partner Jim (full name withheld). Laura was already a member of the pro-Walmart group, Working Families for Walmart, which is a real group with real members, although it was founded with support from Edelman, the leading PR company that advises Walmart.

While Laura insists she wasn't misleading anyone, and the blog did contain a banner advert for Working Families for Walmart, the full extent of Walmart's financial support for Laura and Jim was never disclosed. It is easy to see why Laura may have felt she was acting with integrity: she was a supporter of Walmart before she started writing the blog, and was probably only saying what she really believed. But social media denizens require more than just integrity, they require transparency too. The financial support *should* have been declared, and the fact that it wasn't reflects badly on Walmart and Edelman, as well as on Laura and Jim.

Learnings

Social media are defined by engagement and authenticity. The Trust Barometer – conducted, ironically, by Edelman – regularly reveals that people are inclined to trust "people like me" far ahead of corporate spokespeople. This was both the insight into, and the problem of, this campaign. A blog that purports to be by "ordinary people" will have a high trust quotient, but faking this is likely to be uncovered, and will damage your trust immeasurably. Richard Edelman, CEO and son of the company's founder, has a high profile in the blogosphere and on Twitter, so it is unfortunate that his company was caught out like this.

Being paid for something is not, of itself, a problem. Failing to declare that you are being paid is. Jonathan Rees consults for the AFL-CIO (the umbrella federation for US unions), so is presumably paid by it, but as long as he declares that when he is attacking non-union companies like Walmart, he is behaving ethically.

The rules of social media are only just emerging. Everyone agrees – at least in Western countries – that it would be a clear breach of ethics on both sides if a PR professional paid a journalist to write favorable copy about a product. Any express linking of a reward – such as the gift of a product – to the review that follows is unethical. A journalist should disclose any financial or in-kind relationship with the company they are covering.

But how do these rules apply in the blogosphere? If we are to apply journalistic standards, it would have been down to Jim and Laura to disclose their financial relationship with Walmart – a company that advertised openly on their blog. But lines of reporting and accountability are absent in the blogosphere. Jim and Laura may not have realized that the obligation to disclose fell on them.

> ### ☒ What the parties did wrong
>
> - Jim and Laura, Edelman, and Walmart should all have realized that in any gray area, it is always best to err on the side of transparency.

> ### ☑ What Edelman did right
>
> - Richard Edelman owned up to the misjudgment, apologized, and refused to comment further. It is quite appropriate that the PR company should take the blame rather than try to divert it to the client or the bloggers. It was also appropriate that the CEO – especially given his personal profile in social media – should personally take the hit on this.

SELF BRANDJACK Misjudgment by the company leaves it wide open to criticism.

11 When a multinational fakes a teenage blog
Autumn 2006

From the moment it was launched, the website alliwantforxmasisapsp.com came under fire as a cringeworthy attempt by a multinational to look cool and impersonate user-generated content. The back story was two teenagers – one of whom, most commentators thought, looked about 30 – who were campaigning to get their parents to buy a PSP (PlayStation Portable). The site had embarrassing "user" comments like "this is the best site ever," a view that is not likely to have occurred spontaneously to anyone.

Text on the site was entirely lower case and full of text-style misspellings, such as "ur" and "nxt." (Oddly, the site uses "ur" to mean "your" and not "you are.") Apparently, one of the largest consumer electronics companies in the world didn't know the difference between text speak and web speak. It had the air of a dad who thought he was as cool as his kids and didn't quite get it. The video was especially pilloried in the blogosphere.

Unlike the real blog that Edelman and Walmart supported covertly, this blog was entirely fake. The "teenagers" whose lives it described were fictional, and don't even seem to have been believable. The blog was not only in breach of the principle of transparency but also, based on the contemporaneous criticism, seems to have been done rather badly. It wasn't even well disguised. The domain name was registered to marketing agency, Zipatoni.

None of this is to say that sales of the PSP were not booming in the run-up to Xmas 2006. The product had been launched in North America in March 2005, so 2006 was the first full year of sales, but the second Christmas. The product was generally considered to have sold well. Sales have lagged behind the Nintendo DS, but PSP is the most successful handheld games system manufactured by any company other than Nintendo.

Sony responded very clearly, stating in December 2006:[9]

> Busted. Nailed. Snagged. As many of you have figured out (maybe our speech was a little too funky fresh???), Peter isn't a real hip-hop maven and this site was actually developed by Sony. Guess we were trying to be just a little too clever. From this point forward, we will just stick to making cool products, and use this site to give you nothing but the facts on the PSP. Sony Computer Entertainment America

Learnings

Sony confessed very quickly. You could argue that it had no choice, since the blog was not only a fake, but also a bad one. One criticism was that it underestimated the intelligence of its target market, but the company responded that it had just launched the most complex gaming console ever, so it could hardly be accused of underestimating the intelligence of American teenagers. Perhaps managers there just overestimated their own cool quotient.

Sony has learned from its experience, and is now fully engaged with social media. It has been widely praised for its pioneering use of Twitter games as part of its engagement.

☒ What Sony did wrong

- It faked a blog, in breach of (by then) well-established protocols.
- It underestimated the audience's ability to see through something that was nakedly fake.
- It thought it was cool when really just "dad dancing."

☑ What Sony did right

- It apologized immediately.
- It invested heavily in genuine, and open, engagement with social media.

SELF BRANDJACK	Misconduct by a multinational leaves it wide open to criticism.
FAKE BRANDJACK	A hoax will always reflect badly on you.

12 How passengers slammed an airline from the runway where they were stranded
February 2007

On Valentine's Day 2007, JFK Airport in New York was hit by serious bad weather and numerous flights were canceled or delayed. Many airlines were affected, but none as badly as JetBlue Airways. And it didn't stop when the weather cleared up. JetBlue was slower than other airlines to get its schedule back to normal. But the most devastating aspect for the airline was a single flight, stranded on the runway for seven or eight hours. Conditions were poor, with reports of power failures and flight crew having to open the doors to keep the air breathable. In brandjacking terms, the defining feature of the crisis was the passengers' use of video cameras in their cell phones to record their plight for YouTube.

JetBlue is a remarkable business. It is a low-cost airline, but unlike the low-cost airlines of Europe. Its business plan is built on superior service combined with lower costs. Its staff generally take a fairly friendly and quirky approach (although for an exception to this, see JetBlue CS 45), and the company has generally had high customer satisfaction scores. That it was particularly badly hit by the snowstorms of February 2007 reflected rapid growth and, consequently, a poor communications infrastructure. JetBlue was less good than other airlines at getting replacement crews and equipment into place when scheduled crew could not make it to the right airport.

This all came together in the experiences of passengers on a single flight, who were able to phone the media from the plane and conduct live on-air interviews in which they heavily criticized airline management. As well as the live interviews, passengers were able to record "video postcards" about their experience of freezing on the runway at JFK, including the inadequacy of the toilet facilities and the complete lack of information as to how long they were likely to remain stranded. The airline was unable to arrange a gate, and eventually had to ask the Port Authority to evacuate the plane by bus.

Learnings

JetBlue's response was first rate. First, it focused on dealing with the issues. The passengers affected by delayed or canceled flights were given full refunds and flight vouchers for a free round trip. Those trapped on the runway were given additional compensation, which cost the airline millions.

David G. Neeleman, JetBlue's CEO, described himself as being "humiliated and mortified" by his airline's failure to handle the crisis properly.[10] And he sounded it, with *The New York Times* reporting that his voice cracked several times during the interview. Neeleman was completely open in his interview, accepting that the airline's management was not strong enough and the communications infrastructure had not kept pace with the rapid expansion of the passenger service. Neeleman was also frank about how he was going to solve the problem.

Seven days after the incident, JetBlue launched a Customer Bill of Rights.[11] The first point in the charter is about information, a particularly sore point with the passengers stranded on Valentine's Day. It also promises specific compensation amounts for delays of over an hour. For those delayed on the tarmac, free access to the airline's in-flight entertainment is promised. The Bill of Rights talks about JetBlue's mission to bring the humanity back to air travel, something for which it has been highly praised throughout its existence.

Unsurprisingly, for a company that prides itself on its human engagement, JetBlue is serious about social media including Twitter. A quick Google search turned up a blog by a customer headed "How JetBlue used Twitter to treat me like a human."[12] The headline almost echoes the wording of JetBlue's mission, but if this is a fake, it has been cleverly done as a believable one, and not at all like the unconditional enthusiasm of Sony's fake blog. The customer complains that on a flight from Boston to Denver, the thermostat was set too high and he was hot. He tweeted the complaint on his arrival at Denver, got an almost immediate response: "Thanks for the heads up! (Sometimes flight crews get overzealous flying from cold to cold!)." This is a textbook response to a minor grumble. The company doesn't get defensive, but thanks the customer for the information. It maintains the informal and offbeat style. Even the badly used exclamation points seem to add something to the message. There is no cause to complain about either spelling or grammar. Very well judged.

On the return journey, the same customer arrives at the airport to find no one there to check him in. A quick Twitter complaint, and HQ is on to it. They alert the general manager on site and ask how many others are waiting in line. The interaction is quick, helpful, and human. What could have been an unpleasant experience is leavened by information and feedback.

☒ What JetBlue did wrong

- It failed to realize that its rapid growth left it overstretched and poorly placed to deal with (entirely predictable) abnormal conditions.
- It failed to respond quickly enough, even with information. Later initiatives, such as free access to in-flight entertainment, could have been actioned immediately.

☑ What JetBlue did right

- It confessed, sounding genuine, humble, and apologetic.
- It compensated all the customers affected.
- It acted immediately with measures that could be implemented straightaway, such as enforceable promises of compensation.
- It has engaged with social media, carrying the informal and quirky style over into Twitter, where it is highly appropriate.

CUSTOMER REVOLT BRANDJACK	Mistreated customers have immediate access to platforms to criticize the company.

13 What happens when the media pretend to have filmed rats in your restaurant?

February 2007

They say a picture is worth a thousand words. A video is worth a great deal more. No amount of fast talking and writing can combat the memorable visual image of rats infesting a restaurant. It is hard to put such a video into context, even if the facts are on your side. Worse, what would once have been a local story in New York City clocked 1.2 million hits on YouTube and the worldwide brand took a hit because of a problem in one restaurant.

As it happens, some of the facts were on Taco Bell's side. The clincher is probably that the restaurant was closed at the time of the filming. It was closed for construction work designed to enhance pest control, but while the work was going on, the opportunity to seal the basement was limited. The restaurant had been cited for pest issues – both rats and cockroaches – in the past, but had passed a health inspection less than a week before the video was filmed. The restaurant had scored a 10 on a scale where 0 is good and 28 is a fail. While not perfect, it is better than scores of 14 and 16 in previous years, and these were also passing grades.

But none of these facts is as memorable as a picture of rats running all over a restaurant, albeit a closed restaurant, with the filming being done through the window. The company's response was quick and clear. A widely quoted statement included the following:

> This store will remain closed until this issue is completely resolved. The health department inspected the restaurant yesterday and we will ask them to return when work is complete to give the restaurant a clean bill of health.

Note that this portion of the statement quoted by CNN, Fox News, and others says the restaurant would remain closed, but does *not* say it was closed when the filming took place. An Associated Press (AP) despatch run on MSNBC also did not say this at the time, although a follow-up story on MSNBC the next week, also from AP, did mention this.

Taco Bell is a franchised brand, and the parent company (Yum! Brands Inc.) also owns the brands KFC and Pizza Hut. The company temporarily closed down all the restaurants owned by the franchisee while it arranged for inspections. This seems a little unfair, given that the footage could more accurately be described as rats on a construction site rather than rats in a restaurant. But Yum! was in a situation where it had to be seen to be acting, and setting the news agenda.

Learnings

It is easy to feel sorry for Taco Bell in this situation. The meme started in the MSM – the footage was filmed by a crew working for a breakfast TV program – and continued to be filtered by them. The social media connection was purely the viral YouTube video. And the MSM had no interest in reporting this as a rat infestation of a construction site, because that isn't news.

Nonetheless, Taco Bell has responded pretty well with its social media strategy. By 2010, Taco Bell had 3.5 million fans of its Facebook page, more than Coke and Pepsi combined. Three years later, the figure stood at more than 10 million but, unsurprisingly, the soda brands had shot ahead. Its global Twitter feeds are light and humorous, and it has several subsidiary feeds such as Taco Bell Truck and Taco Bell Foundation. It was early in developing an iPhone app and a popular YouTube channel. It now has all sorts of ways to respond to future unfair media coverage.

☒ What the MSM did wrong

- They presented this story in a very dishonest way.

☑ What Taco Bell did right

- It didn't whine about the unfairness of it all, but acted promptly and firmly.
- It introduced a strong social media engagement strategy.

▐▶ What Taco Bell might do in the future

- Caught in the same situation again, Taco Bell could promote the original video on its own YouTube channel along with its own video, showing that the restaurant is actually a construction site.

| **FAKE** **BRANDJACK** | This story was, quite simply, faked, in a truly gross breach of media ethics. |

14 Greenpeace goes social, and Kleenex pays the price
March 2007

By 2010, Greenpeace had come to set an enviable standard in social media PR, so it is a little surprising that it took the group so long to take its five-year campaign against Kimberly-Clark into social media. Given what Greenpeace itself says about the lessons it learned from "Green my Apple" (CS 9), it looks as though that campaign was absolutely seminal.

Its Kleercut campaign, aimed at saving, in particular, Canada's Boreal forests, was launched in November 2004, with trucks mocked up as Kleenex boxes released into the wild of North America's roads for what would turn out to be a five-year campaign. The first video advert was launched in December 2005, yet it seems to have been a year later that the ad was first uploaded to YouTube. The campaign continued in classic Greenpeace style. There were numerous photogenic stunts, often including the three trucks. At Kimberly-Clark's AGMs, there were demonstrations outside and resolutions placed inside. Reports were issued. Universities decided to boycott Kimberly-Clark products. The Forest Friendly 500 group of businesses joined the boycott. Ads were placed in newspapers, including *The New York Times* and the *International Herald Tribune*. They climbed things. They hung banners.

It was March 2007 that they "punk'd" a Kleenex commercial shoot in New York City. The advertising campaign's theme was Let It Out. People would talk about emotional experiences in their lives. If they cried, and used a Kleenex, their footage might be used in the advert, in which case they would be paid $200. Greenpeace managed to record the slightly cynical briefings being given to participants. It protested, and made its own film, which was posted to YouTube within days. In October 2007, Greenpeace released a new YouTube video of activists disrupting a commercial shoot in Chicago. In November, the famous Greenpeace tactic of scaling a building and hanging a banner from it had become a "digital banner hang." At an address to the University of Wisconsin by Thomas Falk, Kimberly-Clark's CEO, it managed to swap both his PowerPoint presentation (for one rather less flattering, obviously) and the menus at the subsequent dinner. Greenpeace was getting the hang of the social stuff.

The campaign took another two years to be successful, but in August 2009, Kimberly-Clark agreed a new sourcing strategy for its wood fiber with Greenpeace, so the boycott was called off.

Learnings

There is little doubt that Greenpeace learned a lot about social media PR from its Kleercut campaign. The group that now sets the standard was making its first forays into a new world – one where its global network of volunteer supporters could be deployed in asymmetric warfare against its enemies. This was a defining moment for Greenpeace, and thus for the future of digital PR.

Kimberly-Clark was learning at the same time. Ironically, the Let It Out campaign was a new experiment in social media for the brand too. The advertising concept was to create an emotional link with a product that had always been fairly functional. This was classic social media – and therefore PR, rather than advertising – material. People could share their Kleenex experiences, in a way hardly relevant to blowing your nose or, well, other uses of tissue paper.

Now that Kimberly-Clark has reached a deal with Greenpeace, it is allied with an organization that has a tremendously motivated group of social media activists.

✓ What Kleenex did right

- It recognized the value of social media, probably before Greenpeace did, with the Let It Out campaign.

☒ What Kleenex did wrong

- It failed to see Pandora's box. With Greenpeace engaged in social media, the rules have changed forever.
- It took a while for the company to see that it was overmatched and overwhelmed.

☒ What Greenpeace did wrong

- It was surprisingly slow to see the value of social media. Given its assets – highly professional campaigning teams and an extensive network of volunteers – these media could have been designed for Greenpeace. In a sense they were – the Internet was, literally, invented to promote revolution.

✓ What Greenpeace did right

- Once it engaged, it learned very fast, and was pretty soon integrating social media with its established repertoire of visual stunts and media relations.

ETHICS BRANDJACK Greenpeace forces the company to change the way it addresses the key supply issue of wood fiber, ensuring it is environmentally sourced.

15 A CEO engages, but gets caught in anonymous blogging
July 2007

Whole Foods Market is consistently ranked as one of the most environmentally responsible companies in the US. It specializes in expensive (it is sometimes called Whole Paycheck), healthy, organic foods. It is popular in liberal enclaves with a high average educational level, such as college towns, including Austin, Texas, where it was founded. With an educated, trendy, granola-eating customer base, the company has been something of a trendsetter in its social media strategy. Until John Mackey, its founder and CEO, was exposed in an anonymous blogging scandal, that is.

Given the market in which it operates, it is hardly surprising that Whole Foods Market was heavily engaged in social media pretty early on. Especially when compared to other bricks-and-mortar grocery outlets, Whole Foods was a pioneer. This is why the "Rahodeb" scandal was a shock and a particularly serious blow. It led to Mackey facing an investigation by the Securities and Exchange Commission (SEC). Although Mackey was cleared of any illegality, the notion that his behavior was both inappropriate and unethical is harder to dispel.

On July 11, 2007, the *Wall Street Journal* revealed that Mackey was the face behind Rahodeb, the anonymous blogger who had been participating in financial discussions on a Yahoo! bulletin board for seven years.[13] Rahodeb had posted over 1,000[14] contributions to business and financial discussions, all pseudonymously. On occasions, Rahodeb wrote comments that promoted Whole Foods Market and criticized its rival, Wild Oats Markets. He described Whole Foods as "hot" and Wild Oats as a "dud."

In March 2006, Rahodeb wrote:

> OATS has lost their way and no longer has a sense of mission or even a well-thought-out theory of the business. They lack a viable business model that they can replicate. They are floundering around hoping to find a viable strategy that may stop their erosion. Problem is that they lack the time and the capital now.

A year later, Mackey, as CEO of Whole Foods Market, was launching a takeover bid for Wild Oats. None of this is to say that Mackey did not believe the criticism he made of Wild Oats and its management. That might be exactly why he wanted to take the company over – because he believed he could do a better job of giving the business a sense of direction. But should he not have been willing to put his name to both his criticisms of Wild Oats and his praise of Whole Foods? In one particularly embarrassing moment, Rahodeb responded to bloggers who criticized the photo of John Mackey in the Whole Foods Annual Report, saying "I think he looks cute."

More than one poster on the Yahoo! Finance bulletin board had suggested that Rahodeb was a pseudonym for John Mackey prior to his unmasking, although it is unclear in hindsight if they genuinely believed this, or were teasing Rahodeb for his enthusiastic boosting of Whole Foods. When the *Wall Street Journal* broke the story, based on documents filed with the SEC for its investigation of the Whole Foods' bid for Wild Oats, the reaction on Yahoo! Finance was a mixture of anger and amusement.

In August 2007, a Federal Appeals Court allowed the Whole Foods takeover of Wild Oats to proceed, and in May 2008 the SEC cleared Mackey of any wrongdoing. Mackey began blogging again – this time openly – and has admitted to an error of judgment, but not to any ethical breach.

Mackey again came under fire from campaign groups, and Facebook groups were established to call for a boycott of Whole Foods, over his personal – and public – stance on healthcare reform. Mackey's political journey has been a long one. He says that as a student he was a democratic socialist, but his experience as an entrepreneur led him to read the works of free-market advocates, such as Milton Friedman, Friedrich Hayek, and Ayn Rand, who converted him to libertarianism. It is very likely that many Whole Food Markets' customers wrongly assumed that Mackey – a vegan, an outspoken advocate of animal welfare, and one of America's leading proponents of the organic movement – subscribed to a leftwing orthodoxy. His stance on healthcare may therefore have taken his customers by surprise.

In a *Wall Street Journal* article, Mackey was critical of President Obama's plans for healthcare reform and advocated a mixture of catastrophic insurance and health savings accounts for ordinary health expenditures. This is the model that Whole Foods uses for its staff, and the company has been rated as one of the 25 best companies to work for by *Forbes*. He also advocated allowing consumers to purchase health insurance across state lines. (Full disclosure, in a much less high-profile column for *Lake Champlain Weekly*, this author has advocated similar positions.) *Progressive Review* led calls for consumers to boycott Whole Foods over the personal views of its CEO, and a number of Facebook groups issued the same appeal.

Learnings

Social media were never new to Whole Foods. By the time it developed a presence on Facebook and, subsequently, Twitter, there was already user-generated content on the Whole Foods blog. (That's the official one, on the corporate website, obviously.) The original Facebook page was able to replicate that content for discussions about recipes and so on. There are reasons why Whole Foods' customers feel like a community and are clearly connected to the brand and its values. People choose Whole Foods for a number of reasons, but rarely just because it is the closest grocery store and never because it is the cheapest. The largest number of outlets and lowest prices are valuable niches in the grocery market, but Whole Foods does not occupy either of them. People choose Whole Foods for the things that the retailer values: quality products, organic food, animal welfare, and so on. It is probably the case that the healthcare issue became significant for some customers because they assumed that these values arrived as a package with a particular set of political views, and felt genuinely hurt to learn that they didn't.

Given this sense of community, it is not surprising that the Whole Foods' customer base had always included people willing to participate in discussions about recipes and so on. People rank and critique the recipes. If you ask a question about a recipe, you are as likely to get a response from within the community as from Whole Foods itself. There is a sense of identity about choosing this particular retailer, which does not exist to the same extent for other grocery stores. This mass of user-generated content created instant material for the Facebook page.

Twitter came later and, for the first year, the company maintained only one Twitter account. Later, the company decided to develop niche accounts for cheese, wine, and recipes. There are more than 150 accounts for individual stores. Whole Foods has more followers on Twitter than any other retailer. The main account had more than 1.8 million followers by October 2010 and 3.5 million three years later.

Whole Foods has invested in having people available, including experts – the cheese expert is described as having "a quadruple PhD in cheese" – to comment and lead discussions, but the sense of community around the brand was strong before the engagement in social media, which should be seen as reinforcing this rather than creating it.

Whole Foods sees its Facebook presence as being somewhat more passive than Twitter. Content is generally posted to the whole community, and not in messages backwards and forwards with individuals. Twitter can therefore be used for practical information, such as store opening times. Facebook is for longer posts, pictures, and video. Video would seem to be a natural spin-off from the recipe discussions. More than 1.4 million people "like" the main Whole Foods Market Facebook page and, to take a few random examples, over 22,000 like the page for the store in Piccadilly Circus, London, and more than 70,000 the page for New York.

Whole Foods continues to be highly praised for its social media presence. In 2011, Mashable Business listed five social media lessons to be learned from Whole Foods: make content increasingly relevant; go where your customers are; loosen control from the top; decide what channel to use for what purpose; and let the conversation happen.[15]

☒ What Whole Foods did wrong

- As he now acknowledges, John Mackey should have declared his interest in the blogging he did about Whole Foods and Wild Oats.
- He probably should have anticipated that his public stance on healthcare would have been opposed by much of his customer base.

☑ What Whole Foods did right

- Practically everything else. The market position of the company is ideal for developing a community, hence the sense of betrayal over both the anonymous blogging and the CEO's political views. Whole Foods has invested heavily, and wisely, in fostering this sense of community.

 SELF BRANDJACK   A misjudgment by the CEO left the company open to criticism, and even a SEC investigation. Taking a public stand that was out of line with most customers' values compounded this.

16 Brewer invites college kids to "get the party started," college kids get embarrassingly drunk, shock
November 2007

The Canadian operation of Molson Coors – the third largest US brewer – ran an innovative Facebook competition to find Canada's number one party school. It should be noted that "school" in this context refers to university-level education and the promotion was expressly targeted at 18- to 24-year-olds. Facebook, by contrast, is open to anyone over the age of 13. The promotion attracted a great deal of interest, but much of the coverage was negative. The invitation to "show us how you and your crew get the party started" produced photographs of very drunk people engaged in riotous behavior. Surely this cannot have been a surprise? But the image was totally at odds with the official position of the company, which is not to promote binge drinking or irresponsible behavior, but to promote responsible drinking.

The competition was supposed to find the number one party school – not, you understand, in any way to encourage binge drinking, but to encourage school spirit. The prize was a trip for five to Cancún in Mexico, to whoever loaded the largest number of photos. By the time the company canceled the competition, its Facebook page had more than 17,000 friends, but none of the hundreds of photos that had been submitted was on display.

By almost any measure, the contest was a failure. It certainly raised profile, but brewers are not usually short of profile on college campuses. That people would submit the sort of photographs that would embarrass them in later life, or even the following morning, is something the brewer should have considered as a possibility. While maintaining a public stance of opposing binge drinking, every brewer knows that such behavior goes on, and is especially prevalent in the targeted 18- to 24-year-old market. Obviously, the official position of Molson – and every other brewing company – is that alcohol is fun and contributes to a lively party even (perhaps especially) when consumed in moderation. But it is difficult to imagine how it did not see this embarrassment coming. The hostile reaction from college administrators and parents was entirely predictable.

Could it be that Molson absolutely anticipated the reaction? Failing to do so would have demonstrated a complete misunderstanding of this key market segment. Did it, perhaps, want to promote controversy on the theory that any publicity was good publicity? Or that the college administrators would come off as stuffy, leaving Molson looking like the champions of a good time? If so, its hurried climb-down was not only hypocritical but left it looking neither responsible nor as the champions of fun.

On the whole, I think we have to take Molson at its word and assume that it did not anticipate the reaction, or grossly underestimated the strength of it. This leaves Molson looking rather naive and foolish. In addition to the issue of irresponsible drinking, Molson should have considered the fact that Facebook is widely used by students under the legal age for drinking or purchasing alcohol. Indeed, in many parts of the US, Molson's home market, the legal age is 21, whereas this Canadian contest was expressly targeted at 18- to 24-year-olds. The contest would certainly have reached people of high school age and people outside Canada. Again, it is difficult to see how Molson would have failed to anticipate this.

Learnings

Within a year, Molson Coors was being cited in some quarters as an exemplar of good social media practice. In some senses, this should not be hard for it. Alhough a traditional, family-run company, Molson has a long history of engagement with its local communities. It also sees young people as a key part of its market. The company is now fully engaged with not just Facebook but also Twitter, Flickr, blogging, and video blogging.

Perhaps the key learnings from an early social media misstep are that, in social media, you sacrifice far more control than in other media – even in interactive settings such as a contest. This lack of control can lead to your campaign taking a direction that you did not anticipate or wish. Losing control is the price you pay for the engagement and credibility that social media bring. But when your product is controversial and used in ways that you would not wish to promote – and certainly would not wish to be seen to be promoting – the lack of control has clear risks. Molson seems to have been burned, but did not retreat from social media in any way. Instead, it is proceeding with rather more caution.

☒ What Molson did wrong

- It apparently forgot that Facebook operates in numerous juris-dictions with different legal ages for drinking and that its users are age 13 upwards.
- It failed to anticipate that college kids might get seriously and embarrassingly drunk – something completely out of line with Molson's stated purpose of promoting responsible drinking.
- It failed to realize that a competition that involved uploading photos to Facebook could get completely out of control.

☑ What Molson did right

- It moved on and learned, using its experience of community engagement in the real world to extend its engagement, especially with young people, in the digital space.

 In a staggering misjudgment, the company failed to see something completely obvious while its competition got out of control.

 Students provide embarrassing pictures.

Notes

1   BikeBiz, October 6, 2004, accessed online, 01/20/2014.
2   *Bloomberg Business Week*, January 16, 2008, accessed 01/20/2014.
3   Buzzmachine.com, June 21, 2005, accessed 01/20/2014.
4   Interviewed by the author.

5   Brand Autopsy: www.brandautopsy.com/2010/01/tough-love-for-starbucks.html, accessed 01/20/2014.

6   Greenpeace: www.greenpeace.org/international/en/news/features/greening-of-apple-310507, accessed 01/20/2014.

7   IABC: http://evaapp.typepad.com/iabcuk/activism/, accessed 01/20/2014.

8   *Business Week*, October 9, 2006, accessed 01/20/2014.

9   *The Guardian* Games Blog: www.theguardian.com/technology/gamesblog/2006/dec/11/newsonyviral, accessed 01/20/2014.

10   *New York Times*, February 19, 2007, accessed 01/20/2014.

11   JetBlue: www.jetblue.com/p/about/ourcompany/promise/Bill_Of_Rights.pdf, accessed 01/20/2014.

12   Dave's Here and Now: www.daveraffaele.com/2009/01/social-media-case-study-how-jetblue-used-twitter-to-treat-me-like-a-human, accessed 01/20/2014.

13   *Wall Street Journal*: online.wsj.com/news/articles/SB118418782959963745, accessed 01/20/2014.

14   *New York Times*: www.nytimes.com/2007/07/12/business/12foods.html, accessed 01/20/2014.

15   Mashable Business: http://mashable.com/2009/08/25/whole-foods/, accessed 01/20/2014.

The case studies: 2008–10

17 GMnext: greenwashing
January 2008

GMnext was a fascinating innovation by General Motors (GM) to involve publics in discussions about its car designs. Like Chevy Apprentice (see CS 5), it was an experiment in crowdsourcing, with the aim of involving people in discussions about product design and the environmental impact of its products. The site was launched to mark GM's centenary, and the publics were asked how GM should respond to the energy challenges of the next century. As Rainforest Action Network (RAN) put it: "typical corporate greenwashing, but with a new 'web 2.0' spin where the company pretends to care what the public thinks."[1]

Within days, RAN was claiming to have shut down portions of the site, as GM disabled commenting. GM accused some contributors of spamming the site with cut-and-paste abuse. RAN responded by posting a selection of the comments on its own blog, which were clear and reasoned arguments. Christopher Barger, GM's director of global communications technology, joined in the discussion on RAN's blog, claiming that the contributions cited by RAN were not typical of the problem GM had encountered, and GM continued to welcome comments of that type. This doesn't seem to have been precisely accurate, or at least not on the site in question, as GM did not merely introduce moderation to delete spam and abuse, but closed down the comments facility. Incidentally, RAN has a moderation policy on its own blog.

The mixed success of the Chevy Apprentice project should have set off warning bells inside GM before this project was given the go-ahead. Like Chevy Apprentice, it was sure to attract environmental critics of the company, including many who could never be appeased within GM's business model. The Chevy Apprentice project also attracted motoring enthusiasts – apparently in much greater number than the environmentalists – in a consumer engagement campaign with much to recommend it. It isn't clear how GM expected *this* wiki project to achieve the same level of engagement. It doesn't give consumers a feeling of ownership over existing brands, nor encourage brand loyalty in the way that the Apprentice scheme did.

GMnext was a wide-ranging scheme. It included a wiki-based history of the company in which employees and retired employees were particularly active.

It gave communities interested in GM the opportunity to post directly on the GM site and begin discussions there.

The conflict came over just four photographs posted by RAN on GMnext. GM disabled the comments section associated with the photographs but did not – contrary to some media claims – remove comments already posted. It insisted that the reason for disabling new comments was because of cut-and-paste spam comments and personally offensive comments, which were oveelming the site moderators. People participating in these threads were invited to participate elsewhere. This explanation has an odd feel to it. If activists were determinedly trying to shut conversation down, as GM implied, closing comments on those threads would not have helped. They would have shifted to other threads.

Nonetheless, GM did not abandon its attempts to engage. It replaced these discussions with interviews with experts, from within and outside GM. Members of the community submitted questions, not all of which could be put to the interviewee, and thus led to allegations of using only softball questions. GM insisted that it tried to use questions representative of those submitted.

Learnings

GM no longer uses the GMnext branding for its social media presence. The GMnext page on LinkedIn has been closed, although there are still videos on YouTube posted under that name. Although RAN and GM congratulated each other on their respective roles in getting this conversation going, it has not been easy to trace any results of the conversation, and GM's present blogs and Facebook pages seem more based on broadcasting messages than on conversation, although there are comment facilities on the Facebook page. GM has more than 0.5 million likes for its corporate Facebook page and, to choose one of its sub-brands at random, more than 2 million for Chevrolet.

☑ What GM did right

- It reached out and tried to engage with its communities, including staff, retired staff, customers, and activists. Christopher Barger even went on the RAN website to comment there.

☒ What GM did wrong

- It seemed to underestimate, again, the passion that activists were going to bring to the conversation.

A controversial company reaches out, but cannot handle the scale of the response.

 Environmental activists make life difficult for leading company.

 Activists prove more motivated than fans.

18 Target to the blogosphere: you're irrelevant
January 2008

Target is the second largest discount retailer in the US. Its market position differs slightly from Walmart and Kmart, in that it sees itself as slightly upscale and a little ahead of the trend. It doesn't exactly fit with that image to say to a blogger that the company doesn't deal with blogs, because it wants to focus its time on the media that reach its "guests" – which is Target speak for customers:

> Unfortunately we are unable to respond to your inquiry because Target does not participate with nontraditional media outlets … This practice … is in place to allow us to focus on publications that reach our core guest.[2]

As *The New York Times* put it: "Target to the blogosphere: you're irrelevant."

This can hardly be seen as the ahead-of-trend image that Target wishes to portray. Note, this incident came *after* Walmart had already been (falsely) accused of faking a blog (see CS 10). By 2008, blogs had been accepted as a core part of the media. Four years earlier, bloggers had been accredited as journalists by both major political parties in the US at their nominating conventions. By early 2008, Barack Obama was already riding his social media pre-eminence to a victory in the Democratic Party primaries. For Target to be still under the impression that blogs do not reach its target market as late as 2008 was a serious misjudgment.

Blogger Amy Jussel, of ShapingYouth.org, was both influential and a (self-described) loyal Target customer. She was complaining about an ad that showed a target with a woman spread-eagled on it. The bull's-eye was more or less behind the woman's crotch. "Targeting crotches with a bull's-eye is not the message we should be putting out there," she told *The New York Times*. The story raced around the blogosphere – which does not take kindly to being dissed – and was widely reported in the MSM. It was a significant blow to Target's younger, hipper image.

By 2009, Target was already being praised for its engagement with social media. The company has long given 5% of its income to charity under the slogan Bullseye Gives. In 2009, it opened up its Facebook page to let fans vote on which selected charities should receive the most funds. (It was a proportional allocation: if 25% favored a given charity, it would receive 25% of the funds.) This was praised as an innovative move, which makes it surprising that it has been dropped. It was only billed as being temporary, but allowing your publics to engage actively with your CSR plans is a particularly good way of involving them in your brand and generating brand loyalty.

[X] What Target did wrong

- It was slow to realize that blogs are now very significant, especially with younger customers (or "guests," if you must).

[✓] What Target did right

- It is moving, although a little slowly, to engage with customers in social media. That the tie-in with its widely praised CSR campaign was only temporary seems a little odd.

SELF BRANDJACK A misjudgment by the company leaves it open to widespread criticism and even ridicule.

19 Louis Vuitton sues Darfur fundraiser
April 2008

The luxury brand Louis Vuitton (LV) sued an artist selling T-shirts to raise funds for Darfur for breaching its intellectual property rights. The T-shirts showed a starving African child holding a designer bag, the design of which appeared to be influenced by LV. After six months, the company dropped the case.

This whole issue is somewhat bizarre, as LV seems to have dived into this case having considered the legal implications of initiating the action, but without considering the PR implications. Almost everything it did appears to have been a PR misstep.

It is easy to see how LV was genuinely concerned by the case. Its luxury brand was being satirized by its placement in close proximity with a starving child. Nadia Plesner, the artist, was trying to draw attention to warped media priorities, and deliberately accessorized the child in the manner of celebrities to draw attention to the media obsession with celebrities at the expense of serious issues such as genocide in Darfur. She was keeping no money for herself – although at one point a misprint on her website implied that she was – donating 30 percent of the price of the T-shirts, 100 percent of the profits, to the campaign Divest for Darfur. Creating this sharp contrast between the lifestyle of celebrities and starving children in Africa can be seen as having parallels with the spoof Starbucks ad (see CS 8).

Nobody seems to have implicated LV in genocide. The company has done nothing wrong, and it is easy to see why it was offended by an artist linking the brand – albeit peripherally – with something as monstrous as genocide.

It is perhaps worth noting that the money wasn't going to poverty relief in Darfur, it was going to press for a particular tactic – divestment – as a possible solution to the Darfur crisis. Perhaps LV thought this distinction would help its case in the media. If so, it was a spectacular misjudgment. Media and blog coverage largely ignored the distinction, implying and, in some cases, stating that Plesner planned to sell the T-shirts online "to raise money for victims of the Sudanese crisis."[3]

Legally, LV did nothing wrong. Lawyers wrote to Nadia Plesner with a "cease-and-desist" letter, seeking only nominal damages. She published this on her website, along with her reply, in which she made the case that the bag was not expressly a Louis Vuitton as it had no logo and she had a right to free expression. Only at this stage did LV seek substantive damages of $7,500 a day for each day she kept selling the T-shirts, a further $7,500 for each day she kept its letter on her website, and a third payment of $7,500 for each day she continued to use the name Louis Vuitton on her website.

Legally, LV *may* have been right about the cartoon on the T-shirts. The matter is far from clear in law, as the cartoon was plainly a parody and the bag the child was carrying was not labeled as being Louis Vuitton. It was right to assert that it maintained copyright in the letter it sent her. Had LV pursued the case, Plesner would probably have lost on that issue. But did managers ever, for a moment, consider the PR implications of mounting the case in the first place?

LV's desire to be dissociated from the stark image Nadia Plesner created is understandable. But how did it imagine that most people would react to a luxury brand seeking damages of more than $20,000 a day from a student artist? How did it imagine those figures would look in contrast with the poverty in Darfur? None of the media coverage indicates that LV announced it would donate its winnings to charity – poverty relief in Darfur, say – indeed, it was seeking to recoup its legal costs.

Quietly dropping the case seems to have been the only option. The only alternative would have been seeking to take ownership of the issue, by joining with Plesner's campaign, or some other campaign, either to raise funds for Darfur, or to focus on the media's inverted priorities.

In terms of Nadia Plesner's original point, it was not LV that was in the wrong, it was the media. But in terms of the media narrative, which requires a hero and a villain, it is suddenly Louis Vuitton that has been transformed into the villain. Again, surely LV should have anticipated this likelihood?

Learnings

Like Starbucks, Louis Vuitton realized there was no way of fighting this issue and coming out ahead. Unlike Starbucks, it took six months to realize this, and the case generated considerable hostile publicity in the meantime.

Since 2008, the brand has engaged heavily in social media. In October 2010, the Fresh Networks blog rated LV second among luxury brands for its "digital IQ." In particular, the brand has engaged with video blogging and a new trend called the "haul video," where the blogger talks about the goods they have just purchased on a shopping trip.

☒ What Louis Vuitton did wrong

- It reached for its lawyers. It seemed genuinely to imagine that this would help. From the moment that Plesner posted its legal letter on her website, LV should have realized she would call its bluff. Apparently, the company didn't even know it was bluffing.
- It didn't even try to turn itself into the good guy in this, by offering to donate any damages to Darfur, for example. It could even have made the point of donating to poverty relief, in contrast to Plesner's support for a legitimate but debatable political strategy for dealing with the issue.

☑ What Louis Vuitton did right

- Eventually, it realized it could not win, and quietly dropped the case.
- It has moved on to engage cleverly in social media.

Company finds itself linked by association to crimes against humanity.

 Company actively raises the stakes by initiating legal action. Company also creates an explicit link to an issue that was previously merely implied.

20 Greenpeace palm oil campaign 1: "Dove Onslaught(er)"

May 2008

The first of Greenpeace's viral campaigns on palm oil targeted Unilever, one of the largest corporations in the world. Like many other multinationals, Unilever has a range of brands that are much better known than the corporation itself. Much like major rivals, Procter & Gamble, Unilever's name normally turns up in the business pages of the MSM. To be effective, a consumer campaign had to target one of its consumer brands. Greenpeace chose Dove.

Unilever is one of the world's largest purchasers of palm oil. Palm oil is not an environmental bad of itself, but Greenpeace was concerned about the clear-cutting of lowland forests in Southeast Asia, especially Indonesia and Malaysia, to make way for palm oil production. The rainforests being destroyed are habitats for diverse forms of life.

Greenpeace produced a hard-hitting video, "Dove Onslaught(er)," which is still available on YouTube and the Greenpeace website. It shows a crying Indonesian girl and a montage of images of the destruction of lowland forests and the biodiversity these forests support. It claims that "98% of Indonesia's lowland forests will be gone by the time Azizah is 25." Supporters were encouraged to write to Dove – in reality, Unilever – calling for it to end its practice of buying palm oil from unsustainable sources. Greenpeace called for a mass boycott of Dove.

This campaign exhibited many of the features that would become hallmarks of future Greenpeace social media campaigns. It selected one product range by one multinational. It is, in some ways, a test case. It is an example of what Greenpeace can do to Unilever. At this point, Greenpeace was not seeking to associate the campaign with the rest of Unilever's product range, but the implied threat is there. A carefully targeted campaign on a single brand is sustainable. People will remember to boycott Dove. People are much less likely to carry around with them a full list of Unilever products, which would be the only way of sustaining a broad-level boycott of Unilever. But each one of Unilever's brands has a clear monetary value. Hitting one of them costs Unilever a great deal of money. The option of adding other Unilever products to the hit list remains open.

While creating pressure points on the value of one of Unilever's brands, Greenpeace offered a way out. Unilever needed to agree a charter of actions that would relieve pressure on the lowland forests. It was not a matter of abandoning palm oil altogether, but phasing out the use of palm oil from unsustainable sources. In many ways, these campaigns are much cleverer and more targeted than the broad-level campaign against Shell's operations in Nigeria during the 1990s. Greenpeace was not asking Unilever to abandon its core business. The ask was relatively small, one that Unilever could give at a fairly low cost.

A highly professional, targeted campaign such as this is very costly to resist, and relatively cheap to accede to. Unilever acceded in a matter of weeks.

Learnings

The principal learning from Unilever's rapid surrender on this issue is this: some things are worth fighting for and others are not. This is not to say that Unilever and its brands, including Dove, are not heavily engaged in social media. They certainly are. Social media are essential for Dove's campaign to get men to take more of an interest in personal grooming. Unilever has identified this as an underexploited market. It seems doubtful that it will persuade men to talk about their moisturizing routine with the same enthusiasm that women sometimes do, but social media "lurkers" are likely to gain reassurance from the notion that other men are increasingly using such grooming products. As with all social media campaigns, active participants in the media are only a small part of the market. Those who learn from other people's participation are sure to be a much larger group.

☑ What Unilever did right

- It recognized that this was not a fight worth having, and acceded to Greenpeace's demands fairly quickly.

☑ What Greenpeace did right

- It picked off a single Unilever brand and applied strong pressure to it.
- It produced a creative video.
- It mobilized its supporters to pressurize and boycott Dove.

Campaigners put an environmental issue at the heart of debate and forced company to back down.

21 "Speed dressing" ad wins award, but the client knew nothing about it
June 2008

What do you do when a controversial ad for your brand wins an award at the Cannes Lions International Advertising Festival? Deny that you knew anything about it, of course.

The storyline of the ad was simple. Two attractive young teenagers at home in their bedrooms practice putting their clothes on as quickly as possible. Then the boy calls round on the girl, and she announces "hey, Mom, we're just going to go down to watch TV in the basement." The ad ends with the JCPenney logo and the phrase "Today's the day to get away with it," echoing the retailer's use of the phrase "Today's the day …" in its advertising over the previous year.

Whoever came up with the concept could have anticipated the reaction. It was praised as realistic in some quarters and condemned for promoting teen sex in others. The reactions are as knee-jerk as they are silly. Why is realism to be praised in an advertisement? And since when did teenagers need to be encouraged to think about sex?

The predictable arguments led to speculation that the US retail chain JCPenney – or its advertising agency Saatchi & Saatchi – had created the ad in order to stoke up controversy. In fact, the incident led to a major falling out between the retailer and its advertising agency. Mike Boylson of JCPenney strongly condemned the use of JCPenney branding in the ad: "It's obviously inappropriate and nothing we would ever condone. We're very disappointed that our logo and brand position were used in that way."[4] JCPenney is based in the conservative Dallas suburb of Plano, Texas. So, the client didn't like it. But nor, it seems, did the ad agency. The ad was entered for the industry award in Cannes by the third-party filmmaker, Epoch Films. According to Saatchi & Saatchi, it was entered "without J.C. Penney's knowledge or consent … Saatchi & Saatchi did not enter the spot and deeply regrets the message this ad presents."[5] Unsurprisingly, the critically acclaimed but highly controversial ad developed a cult following on YouTube.

Is any publicity good publicity? Was JCPenney, even without its consent, benefiting from this controversy? Were Epoch Films and Saatchi & Saatchi benefiting by showing off their controversial cleverness? It is difficult to be certain, but I can't help suspecting that the client was a clear loser here. It managed – inadvertently – to offend cultural conservatives while also appearing sanctimonious and censorious to cultural liberals. It is unlikely that either side in the debate emerged with an enhanced opinion of the retailer. Taking controversial stances can sometimes position a client well with its target market – if the target market disproportionately takes one side in the controversial debate in question. A general retailer such as JCPenney should probably not offend either side in the divisive culture wars, but probably ended up offending both.

Overall, this artistically clever ad can only be judged a branding failure, despite being dubbed one of the best viral videos of 2008 by the ViralReality blog.

Learnings

By 2008, JCPenney was making waves with its pioneering use of blogs. It used its own site as an aggregator of material from some of the leading mom blogs to create discussions around subjects of interest to its publics. This is one of the best ways to optimize your site for search engines. New and relevant content drives search engine optimization (SEO), and blogging, especially drawing content from a variety of trusted peer-to-peer sources, is at the cutting edge of SEO. It pushed JCPenney to fifth on a search for "fall shopping" and second for "fall shopping guide."

In 2010, the BizWorks360 blog picked up on JCPenney's social media integration to its advertising around the Academy Awards. The Oscars are still the second largest US TV audience of the year. Although well behind the Super Bowl, the Oscars have a much higher proportion of women in the audience, so it is a key – and very expensive – TV advertising spot. BizWorks360 praised JCPenney for using its social media presence to talk about its sponsorship of the Oscars in the days running up to the ceremony, but felt there could have been much better integration between social media and the advertising on the day itself. There could, for example, have been a separate Oscars landing page on the website.

The Word of Mouth Marketing Association has praised JCPenney's initiative in creating Ambrielle Team for its Ambrielle lingerie line. The community involves customers in product testing, including wear tests, and discussions as part of a private online community. Live online chats and postings to a discussion board produced considerable consumer feedback to the Ambrielle team, leading to significant product changes in terms of the bra straps and sizing of the product range. Such live interaction between the product team and consumers is much more than just a new way of organizing market research. It is a way of creating communities of brand champions who will advocate for the product.

Another area in which JCPenney has been praised by experts in online communication management is in the use of augmented reality (AR). AR is a relatively new area of online communication, depending on webcams, high bandwidth, and fast processing speeds at the user end. Such things are now commonplace, after several years during which such a program would have been impractical. In AR, your computer screen can show a webcam image that does not, in reality, exist, combining images from two locations to create new – augmented – reality. AR as an e-commerce and social media tool was rather overhyped in 2009, with the available technology not really living up to its promise, but by the summer of 2010, it was already meeting and even exceeding the hype.

In JCPenney's case, AR can be used to create a "virtual dressing room." You and the clothes may be in different places, but through the fast processing speeds of AR, you can see an image of yourself wearing the clothes and moving around in them. In August 2010, Racked was calling JCPenney's AR (produced in partnership with seventeen.com): "one of the coolest online shopping tools we've ever seen."[6] In 2013, Wipro was still calling AR virtual dressing rooms "state of the art" and reporting that JCPenney planned to use radio-frequency identification tags to eliminate checkout stations before the end of the year.

☒ What Epoch Films did wrong

- It entered the contest without the permission of either the agency or the client. It showed off artistic cleverness, but must have left people less willing to trust the company.

☑ What JCPenney did right

- It disowned the ad. It had no choice, given the customer base.
- It has invested heavily in social media tools, setting high standards with its Ambrielle Team and its use of AR, which competitors will have to follow.

 SELF BRANDJACK Ultimately, the relationship between JCPenney, its ad agency, and the agency's suppliers broke down. As a result, the client ended up alienating both sides of the culture war.

22 ExxonMobil: victim of the first Twitter brandjack
July 2008

In what seems to have been the first Twitter brandjack, a Twitterata[7] called "Janet" simply began tweeting as though she was an official spokesperson for the ExxonMobil group. This was groundbreaking, although not in the way it first appeared. For several days, ExxonMobil was praised by social media commentators such as Jeremiah Owyang, who at first assumed that "Janet" was a real ExxonMobil spokesperson. Twitter was only just rising to high levels of public consciousness in 2008, partly as a result of Barack Obama's groundbreaking use of social media in his presidential election campaign. As of July 2008, the Iranian elections – one the key breakthroughs for Twitter in the MSM – remained in the future. For a generally cautious company such as ExxonMobil to be leading the way into the Twittersphere seemed too good to be true, as, indeed, it was.

On July 28, 2008, when Owyang still believed Janet to be an official spokesperson for ExxonMobil, he praised her for the good practice of responding directly to the storm of criticism that, understandably, greeted ExxonMobil's presence on the microblogging site.[8] Janet's engagement on ExxonMobil's behalf is interesting. She was not a satirical brandjacker like Leroy Stick (see CS 40), and seemed to be genuinely partisan on ExxonMobil's part, posting: "@1WineDude, did you know that the Valdez spill wasn't even one of the top 10 worst spills in history? Like the Nowruz Oil Field spill in '80." She was right. Despite the high profile of the Exxon Valdez spill, with a general impression that it was the biggest or at least one of the biggest oil spills of all time, it was not even the biggest oil spill of that winter, as there had been a larger one off Nova Scotia less than six months earlier. Despite that, it seems unlikely that pointing out the existence of larger oil spills than the Valdez was ever a key part of ExxonMobil's defense strategy. As a general rule, telling people that, although you are bad, some other people are worse is not an effective strategy. In social media, where people expect transparency and engagement, it is a particularly poor approach.

While making true but inapt comments about the Valdez, Janet was describing ExxonMobil's positions on matters of political and legislative controversy. The corporation denied that it had ever taken such positions. On the other hand, Janet spoke up for ExxonMobil's corporate philanthropy in supporting the Save the Tiger Fund. It seems difficult to ascribe any malicious motives to this brandjacking.

On 1 August, Owyang published a further blog,[9] exploring the fact that Janet was not, in fact, an official spokesperson for the ExxonMobil brand. He even made one of the earliest uses of the word "brandjacking," although he spelled it as two words. Owyang explored with Alan Jeffers, the real ExxonMobil spokesperson, how the group felt about Janet's Twitter identity. Among other things, he wanted to know if ExxonMobil's attitude would be different if Janet was entirely unaffiliated with the corporation or an employee, but not an authorized spokesperson. Jeffers was clear that he regarded this distinction as irrelevant. In the sense that Janet seemed to be portraying herself as speaking on behalf of the brand, he is right. But corporations are going to have to get used to the fact that their employees *are* going to tweet, and real information about the business is going to get outside. In any case, as Jeffers pointed out: "It's our perception that social networking is based on honesty, transparency and trust, it's important that they become forthcoming about who they represent." Quite right, and remarkably adept for a corporation that wasn't actually engaged with social media, and not expressing any interest in becoming so.

Learnings

Owyang, one of the most intelligent, informed commentators on the corporate use of social media, immediately identified several critical learnings from the episode. He called for Twitter to support identity confirmation – which it now does. He advocated that organizations need to monitor the use and abuse of their brand in social media and suggested that the real ExxonMobil should step forward to engage with its publics.

ExxonMobil does now have a blog, Perspectives, in which it has commented on, among other things, the BP oil spill in the Gulf of Mexico. There is also an official Twitter feed, although it was not launched until October 2009, and with a grand total of 346 tweets in its first year, it was not exactly active. With 41 tweets in October 2010, it did seem to be, slowly, picking up pace. By June 2013, however, the activity on the main (verified) account had fallen to just 5 tweets. The group had 45,000 followers but was following just 176. The spoof account Exxon Cares was actually following more people, although it only had 4,000 followers and had tweeted just twice in the preceding month.

ExxonMobil remains rather poorly engaged with social media. It has long had a reputation for caution and centralized control. Long-term thinking – exploration and production projects are investments that pay off over decades rather than years – is inherent in the company's business model. Social media, which require rapid and open engagement, are alien territory.

☒ What "Janet" did wrong

- She spoke as though she were tweeting on behalf of ExxonMobil, and never made it clear that she was not.
- She ascribed to ExxonMobil positions on controversial issues that did not represent the group's position.

☒ What ExxonMobil did wrong

- It remained slow to fill the gap, waiting more than a year to launch a real Twitter account, and even then using it sparingly.

IMPERSONATION BRANDJACK A clear case of someone, still unknown, seeming to speak on behalf of a brand without any actual authorization to do so.

23 Motrin patronizes and offends its target market
November 2008

In November 2008, people were still getting to know Twitter, and were unsure of its power within social media. Many organizations didn't monitor the microblogging site, and could thus be completely taken by surprise by a Twitterstorm.

Certainly, Johnson & Johnson (J&J) was blindsided by the Twitter reaction to a viral ad it produced and put on its website for Motrin, its ibuprofen brand. The reaction was ferocious. The message of the ad was that many mothers were carrying their babies in slings for reasons of fashion, that this could put stress on a mother's back and neck, causing pain, but using Motrin could control the pain, thus allowing them to look like an "official mom," so that if they looked tired and crazy, people would understand. Every single stage of this argument was not only rejected by groups of mothers, but often declared offensive. First, they insisted, mothers don't wear their babies in a sling or front carrier for fashion reasons. Second, it doesn't put particular stress on the back and neck – at least no more so than carrying a baby in some other way. Third, they don't do it to look like "an official mom," and fourth, moms are not necessarily more tired and crazy than anyone else.

The merits of the #motrinmoms case are debatable, but seem to be generally sound. After all, people carry around heavy objects such as laptops and sports gear in a variety of different ways, and some people find one method more comfortable than another. There is no right or wrong posture for a laptop, so why should Motrin designate one particular method of carrying babies as being motivated by fashion, as opposed to either the comfort of the mother or a desire to promote intimacy and bonding? Why would J&J think it is Motrin's role to second-guess and trivialize these choices? Do mothers get more tired and crazy than other people? Not generally, and if they do, it is both impolite and unwise to mention it.

The ad drove a great many mothers crazy, that is, it angered them. It is the nature of Twitter – like the Dell Hell blog (see CS 4) – that it gathered together the aggrieved parties, and they tended to reinforce each other's grievances. This is what makes a social media storm quite different from controversies in the nondigital world. Groups like Greenpeace can use social media – very effectively – to mobilize campaigns that would have existed anyway. Social media are a new way for such groups to organize their campaigning and advocacy. But #motrinmoms would not have existed at all without social media. Individuals might well have been annoyed with Motrin, but there would have been no campaign. The disaffected would have remained isolated.

Using Twitter, the group coalesced in a short space of time, and disappeared fairly shortly after winning its case. Without social media, this would never have happened. Groups exist, in the real world, to campaign for long-term shared objectives, such as protecting the environment. They don't spontaneously arise to fight battles that are likely to be over in a week. The actions necessary to organize a campaign are disproportionate to the benefits.

The #motrinmoms were able to organize their own video responses on YouTube, expressing considerable anger towards the corporation. At one point during the controversy, bloggers were reporting that the Motrin website appeared to be down. The anger appeared to be feeding off itself, although quite a few of the Twitter and some YouTube responses were more mocking than angry. At one point, #motrinmoms was the top trending topic on Twitter.

J&J was slow to react to the #motrinmoms Twitterstorm – slow, that is, by the standards we expect today. Twitter was still new and had a low profile. Nonetheless, the ad was pulled within a few days and J&J apologized for the offense.

Learnings

This problem could have been avoided if the ad had been tested with a sufficiently large segment of the target market. People are much less likely to get angry if told: "this is an ad we have been thinking about, what do you think?" If the plan was to generate controversy – and I rather doubt it, although the whole thing was great for Motrin's *profile* – it certainly worked, but at the cost of a mounting anger in the target market. The main learning from this was that businesses were still focused on blogs, YouTube, and MSM, and had not yet spotted the significance of Twitter.

☒ What Motrin did wrong

- It failed sufficiently to test the ad either by a focus group or an appropriately large e-test market.

☑ What Motrin did right

- It backed down quickly.
- It learned that Twitter is a key part of social media.

CUSTOMER REVOLT BRANDJACK A lack of adequate market testing left the company with an ad that irritated the target market.

AGGREGATION BRANDJACK The issue is one that would probably not have taken off in an offline campaign.

24 Virgin Atlantic staff insult customers and cast doubt on plane safety

November 2008

Virgin Atlantic fired 13 flight attendants for participating in a Facebook exchange in which they brought the company into disrepute in a number of key respects:

- They queried safety standards, saying one plane had had to have an engine changed four times in a year.
- They said the planes were infested with cockroaches.
- They referred to passengers as "chavs" – a British term referring to rowdy, white, working-class people, roughly equivalent to the US term "trailer trash," although normally indicating young people and associated with antisocial behavior such as street drinking.

Virgin Atlantic stated to the media:

> Following a thorough investigation, it was found that all 13 staff
> participated in a discussion on the networking site Facebook, which
> brought the company into disrepute and insulted some of our
> passengers.[10]

The Virgin Group is an unusual company, active in many varied markets, including print, broadcast, and online media, financial services, and air travel. It began as a music publisher and owner of a chain of record stores, although the record business was sold some time ago. The unifying theme, apart from the name, is the leadership of Sir Richard Branson, the high-profile British entrepreneur. Even the name isn't an absolute, as Sir Richard's brand of condoms is marketed as Mates – the Virgin name being inappropriate to that particular product line.

Sir Richard is fundamental to the Virgin branding, which is always cheeky and friendly. The company likes to be seen as the upstart challenger, principally, in the case of the airline, to British Airways. One of the main advantages in building the reputation around Sir Richard is that it puts a friendly face on the enterprise. People find it easier to trust a person than they do a faceless corporation. Virgin has carefully cultivated the image of a company run by a man you might actually like if you met him – a branding element generally absent from other corporate strategies.

It follows that staff showing contempt for customers is probably more damaging to Virgin than it would be to some other businesses, whereas at Ryanair, it sometimes seems as though it is actively encouraged (see CS 48). In some ways, Virgin was rather lucky with the "chav" comments. They meant that firing the cabin crew was uncontroversial. If it had fired people for the cockroach and engine remarks, Facebook would have been in uproar about "censorship" and Virgin suppressing discussion about serious issues. As it was, the company could not afford to ignore the other issues, even though media coverage did tend to focus on the "chav" comments.

The company statement about the firing said: "We have numerous internal channels for our staff to feed back legitimate and appropriate issues relating to the company."[11] Virgin was also at pains to point out that its 747s flying out of London Gatwick (the planes on which the 13 cabin crew had been based) were among the newest in service.

Learnings

Virgin reacted in exactly the right way, dealing with the issue within days and going to the media as soon as the cabin crew were fired. By June 2013, Virgin Atlantic had over 160,000 followers for its main Twitter feed and another 80,000 for the Virgin group. There are over 250,000 fans for Virgin Atlantic's Facebook page. That said, BA North America had over 300,000 followers on Twitter and almost 900,000 likes on Facebook.

Virgin Atlantic's web-based community, vtravelled.com, is an award-winning site in which customers can engage with each other. There is a real sense of community, and a full-time blogger. The site generates lists of the top 50 things going on in the city you are visiting, and a list of events that other people with a similar customer profile have enjoyed.

In general, Virgin has carried its friendly offline image into social media rather well.

☑ What Virgin did right

- It fired the staff concerned.
- It responded to the substantive criticisms of the airline, while reserving its outrage for criticism of customers.
- It continued its expansion into social media, developing the cheeky upstart image in building its digital communities.

STAFF BRANDJACK A clear case of staff misconduct that damaged the company. The company was lucky that staff had alienated customers, thus leaving them with little sympathy, and deflecting attention from other, more serious issues.

25 When customers remain attached to a logo the company wants to drop
February 2009

PepsiCo decided to rebrand its popular Tropicana juice range, only to encounter a wave of protest from people who liked the old look and feel. The protests gathered pace in social media to the point where Pepsi backed down.

Rebrands are often unpopular. You would imagine, as a media consumer, that they are *always* disastrous and ludicrously expensive, and never succeed in their stated goals. This is merely an observer error. "Client paid reasonable fee for rather attractive rebranding" has never been used as a headline. While, at first glance, it seems astonishing that all stories about rebranding and new corporate identities are negative, the explanation is simply that good news is not news. Whenever corporate ID stories hit the headlines, it is because of some catastrophe.

When these stories occur, the reactions are predictable. Someone will say it was an absurd amount of money, someone else will say "my five-year-old could have drawn that," and everyone will agree that the old branding was better. These are all good reasons for only redesigning your corporate graphics when it is clearly necessary. The fact that a new head of brand wants to make a mark is not a good enough reason.

Tropicana's circumstance was specific. It was a premium brand with an instantly recognizable graphic: a straw poking into an orange. It was losing market share to generic store brands. One of the leading criticisms made of the new branding was that it was bland and generic. It made Tropicana harder to pick out on the shelf. If you look just like all your competitors, why would people pay a premium price?

One possibility is that people don't know the price of fruit juice in the first place, and don't look at the price. Maybe people just pick up the juice that *looks like* a generic brand, assuming that it will be cheap. That certainly seems possible, but if you have a distinctive market position based on a premium price for a premium product, the value of looking distinctive surely outweighs this. It also has to be worth considering how much consumer attachment there is to existing designs.

In this case, people were able to bombard PepsiCo with complaints via Twitter, Facebook, blogs, and email. It is another example of a relatively trivial and entirely one-off issue around which people can coalesce. In the pre-digital world, Tropicana didn't have fans, it just had customers. The relationship was purely transactional. But in the Facebook world, we can all become fans of brands. This is the route by which organizations can help build brand loyalty, but it is also a platform your fans can use to organize in opposition to corporate policies. Suddenly, orange juice drinkers are behaving like sports fans. They want to second-guess the coach, and call for his sacking when the team is underperforming. The result of this rebellion by "fans" of the juice brand was a PepsiCo climb-down in just weeks.

Learnings

The first thing Tropicana learned from this fiasco is that it had more fans – and fans who were more devoted – than it had realized. This is an astonishingly valuable piece of information, and social media channels open up new ways of reaching this audience.

Tropicana has made great use of a tactic called "game seeding." This involves linking your brand with games or Facebook apps that will be attractive to users in your target market. An association with a successful game can mean exposing your branding to consumers for hours at a time. In Tropicana's case, this is used to reinforce the company's CSR program under the branding "Tropicana Rainforest." Such consumer engagement enhances the brand's premium position. It seems unlikely that generic and store brands can generate the same degree of loyalty.

☒ What Tropicana did wrong

- It seemed to rush into a rebrand without considering its premium position in the market.
- It seemed not to research the question sufficiently.

☑ What Tropicana did right

- It backed down quickly.
- It invested in building relationships with its loyal fans.

CUSTOMER REVOLT BRANDJACK — Customers retained surprising attachment to the old logo.

AGGREGATION BRANDJACK — A relatively trivial issue engages people in a Facebook campaign. It is difficult to imagine street demonstrations on this question.

26 A fan impersonates a comedian and forces the comic onto Twitter

Early 2009

If you Google "Quentin Langley," you find this author and, more or less, no one else. My parents had the foresight to give me a very Googlable name. If, on the other hand, you Google "David Mitchell," good luck in finding the one you were looking for.

David Mitchell, British actor/comedian, shares his name with, among many others, a bestselling novelist and a former Conservative MP – and that is when you limit your search to the UK. The actor regards himself as a technophobe, with a website that has been "under construction" for more than a decade, and writes of the social humiliation of never having heard of Facebook as late as 2007.

Of course, even the least Internet-savvy of people eventually has to catch up. As Mitchell put it in an article in *The Guardian*:[12] "My solo attempt to snub the worldwide web went badly." Such a notorious technophobe could hardly expect to be the first "David Mitchell" to sign up to Twitter, but he was beaten onto the microblogging site not merely by other people who happen to share his name but also by a dedicated impersonator. Mitchell explains:

> This was not just another David Mitchell going about his business. He was saying things like: "Went to Peep Show [in which Mitchell stars] production meeting today" and: "Don't know what to get Robert [Webb, Mitchell's comedy partner] for his birthday" and making terrible, eye-watering, embarrassing attempts at wit. So he'd really done his homework.

A dedicated impersonator is rarely harmless, even if that is the intention. At one point, the impersonator started tweeting in unflattering terms about the management of the BBC. Since the BBC broadcasts the TV show *That Mitchell and Webb Look* and employs Mitchell to present a radio program, as well as having him as a frequent guest on other shows, it is potentially damaging to his career to have his name linked to attacks on the corporation.

Learnings

Mitchell surrendered to the inevitable, and created his own Twitter account and became an active user. He makes generally intelligent and usually funny (that is his job) comments and has attracted a strong following. By the end of 2010, he had more than 300,000 followers and had been listed almost 8,000 times. By mid-2013, his followership had risen to more than 1.1 million. His tweets support his acting and writing career, with frequent comments about upcoming shows. He remains a bit of a Facebook newbie, though, with only 21,000 likes.

✓ What David Mitchell did right

- He embraced the technology, not only creating an account, but becoming an active user.
- He has written articles in the MSM about his struggle with technology and the experience of being brandjacked.
- He has used his humor as a tool to attract a large following, thus taking "ownership" of his rather unremarkable name.

IMPERSONATION BRANDJACK There seems no doubt this was a deliberate attempt to impersonate a celebrity, possibly for malicious reasons, and certainly risking the man's reputation.

27 The voluntary brandjack: Skittles cedes control
February 2009

Skittles engaged in what might be considered the first voluntary brandjack. It was an astonishing experiment, which garnered tremendous coverage on the basis of first mover advantage. Put simply, Skittles ceded control of the brand to the social media community. The entire Skittles website was replaced by a feed of all mentions of Skittles on various social media platforms, most significantly, Facebook and Twitter.

The navigation on this site was simple. The home page was a Twitter stream. Go to "Friends" and you got the Skittles Facebook page. Go to "video" and it was a YouTube channel. "Pics" was hosted on Flickr. There was almost no standard information at all. It was all user-generated content.

The first thing to point out is that Skittles.com was never a corporate site, only a brand site. The brand is wholly owned by the Mars Corporation, and Mars continued to maintain its own corporate site, which was entirely separate.

Nonetheless, even with a separate corporate site, turning over the whole of your home page to Twitter feeds is remarkably brave. Anyone who mentioned Skittles in their tweets was immediately on the Skittles home page. It was not just the obviously spoof tweets, such as "Skittles give you cancer and is [sic] the cause of all world evil" posted by TechCrunch blogger, Mike Butcher, that could reflect on the brand. Skittles – a candy brand, after all – had to protect its page against access by children by asking for a date of birth declaration, because it could not control the content of Twitter. Locking children out of a candy product's website is rather strange, but it was essential to the project. Twitterati quickly began to test the system, by posting some very blue comments, which duly appeared on the Skittles home page. Skittles had upped its social media volume immensely, but completely ceded control of the brand narrative.

Being pioneers in this voluntary brandjacking attracted all sorts of attention. As the first user of this strategy, the brand was written up in the MSM and on social media. Much of the commentary was favorable. But as pioneers, Skittles inevitably attracted much more of the blue testing of the strategy than future users would. On balance, the blue language probably didn't damage the brand in any serious way. It hasn't created any lasting linking of the brand to scatological or sexual functions. And ceding control is exactly what social media mavens urge onto brand managers. As Jeff Jarvis puts it, credibility is inversely proportional to control.[13] This self brandjacking is a great example of a company allowing its publics to build the narrative around the brand.

Skittles took the risk of handing its website over to user-generated content earlier and in a bigger way than other brands, but it is not the only organization to run into this type of issue. In April 2009, the British newspaper the *Daily Telegraph* included a real-time Twitterfall on its website for its coverage of the UK national budget: an unmoderated display of all tweets with the hashtag #budget. Among the tweets displayed on the website before it pulled the plug on the experiment were "Telegraph wankers #budget Didn't work" and "Silly paper messing with technology it doesn't understand #budget."

Does it make sense for a candy brand like Skittles to lead the way in this manner? Certainly, a social media strategy that locks out children is a peculiar choice. And we need to ask the extent to which customers have a genuine relationship with a candy brand. Purchases of this type are frequently undertaken on impulse and are nearly always transactional. A bag of Skittles is bought to be consumed. It does not become a treasured possession that one is proud to own.

Learnings

The boldest part of the experiment – making the Twitter search for the word "skittles" the home page – was abandoned in a few days. It isn't clear whether this was a climb-down, or a gimmick designed to launch the new social media-friendly site. The Twitter feed remained a part of the site, but was no longer the entry portal. Probably, the level of blue language was greater than anticipated, and Skittles felt it needed to reinstate some measure of control over the site, if only the home page.

Moderation of the Twitter feed would have undermined the authenticity, no matter how many times editors proclaimed they were only removing offensive language. Automatic moderation software always produces false positives for offensive language – known as Scunthorpes, after the English east coast resort – and is therefore not ideal either.

The learnings from this experiment are as much about social media as they are about Skittles. As brands cede more control, they need to be aware of the key issues.

Questions to ask if you are considering this strategy

1 You will still need a corporate site. Is your corporate site separate from your brand-building site?

2 How much blue language can you tolerate, given the demographics of your publics? Is it serious if you have to exclude children from your site?

3 Are your publics likely to engage, talking about your brand? Frankly, is your product one that is worth discussing?

4 Will your key messages even be a part of the discussion if you cede control in this way? Are there brand champions out there, talking about the merits of your product?

5 Will your staff engage, and what will they say if they do? How big a part of the debate are they likely to be?

6 Do you have motivated groups of activists ready and willing to criticize you? If so, for what? Do they fundamentally object to your business model – as with most energy companies – or are they pressing you to change one aspect of your sourcing policy (see CS 14)?

| SELF BRANDJACK | The rare voluntary self brandjack. This was not something Skittles created by misjudgment, but by design. |

28 How a pizza co. reacted to unhygienic practices filmed at one of its franchises

April 2009

An unidentified Domino's Pizza franchise was the scene of a video posted on YouTube, which showed staff doing some extraordinarily unsanitary things with food and utensils. It isn't necessary for you to know what they were doing to understand why this was rather off-putting to potential customers, so the description is included in a footnote, which you can read, or not, as you choose.[14]

Domino's, in conjunction with the local authorities, took all the basic remedial actions that you would expect. The employees were fired and subsequently prosecuted. One was sentenced to 24 months' probation. The outlet was shut down while all food not in its original packaging was disposed of. All utensils were sterilized. The franchise subsequently closed.

Domino's responded to the gross-out with a video recorded by the group CEO. Cleverly, Domino's gave its film the same title as the original, so anyone searching for the gross-out video would also find the CEO's response. During the resulting publicity, it emerged that one of the employees – a woman providing commentary on the video – was on the sex offenders' register. Domino's corporately deflected questions as to why she had been hired, saying this was a matter for local franchise owners. The franchise owner refused to comment to the media.

The buck-passing by the company on the question of staffing decisions is unfortunate, and obviously looks like an inadequate response. In reality, it is an inevitable consequence of the franchise structure. There will always be things the franchisor controls and things left to the discretion of the franchisee. It makes it difficult to respond centrally to crises that hit the brand as a whole. Customers have a right to expect that the franchisor will lay down standards of behavior that the franchisee will be contractually obliged to monitor as a condition of being allowed to use the name. Clearly, the staff in the video breached reasonable standards of behavior. It is less clear that the franchisor had any duty to impose an obligation to check staff against the sex offenders' register. (Domino's, unlike McDonald's, doesn't host children's parties. It is a pizza *delivery* operation.)

Learnings

Social media crises pose challenges to all organizations, but particular challenges apply to the franchise model. There are now additional risks that apply to the brand and will, potentially, hit all franchisees, even if the inciting incident applies only at one branch, as in this case. The franchisor has the responsibility to protect the value of the brand as a whole, and it is possible that franchise contracts will increasingly have to take account of such risks. This is not to say that risks apply more to the franchise model than elsewhere. This particular example could have arisen at any food preparation chain. In many cases, a franchisor may have additional sanctions – such as revoking a franchise – which are not available to a chain that owns its restaurants directly. The point is that social media challenges may increase the number of risks that apply to a brand as a whole, and franchisors may have to monitor and manage in a slightly different way.

Domino's rapidly applied some social media lessons learned from this crisis. By July 2010, *New Media Age* was reporting that Domino's engagement with social media had led to a 61.4 percent growth in the outlet's online sales. Promotions were being offered to customers who checked in on FourSquare. People were incentivized to get their Facebook friends to order a pizza (the pizza "holdouts"). It even tied up with YouTube to release the lunchtime menu.

☑ **What Domino's did right**

- It acted immediately against those responsible and took action to sterilize the brand.
- It put its CEO's response on YouTube.
- It invested heavily in new digital and social media strategies, including community building to promote online ordering.

STAFF BRANDJACK | Gross misconduct by staff damages the reputation of the company.

29 A retailer spams serious discussions on Twitter
June 2009

Habitat, the trendy UK furniture store, found itself in trouble for Twitter hashtag spam. It was a serious black mark for a company that had otherwise been doing rather well in social media.

For the benefit of the non-Twitterati, there are two principal ways in which users can follow things on Twitter. You can either follow a particular user – in this case @habitatuk – or you can follow a particular subject, identified by a hashtag, for example #habitat. Without hashtags – it now seems as though Habitat is not using hashtags – your tweets only go to your followers, unless one of them retweets to their followers.

Hashtag spam is when you include an irrelevant hashtag in your tweets. It is easy to do. Twitter helpfully tells you which hashtags are "trending," that is, popular. So if you want your tweets to be seen by large numbers, simply include a popular hashtag in your tweets – at the cost of irritating everyone immensely. Because hashtags are not like the metatags on websites. Metatags are invisible coding, whereas hashtags are included in the body of your tweets. This makes it rather surprising that anyone thinks they can get away with hashtag spam.

Habitat's offenses were especially egregious. Spamming trivial trends, or even competitors, might be regarded as cheeky, but Habitat spammed several threads relating to the Iranian elections, the principal serious news story of the day. There are, obviously, different levels of spam. For Habitat to use #ikea would have probably raised a giggle more than anything. The hashtags #iphone and #trueblood were likely to raise protests, but it was intruding on the serious news from Iran that provoked such anger.

In June 2009, Iran held its tenth presidential election. Incumbent Mahmoud Ahmadinejad was facing a number of serious challengers. Mir-Hossein Mousavi was the leading challenger, endorsed by Mohammad Khatami, the popular former president. Mousavi was widely expected to proceed to the second round against Ahmadinejad. The day after the first round, however, the Islamic Republic News Agency reported that Ahmadinejad had won 62 percent of the vote, meaning that there would be no runoff a week later. Initially, Western governments and media seemed to accept this. Ahmadinejad's victory seemed decisive. But mounting coverage on Twitter seemed to cast considerable doubt on the results. Ahmadinejad was reported as winning inconceivably high numbers of votes even in the home areas of his opponents. People in Iran began to mobilize and protest against the "stolen" election.

The Iranian elections were not only dominating the news, they were also bringing Twitter into the mainstream for the first time. The Twitterati were proud of their role in bringing this story to the attention of the world, so spamming it with offers on designer furniture was a particularly bad move.

Learnings

☒ What Habitat did wrong

- It engaged in a blatant spam, intruding into serious discussions.

☑ What Habitat did right

- It apologized immediately. This was the minimum that could be expected in the circumstances. The offense was monumentally bad judgment, and it is not as if it could possibly have been accidental.

What Habitat could have done differently

- It could also have sent @replies – messages sent publicly, but addressed to individuals – to the people who complained about its behavior. That would have been a graceful way to apologize.
- It would have been sensible for it to have tried to engage the Twitterati in discussing what sort of behavior *is* acceptable. While Habitat's spamming was outrageous, and well beyond the line, exactly where the line should be drawn is a matter of legitimate debate.

SELF BRANDJACK Serious misconduct by the company provoked a wholly predictable backlash.

30 **Washington DC rail crash**
June 2009

When two trains on the Washington Metro system's Red Line crashed, WMATA, the metro operator, and Adrian Fenty, the mayor, immediately faced two crisis communications issues: casualties and disruption to the system.

Obviously, the fatalities and injuries were the more serious issue, but not one that effective communication after the fact could actually alleviate. This should not, of course, be taken as an indication that effective crisis communication around casualties is not important. But communication around the disruption, while less important, is more immediate. By communicating to passengers that the system is disrupted, WMATA (Washington Metropolitan Area Transit Authority) could discourage people from arriving at stations and encourage them to find other routes home. It could also communicate effectively to passengers whose planned route was *not* disrupted: an equally important message in an atmosphere of confusion.

Accurate information in any such crisis is critical. A person arriving at a Metro station in the midst of the crisis does not know the cause of the disruption. Is it a signaling problem or passenger incident, potentially cleared up in minutes? Is it a terrorist attack, which might lead to the whole system being closed through fear of further attacks, and not just those parts directly affected? It will not be clear to a person at the station whether the issue affects one station, one line, or the whole system. The information that becomes known afterwards is not known to those who are caught up in the issue at the time.

As regards the crash itself, the mayor arrived at the scene fairly quickly. This communicates the message that someone is in charge and the authorities are dealing with the situation. In the world of social media, this is more important than ever. It is a way of dealing with the rumors that inevitably spread on social media. Mayors in this situation no longer have to arrange their own publicity surrounding it, which can undermine the message by making the mayor seem self-aggrandizing. You can generally expect that, at any incident where hundreds of people are gathered, someone is filming the incident on a cell phone and uploading it to YouTube. (Although, as of 2012, no such videos of Fenty at the crash are discoverable. Had the crash occurred even two years later, far more of the passengers present would have been likely to be carrying cell phones with video capability.)

WMATA's communication with its customers was focused on its website, email, and text messaging. A few years later, and it would probably have focused more heavily on Twitter and Facebook. Part of the problem is the transactional relationship that a rail system has with its customers. Most customers either buy a season ticket, or one-off, small-scale purchases such as single-use tickets. Season tickets give the operator only one opportunity a year to gather information such as email addresses, cell phone numbers, and social media handles. Small-scale purchases are usually for cash, so there is no information-gathering opportunity. Both situations make broadcast communications, such as websites and mass emails/texts, the best available option.

More sophisticated computerized ticketing allows rail operators to analyse passengers' regular journeys. Potentially, individual passengers can be advised that their journey has been disrupted and free shuttle buses (which WMATA did arrange) have been laid on. Equally, other passengers can be advised that their normal line has not been affected.

Even without gathering data on passengers, WMATA could use social media to send targeted messages. It has just one official Twitter account, although there are numerous critical accounts, such as @wmataFAIL, @WMATAHarassment, @MetroShutsDoors, collecting stories to embarrass the authority. It would be perfectly simple for the authority to create Twitter feeds for each line and/or for each station, enabling it to deliver targeted messages as well as broadcast ones.

The use of the WMATA Twitter feed was heavily criticized by crisis experts during the delays surrounding the crash. Unlike the email and text messages or the website, the Twitter feed spoke of a "situation" and "disruption," without making it clear that the cause was a crash between two trains, for which WMATA had overall responsibility. In fact, there were reassuring messages that the authority could deliver. While the number of casualties may not have been clear at the time, what was clear was that the trains involved were traveling *into* central Washington at the start of the evening rush hour, a time when the majority of passengers were traveling in the opposite direction. A crash in the same place in the morning or between trains traveling in the opposite direction in the evening would have been likely to have killed far more people. At nine fatalities, the crash was nonetheless the deadliest in the history of the Metro system, and the Twitter feed should have acknowledged that the delays were caused by a *fatal* crash.

Learnings

While the shift to social media usage and especially cell phone access to social media has accelerated since June 2009, there is much more that WMATA could have done, even at the time.

☑ What Fenty did right

- He arrived at the scene quickly and gave reassuring interviews to the media.

☑ What WMATA did right

- It laid on shuttle buses for passengers and communicated well via website, email, and text.

☒ What WMATA did badly

- It failed to acknowledge the seriousness of the incident on Twitter.
- It failed to establish differentiated Twitter accounts for more targeted information, and, as of February 2014, still has not done this.

SELF BRANDJACK WMATA's own system failed and the communication response was patchy.

31 Maytag offends a leading blogger
August 2009

Dooce is the handle of blogger and writer, Heather B. Armstrong. She has 1.5 million followers on Twitter, which is 50 percent more than Sarah Palin. Granted, Palin does most of her social media engagement through Facebook (3.9 million likes), but you will have got the picture that Heather has a following. Heather is one of the people that *Time* had in mind when it named "You" as its person of the year 2006, and she has been named as one of the most influential women in the US media. She should wear a sign visible to all customer service people that says "Don't mess with Heather." The guys at Maytag may wish that she did.

Heather and her husband Jon paid $1,300 for a top-end Maytag washing machine. Their expectation was that it would wash their laundry. It didn't, and that caused them some distress. It was three days before the repairman came, and he estimated 7–10 days for parts. When he came back with the parts, they were the wrong ones, which meant ordering parts again, and another 7–10 days. The machine was still brand-new, so you can imagine that Heather and Jon thought Maytag was most definitely in breach of the imaginary instruction not to mess with Heather.

At this point, Heather got on the Maytag helpline and started demanding that something be done – such as providing her with a washing machine that worked until it could repair the brand-new one that didn't work. Maytag did not think this was a good idea. That was when Heather snapped and demanded "Do you know what Twitter is, because I have over a million followers on Twitter?" It turned out the person on the other end of the phone did know what Twitter was – or thought she did – but expressed the view that this would make no difference. Her supervisor thought the same. It turned out that they were wrong.

Heather posted a series of tweets about Maytag, making it clear that her brand-new machine did not work and that her experience with customer service had been appalling. She was rapidly contacted by several retailers, such as Whirlpool (Maytag's parent company) and Bosch. Whirlpool quickly made arrangements to sort out the problem. Bosch offered her a brand-new machine. She tweeted about the offer, saying she didn't feel able to accept it. Another Twitterata suggested she donate the Bosch to a shelter, which, with Bosch's agreement, she did. Apparently, Twitter did make a difference.

Learnings

Some people have suggested that Heather is a bully. She addressed this issue herself in her lengthy blog on the subject,[15] and in one sense they have a point. Heather reached a point in her dealings with Maytag where she was demanding special treatment because of her position in Twitter. Special, that is, in comparison with what Maytag was prepared to do for lesser mortals. But what she was asking was not really all that special. She wanted her brand-new top-of-the-line washing machine to, er, wash her laundry. How special is that? She wanted the 10-year service contract she paid for to mean that it could rapidly repair a product that didn't even work for 10 hours. Not that special, really.

If Maytag wants a reputation for quality, it has to communicate that circumstances such as this – where an expensive washing machine simply doesn't work on day one – are exceptional. This means saying to the customer that while it would normally take a few days to get a repairman round and another 7–10 days to get parts, it recognizes that in these circumstances that falls well below the mark.

There is a story about a man driving a Rolls-Royce abroad who suffered a breakdown. The camshaft broke. Rolls flew out an engineer and replaced it. No invoice was sent, so he phoned up and asked how he should go about paying for the service. Rolls said "Sir, there must be some mistake. Camshafts on Rolls-Royce motor cars don't break." The story may be apocryphal, but what does it tell you about the reputation of Rolls-Royce? It can move mountains for you if something goes wrong, *because things hardly ever go wrong*.

Dealing with an exceptional breakdown in product reliability and customer service through the ordinary system implies that it is perfectly ordinary for expensive washing machines to simply not work. The Rolls-Royce approach, which implies it is making things up as it goes along, is superior because of the clear message: Rolls does not have a procedure for dealing with issues like this, because these things don't happen.

Whirlpool is now well regarded for its social media strategy. In presenting case studies at conferences, Bryan Sneider and Scott Spiegel of Whirlpool make the following recommendations:[16]

1 Remember that consumers interact with your brand – they don't interact separately with customer services, PR, and marketing. They expect you to behave as though you are a single organization.
2 Your brand experts need to be available in social media to answer questions from Twitter and Facebook fans.
3 Different brands have different objectives. The different brands within the Whirlpool group have different priorities.

☒ What Maytag did wrong

- It failed to recognize that it was dealing with a powerful blogger.
- It wasn't investing in the reputation of its premium brand. Sneider's point about priorities is relevant here: a premium brand needs to be backed by quality.

☑ What Maytag did right

- It moved quickly to correct the situation once the story became public.

▥▶ What Maytag could have done differently

- It could have reacted as though such poor performance was exceptional, and required an exceptional reaction.

32 "United Breaks Guitars"
July 2009

This is the story of one of the purest and most effective viral brandjacks ever. In July 2009, a major corporation faced a crisis in its reputation through the action of a single dissatisfied customer who wrote a song about his experiences and posted it on YouTube.

Dave Carroll – a singer-songwriter and part of the group Sons of Maxwell – was traveling from Halifax, Nova Scotia to Omaha, Nebraska, with a layover at Chicago O'Hare airport. He was flying United Airlines with his $3,500 Taylor guitar checked in as luggage. Both Dave and several other passengers had seen ground staff at O'Hare throwing guitar cases to each other on the runway. He immediately alerted cabin crew to the issue, but no one was helpful. Dave tells the story very effectively in song, and the video is well worth reviewing. As he puts it, the employees "showed complete indifference towards me."

On landing in Nebraska, Dave "confirmed what I'd suspected." The guitar was damaged beyond repair. (Dave's video shows the chalk outline of a guitar with a broken neck.) As a result, he submitted a claim for compensation, but this was rejected as he had failed to apply within 24 hours of landing. For the next nine months he remained in dispute with United, but the airline insisted that there was no possibility it could pay compensation. So Dave wrote a song about the incident and posted it on YouTube.

One of the main factors in the subsequent development of this story is the quality of the material. The song is very funny, as is the video. The whole thing is brilliantly put together. The "year-long saga" concludes with the airline giving him a "final word" of "no." Dave says his inspiration for producing a song was to ask himself "What would Michael Moore have done?" It says a lot about the success of this brandjack that customers in dispute with corporations these days are likely to ask themselves, "What would Dave Carroll do?"

Dave posted his video on July 6, 2009. In the first 24 hours, there were 150,000 views. Dave Carroll and Sons of Maxwell had an existing fanbase, but as the song went viral, the circle extended far beyond the usual range of website visitors. People who liked the song sent the link to friends. The day it was posted, Rob Bradford, managing director of customer solutions at United Airlines, personally telephoned Dave to apologize for the incident and ask if the company could use the video as part of its staff training program. By July 9, the video had over 0.5 million views and by mid-August some 5 million. A year later, it had been seen by 9 million people.

Initially, Bradford had offered a cash payment from United as compensation for the broken guitar, along with some flight vouchers. Since Bob Taylor, of Taylor Guitars, had already replaced Dave's guitar, the cash was donated to a charity instead. Taylor Guitars must have benefited tremendously from the viral success of "United Breaks Guitars," as the company's product is repeatedly mentioned in the chorus.

On July 22, *The Times* newspaper in London wrote:

> within four days of the song going online, the gathering thunderclouds of bad PR caused United Airlines' stock price to suffer a mid-flight stall, and it plunged by 10 per cent, costing shareholders $180 million. Which, incidentally, would have bought Carroll more than 51,000 replacement guitars.

It is worth noting that the causal link implied by *The Times* is speculative. The stock price had shown volatility in the preceding months and other airlines showed a decline in valuation at the same time, so the extent to which the video may have caused the decline is questionable.

Since the original video, Dave has produced two new songs in the series, one about his dealings with the United employee Ms Irlweg. *The Times* article quoted above, which was published before the second song, speculated that no one would want to be Ms Irlweg with the second video due out, but the mood of the song is not personal, blaming the airline's policy.

Dave also produced a third, more conciliatory song, in which he talks more about general customer service at United and how the airline claims to be changing. There is also a YouTube response from an angry young woman claiming to be Ms Irlweg. The response is almost certainly a hoax: there is no evidence that the video is genuinely from a United employee.

In addition to securing a complete and satisfactory settlement to his original dispute, Dave Carroll has significantly raised his profile and that of his group, Sons of Maxwell. Furthermore, he has developed a whole new career as a speaker on customer service issues. In itself, this is a considerable testament to the power of brandjacking.

In the original song, Dave says that he would never again entrust his luggage to United. His dispute now seems to have been satisfactorily resolved. According to postings on Wikipedia, Dave has indeed flown with United again – presumably using the flight vouchers he was given – while touring the country speaking on customer service issues. On one of Dave's trips, United lost his luggage. I am guessing that, on this occasion, customer service staff were accommodating. All he would have to say to them was "I am Dave Carroll."

Learnings

First, humor is an especially valuable weapon in the irreverent world of digital media. Second, look at the power of the viral. People liked the video, so they referred it to their friends. That is the sole reason this video spread so far and fast. By underestimating these factors, and seeking to stand firm on a restrictive company policy, United may have cost its shareholders $180 million in value.

☒ What United did wrong

- It developed a set of restrictions designed to make it difficult for customers to claim compensation.
- It doesn't seem to have empowered staff to exercise discretion.

☑ What United did right

- It acted promptly to correct the situation. That call to Dave from a company managing director shows that United was taking the crisis seriously, although it may also reflect the fact that people below that level have little power to make decisions.
- It has made use of Dave Carroll and his video in staff training to prevent future problems.

| CUSTOMER REVOLT BRANDJACK | Customer loses patience and asks "What would Michael Moore do?" His answer is better than any of Moore's work. |

33 Soft drinks co. helps young men score, then women get to hear about it
October 2009

This is a great example of the self brandjack. PepsiCo launched a marketing initiative that came to dominate the social media conversation, in an unflattering way. Pepsi launched a sophisticated, useful, interactive iPhone app linked to its Amp Energy brand. It was selling a lifestyle, targeted at young men. Amp

Energy is a popular soft drink aimed mostly at younger people. It is a sponsor of NASCAR driver Dale Earnhardt Jr and a number of athletes and has partnered with prominent DJs. It was the sponsor of World Extreme Cagefighting. The iPhone app caused an immediate stir and big brand profile. If it hadn't been for the whole alienating women thing, it would have been a major hit.

The iPhone app, "Amp up before you score," seems to have been technologically complex and in some ways rather insightful. For example, imagine you are a young man seeking to score with women. You spot a likely target. You whip out your iPhone and select from the supplied list the type of woman she is: Sorority girl? Foreign exchange student? Tree hugger? Political girl? The app will then connect you with a series of chat-up lines targeted at her type, as well as actual interactive information. For example, if she is a tree hugger, it will give you a live Twitter feed of any tweets mentioning "carbon footprint." If she is a punk, it will give you the Wikipedia history of punk rock. I suppose this puts it well ahead of websites offering the neurolinguistic programming way to score with women.

So what was the app? Was it a way that sensitive young men could become informed on subjects of interest to a young woman before approaching her? Or was it a way for some guy to fake an interest in tree hugging so he could score? Presumably, it could be used for either purpose. *Information* is neither of these things: it is morally neutral. The moral judgments come to bear on what someone does with the information. That said, the name of the product, the rather patronizing way it classified women, and the fact that it included a bragging list – digital notches on your bedpost – implied that it was aimed at the second market.

Does that mean PepsiCo could have tweaked the product and been praised for its sensitive and sophisticated handling of the perennial young person's dilemma? It seems unlikely. The classification was integral to the operation of the app. And people's fear of technology means that any digital application is always going to be judged by the worst thing someone could do with it. There are still a great many people in positions of power in the MSM who are happy to blame new technology for every dubious application to which it is put. Look at the way Facebook is blamed for the fact that pedophiles can use it to find children, when parks are generally thought of as morally neutral. Think of the media outrage when a crime is plotted *on the Internet*, when nobody thinks that Starbucks is to blame if people plot their crimes in a coffee bar. It was always inevitable that PepsiCo would be blamed for every clod who used the app in an insensitive way. It would probably have been blamed if someone had used the app and then gone on to commit rape, as if the failed seduction and not the rape were the problem.

In some ways, none of the issues raised by the app was all that new. Branding strategies have been implying that, by associating yourself with a particular brand, you can suddenly live the lifestyle of the good looking and successful since, well, since there have been branding strategies. And right at the heart of this lifestyle is your access to hot young people of the opposite sex. Advertising and reputation management around the principal soft drink rivals have been consistent for more than a century. The ads often involve good-looking young people consuming the product.

Nor are offensive "strategies" for scoring anything particularly new. "Guaranteed" lines for chatting up your target can be found in numerous books and magazines and, in even greater number and with less elegance and tact, online.

Nonetheless, the reaction to the Pepsi app was wholly predictable. It was widely considered to be offensive. Blogs, Twitter, and the MSM took up the issue. Mashable's article on the subject was headlined "Alienate Your Female Customers? Pepsi Has An App For That."

As Hortense put it on Jezebel.com:[17] "This is a program sponsored by a major corporation that encourages men to look at women as objects to be won, used, and tossed away after a 'victory' is obtained." She continued by promising to keep on mocking the program, in the same vein as her earlier comment: "Don't you wish your date was gross like me? Don't you wish your date was a creep like me? Don't cha?!"

Before long, Pepsi removed the video promoting the app and then removed the app itself from the app store. This was followed by the inevitable apology on Twitter. Interestingly, Pepsi's tweet on the subject included the hashtag #pepsifail, which ensured the tweet came to the attention of those most active in discussing the issue, but involved Pepsi actively associating its brand name with the word "fail."

Learnings

☒ What Pepsi did wrong

- There was not enough research done into this product. It is easy to imagine that Pepsi researched the product with young men, and found that they liked the idea. But it must have been obvious from the start that women would get to hear about the app. It is inconceivable that it could have advertised the product to half of America's youth without the other half even learning of the app. And surely any observation of the way young people behave would have revealed that while young men often talk in an insensitive way about young women, they almost never do it in front of them. That would be self-defeating.

✓ What Pepsi did right

- It withdrew the product promptly when it started to generate controversy. There was no serious attempt to defend the product.
- It apologized quickly. Using the hashtag #pepsifail was always going to be controversial, but it was the right call. It spoke directly to the people who were criticizing the company.

SELF BRANDJACK Bizarre misjudgment by company leaves it open to massive, and wholly predictable, backlash.

34 The world's biggest cell phone provider tweets homophobia

February 2010

Vodafone was the world's largest cell phone operator by revenues in 2010, but China Mobile has since overtaken it. Although it has a secondary listing on the NASDAQ, its HQ is in Newbury, UK and its main listing is on the London Stock Exchange, where it is ranked fourth in the FTSE 100.

In February 2010, a tweet was issued on the VodafoneUK Twitter feed saying: "VodafoneUK is fed up of dirty homo's [sic] and is going after beaver." The natural assumption among the Twitterati was that Vodafone's Twitter account had been hacked. Surely, the company cannot really have issued that tweet? However, Vodafone quickly confirmed that its account had not been hacked, and the tweet had indeed been sent from inside its building, albeit not by someone expressing the corporation's official position.

The apology, published again and again, both as a general announcement and as an @reply to individuals who had commented on the offensive tweet, said: "An inappropriate message. Severe breach of rules by staff in our building, dealing with that internally. We're extremely sorry."

Intriguingly, almost all the blogs and MSM articles I have located have focused exclusively on the homophobic aspects of the tweet, as though saying "VodafoneUK is going after beaver" would have been uncontroversial – a rather unlikely proposition, I am sure we can agree.

"Dealing with that internally" turned out to mean, in the first instance, an indefinite suspension for the employee concerned. Some media commentary has suggested this should have involved summary dismissal. This ignores the fact that UK employment protection law, while almost certainly allowing summary dismissal for a breach of discipline this severe, requires fair procedure. Asking why the employee was not fired immediately is a bit like asking why the murderer was not executed on the day of the murder. No matter how serious the offense, you still have to hold a trial.

Learnings

At the time of the incident, Vodafone UK had 11,000 followers on Twitter and tens of thousands of fans of its Facebook page. By 2013, this had risen to 20,000 on Twitter and 670,000 on Facebook. Open and transparent operations need to encourage employees to participate in social media. That said, only limited numbers of people should be able to speak on behalf of the organization. Both groups of people will need training in what is and is not acceptable behavior. In this case, it is difficult to believe that Vodafone was caught out because of lack of training or procedures. It seems certain that the employee concerned knew perfectly well they were breaking the rules. The explanation seems to be that the offending staff member thought they were leaving a spoof message on a friend's computer, which would only be seen by the friend. It was not their intention to publish it to the whole Twittersphere.

Vodafone has an active profile in social media – as befits one of the largest providers of cell phone services. Increasingly, social media are accessed on mobile devices, and Vodafone is right at the heart of this. It claims to be active in around 95 percent of social media debates about Vodafone. It claims resolution and customer satisfaction rates of more than 85 percent for queries raised in social media. Its social media are not merely for customer relations. It also has clear objectives for market intelligence, such as competitor monitoring and handset trends. (NB: Vodafone is not a handset manufacturer.) Another priority in social media strategy is advance identification of issues.

☑ What Vodafone did right

- It acted immediately to discipline the rogue employee and apologize to followers and everyone who commented on the tweet.
- It moved on, and has not commented on the issue since.

Clear breach of established procedures by a staff member endangers the company's reputation.

35 An airline bumps a passenger for being too fat
February 2010

Kevin Smith was already seated for his flight from Oakland to Burbank when he was ordered off the flight by the captain for being too fat. Kevin Smith is also an outspoken film director and blogger with more than 1.6 million followers on Twitter. Southwest Airlines should probably have seen this one coming.

According to Southwest Airlines, the policy affected anyone who was unable to put both armrests down, and was introduced following customer complaints about fat people encroaching into their space. According to Kevin Smith, he was also told that he was a safety risk. Some of the facts are not disputed. Kevin Smith concedes that he is fat: "I know I'm fat, but was Captain Leysath really justified in throwing me off a flight for which I was already seated?"

After a Twitterstorm of complaints, Southwest Airlines apologized, some six hours after Smith's first tweet on the subject. Smith was in no mood to accept the apology, telling the "PR-challenged fatty-haters" that "Your 'apology' blog is insulting, redacted, bullshit."

Within a day, Southwest was blogging about the subject. It apologized, again, for the way the issue was handled, and divulged some additional information about its longstanding relationship with Kevin Smith. Apparently, the customer of size policy is 25 years old, and applied by many other airlines. Kevin Smith has long known all about it, and usually purchases two seats. In fact, he had booked and paid for two seats on this occasion too, but chose to fly on an earlier flight, which meant he was a standby customer. As a standby customer, he could not be seated until all the booked customers were seated. It turned out that there weren't two seats together, so he couldn't be accommodated. Even as he was ejected, to take the flight he had in any case booked, he was given a $100 flight voucher. It also turns out that Southwest Airlines has a different policy to most other airlines – in fact, it claims the policy is unique. If a customer of size has booked two seats and there are spare seats on the flight, the airline refunds the price of the second seat.

So, what was the fuss about? Let's give Kevin Smith the benefit of the doubt and assume it wasn't all a publicity stunt for his career as a filmmaker. If a customer requires, under your rules, two seats, and has actually paid for two seats, why were staff trying to accommodate him on a flight for which he had no booking and they didn't have enough seats? It sounds as though there was an administrative cock-up. They thought they could accommodate a standby passenger, without realizing this particular passenger needed two seats. This meant that Kevin Smith had to be ejected from the flight, even though he had already been seated. And, from his original tweet, this seems to be his complaint. It wasn't that Southwest required him to pay for two seats. Apparently, he had done that. It was that he was ejected from the flight, which must have been humiliating.

Staff probably should have realized immediately that humiliating a regular customer in this way was going to be a problem, and required rather more than just a $100 voucher. They also don't seem to have anticipated the social media reach of a successful filmmaker with 1.6 million followers on Twitter, which has to be a major error of judgment.

Learnings

Southwest has been held up as an example of good practice in social media. It makes consistent, light-hearted use of social media channels. Each channel has a separate voice and a clear purpose. Blogs are used to delve into issues, Twitter as a teaser for news and other channels, and Facebook for its promotions. This issue did not arise because of any failing in Southwest's social media strategy, rather because an operative on the ground failed to spot the social media ramifications of a decision that humiliated a regular customer.

☒ What Southwest Airlines did wrong

- This is a sensitive issue, and the employee on the ground made an administrative error, which led to humiliating treatment of a regular customer. Having made the error, more profuse apologies and more generous compensation should have been arranged.

 A customer with a strong existing base in social media created a storm of protest over a personal slight.

36 A chain store uses plagiarized artwork
February 2010

British-based multinational stationery chain Paperchase came under fire in blogs and on Twitter in plagiarism claims, which it strongly denied. However, as the story gathered pace, the artist from whom the chain had purchased the design admitted to being "influenced" by the artist claiming plagiarism, forcing an apology from Paperchase.

The story began when an independent artist saw a design on sale on Paperchase notebooks that bore a striking resemblance to her work. She says she approached Paperchase and the company ignored her. Paperchase denies this. It says it was in touch having investigated the matter and concluding that there had been no plagiarism. Then the artist – who blogs and tweets under the name @hiddeneloise – wrote about her experience. The story gathered momentum when it was picked up by Neil Gaiman, US-based British SF and fantasy writer, who took the artist's side.

At this point, Paperchase began to defend itself publicly. Timothy Melgund, CEO of Paperchase, denied any wrongdoing. He insisted that staff had fully investigated the allegations, which they had taken seriously. Paperchase had purchased the designs from an independent agency and put the agency "under considerable pressure" over the matter, but was eventually convinced that there was no plagiarism.

Paperchase was, understandably, defensive. It had received hundreds of complaints, some very aggressive, and calls for boycotts of the company. Melgund insisted he could understand the strength of feeling, which would have been justified if Paperchase had engaged in plagiarism. The issue raised for him questions about the "powers, and there in the danger of Twitter. I am sure it can be beneficial but if you get an untruth (on it) it can be very dangerous."[18] This seems to have been the first time Melgund considered the risks of Twitter, as Paperchase had almost zero engagement on the microblogging site at the time.

Unfortunately, Melgund's line of defense soon fell apart. Indeed, in his interview with the *Daily Telegraph*, published on February 11, 2010, he seemed to be pursuing two lines of defense: that Paperchase had purchased the designs "in good faith" and also that the work wasn't plagiarized anyway. Using the phrase "good faith" implies that Melgund was already entertaining doubts about the design and wanted to make sure that people understood that if there had been any theft of intellectual property, Paperchase was an innocent victim.

The chain of purchase seems to have been this: a freelance artist sold the design to an agency called Gather No Moss, which sold the design on to Paperchase. As the Twitterstorm escalated – at one point #paperchase was the top trending search on Twitter – the artist came forward and apologized to both @hiddeneloise and Paperchase, admitting that her design had indeed been influenced by @hiddeneloise. Paperchase promptly apologized and withdrew the products from sale.

Learnings

In terms of its actions, Paperchase does seem to have done more or less the right thing. It purchased the design in good faith. It investigated when the matter was raised with the company. It apologized when it turned out that the design had indeed been stolen. There is a question mark over the quality of its communication with @hiddeneloise, with the parties simply giving contradictory accounts. Paperchase *should* have been in personal and direct communication with her about its investigations. The company insists it was and she insists it wasn't.

Where Paperchase was caught unprepared was in its engagement with social media. It had no existing goodwill on which it could rely. Its Twitter account was effectively dormant, and made almost no contribution to the debate about the company. Twitter was alive with a conversation about Paperchase, and Paperchase was not participating.

Eight months later, Paperchase, which has more than 100 stores in the UK and over 300 concessions in Borders stores across the US, had just 212 followers on Twitter. This compares with over 1,600 for @hiddeneloise and over 1.5 million for Neil Gaiman. Even before the celebrity involvement, the major corporation was a social media minnow compared with the freelance artist. By 2013, the Paperchase account had overtaken @hiddeneloise and has almost 9,000 followers, but (although it appears to be genuine) has still not been verified by Twitter. This is still a very small number for a major retailer. Gaiman now has almost 2 million followers.

☒ What Paperchase did wrong

- It seems the store was not as able as it thought it was to guarantee its supply chain.

- It tried to hedge its bets in its defense, claiming there had been no wrongdoing, while also claiming "good faith." This is normal in legal disputes, but hard to defend as a PR strategy.
- It may have failed to engage after Hidden Eloise made her first contact with the company, although Paperchase denies this.
- It had no existing engagement or credibility in social media.

☑ What Paperchase did right

- It investigated immediately.
- When it turned out to be in the wrong, it immediately apologized and withdrew the products from sale.

▐▐▶ What Paperchase might have done differently

- Offered Hidden Eloise some work. The company obviously liked her work, and has reason to doubt the reliability of one of its suppliers. Why not buy artwork directly from Hidden Eloise and also employ her to boost the company's social media profile?

SELF BRANDJACK	Somewhere in the supply chain, there was clear misconduct or misjudgment. Paperchase itself was more of a victim than a malefactor, but needs to make it clear that is has rigorous procedures to protect itself and artists.

37 A multinational calms critics with an appearance on Digg Dialogg
November 2009–February 2010

Toyota is the world's largest automobile manufacturer by sales and volume. Traditionally well regarded for quality and safety, it was forced to initiate three separate but linked product recalls in four months.

In November 2009, Toyota began to recall some models affected by an issue with the floor mat on the driver's side. The mat could become entangled in the accelerator ("floor mat incursion"), causing "sudden unintended acceleration." By January 2010, it was clear that not all the cases of sudden unintended acceleration were caused by floor mat incursion, and some models were prone to mechanical sticking of the accelerator. Then, in February 2010, Toyota issued a recall relating to anti-lock brake software.

Three separate recalls in such a short space of time is extremely damaging to the reputation of any company, and, in the case of an automotive manufacturer, raises serious issues of liability. The automotive industry has struggled for some time with allegations of sudden unintended acceleration, with considerable disputes as to the extent and even the existence of the problem. In the 1980s, America's National Highway Traffic Safety Administration concluded that the problem must be due to driver error. Other explanations offered at different times have included mechanical and electrical problems with the cars.

The climate of public and political opinion within the US was also not favorable to a Japanese-owned automotive company with difficulties. Although Toyota manufactures in the US, it is generally still thought of as a Japanese company. The big three Detroit manufacturers were all in considerable difficulty at the time, with GM and Chrysler filing for Chapter 11 bankruptcy protection in 2009, and the federal government ultimately taking a stake in GM as part of the reorganization. Given the political connections of the big three and the automotive unions, any issue with any of their competitors was sure to be magnified in the political and media debate.

Toyota responded by engaging heavily in social media. Its most striking innovation was the use of Digg Dialogg as a means of driving the conversation. Digg describes itself as a social news site. Its core method of operation at the time of the Toyota crisis (a new version was launched in August 2010) was that it allowed members to either "digg" or "bury" stories and thus vote them up or down a popularity list. The most "dugg" story would adorn the front page of the site as the lead story of any news site does. Digg Dialogg is a video interview based on this core technology. Questions are submitted in advance by members of the Digg community, who then vote the questions up or down the list. The 10 most popular questions are then put to the guest.

Learnings

Toyota's first lesson from this crisis was rather basic: when you are obsessing about something internally, your publics are not necessarily obsessing about the same issue. Jim Lentz, president and CEO of Toyota North America, was interviewed on Digg TV on February 8, 2010 – the very height of the recall crisis. The recall had triggered Digg's interest in Toyota and Toyota's desire to engage with Digg. Yet 6 of the 10 most popular questions were not about the recall.

The single most popular question was "What do you drive?" For the president of an automotive company, this is a great question. It enabled him to talk about his full range of products. His answer was that he drives his full product range fairly frequently, and also drives competitor models. He was able to talk about what he likes about different models, and how they compare with competitor products. You could see that he was enjoying the question. It seems that, unlike journalists, the audience occasionally wants to learn something from interviewees, and is much less obsessed with catching them out.

Toyota was extremely pleased with the result. Not only did Scott DeYager, Toyota's social media supervisor, choose to talk about his company's experience with social media during the recall crisis at the Public Relations Society of America's Digital Impact Conference in May 2010, but Dino Triantafyllos, VP of quality, went on Digg TV in June 2010. DeYager advises companies that potential advocates are waiting for you to reach out for them. You should not wait for a crisis before engaging with them. Your availability to engage with your publics – and listening as well as talking – are critical to your process. Transparency is a key goal, as is humanizing the brand. Both are challenging, but achievable. Finally, DeYager recommends that you need a radar to keep an eye out for your brand haters.

☑ What Toyota did right

- It engaged with the community.
- It humanized its brand.

SELF BRANDJACK A voluntary self brandjack in which the company invited the Digg community to set the agenda for its interview.

38 Greenpeace gets Nestlé to "Give the orangutan a break"

February 2010

"Give the orangutan a break" was the next stage in the Greenpeace campaign on palm oil (see Dove, CS 20). It was a creative, well-planned, and well-resourced PR campaign designed to achieve a specific behavior change – to get Nestlé to stop buying palm oil from companies that engage in deforestation in Southeast Asia.

Greenpeace typically portrays itself as being the plucky little guy taking on the giants, rather like Dave Carroll and his campaign (CS 32). The contrasts are, in fact, extreme. Greenpeace is a global leader in PR, with worldwide representation. Its total budgets are smaller than Nestlé's, but PR campaigning is Greenpeace's core business activity. Most of its resources are devoted to that specific goal and not, for example, to manufacturing chocolate. Greenpeace also has huge off-budget resources – the time of its volunteers around the world, who are critical to the success of its business model. United Airlines could not have anticipated Dave Carroll's success, but any business taking on Greenpeace knows that it is in a fight with one of the most professional and effective PR operations in the world.

As with other Greenpeace campaigns, it was long in the planning. The implementation stage turned out to be much shorter than the group anticipated. An insider told me that all the planning was built around the assumption that Nestlé would be a tough nut to crack. The company had been resisting campaigns on the marketing of formula milk for more than 30 years.

The creativity at the heart of the campaign was a mock ad for one of Nestlé's premier products: Kit Kat. As with Unilever, Nestlé is less well known than the brands of its individual products. Kit Kat is a long-established chocolate brand, first created by the British company, Rowntree. In the major North American market, Kit Kat is not even a Nestlé product, and is manufactured under license by Hershey. When Nestlé took over Rowntree in 1988, it acquired control of the Kit Kat brand everywhere except North America, where the licensing arrangement persists. Nestlé added new manufacturing, including in Southeast Asia, and began to develop the brand in new markets. Since the 1990s, Nestlé has also been stretching the brand by adding variants to the familiar chocolate and wafer formula, the first of which was orange Kit Kat.

Kit Kat's advertising has incorporated the "break" theme since 1937 and the familiar "have a break, have a Kit Kat" slogan has been in use since the 1950s. The Greenpeace version of the Kit Kat ad is still available on YouTube and is well worth watching. Just search for "Give the orangutan a break." The ad is closely modeled on a real Kit Kat ad. It shows a bored young office worker engaged with the mind-numbing task of shredding documents. This cuts to the red background and familiar font of Kit Kat and the tag line "have a break." But when the young man opens his Kit Kat, the finger he breaks off is not chocolate and wafer: it is an orangutan's hairy finger. As he bites into it, blood spurts out and drips down his chin onto his desk. The imagery is consciously disturbing. The scene then cuts to a new tagline: "give the orangutan a break … ," then footage of an orangutan in his natural habitat, on to a scene of chainsaws laying waste to a forest, and finally a new tagline: "Stop Nestlé buying palm oil from companies that destroy the rainforests." The ad was beautifully crafted and highly effective. It is short, and Greenpeace's army of volunteers was happy to forward it on to their contacts.

Nestlé is a somewhat cautious, old-fashioned company. Its first reaction was to reach for the lawyers. If such an approach ever made sense in crisis management, it has long been superseded in the world of social media. Nestlé insisted that YouTube – a Google company – remove the offending ad on the grounds of copyright infringement. YouTube immediately complied. But suppressing videos on YouTube is a game of Whac-A-Mole. Members of the YouTube community kept reposting the video. As Facebook users started posting messages on Nestlé's Facebook page, Nestlé started deleting them, aggravating the social media community even more.

The release of the viral video, and its promotion through Greenpeace's extensive networks on Twitter and Facebook, was only one stage in the campaign. Supporters were urged to descend on the Nestlé Facebook page, to send emails to the corporation, to threaten boycotts of Nestlé (and even Hershey) products.

Learnings

It must have become apparent, almost immediately, that this battle could not be won by lawyers. Winning it by PR techniques and social media engagement would be a long, unlikely, and expensive process. Ignoring the campaign was out of the question. By far Nestlé's most sensible option was surrender. Palm oil is not Nestlé's core product, and it could drop it, or re-source it at relatively low cost. If Nestlé was to take any lesson from this, it would probably be that it should have surrendered more quickly. Deploying the lawyers was a huge strategic error, and turned the conversation onto the question of censorship, which always infuriates social media users. I am in no doubt that more people forwarded the link to the video, or embedded it in their website, precisely *because* Nestlé tried to get the video removed.

To object that social media users completely misunderstand the concept of censorship – which is government trying to suppress debate, not YouTube deciding what can and can't be posted on its site – is little more than a debating point. People will be infuriated by such actions whether or not "censorship" is the right word to describe them. (People accused Vodafone of "censorship" for initiating disciplinary action against the employee who abused the corporate Twitter account (CS 34). It was almost the only point cited in defense of the person in question.)

☒ What Nestlé did wrong

- It reached for its lawyers. It should have been obvious that this would be self-defeating, and so it proved.
- It imagined it could tough it out, when there was really little reason to do so.

☑ What Nestlé did right

- It quickly realized that there was no value in fighting this, and surrendered.

☑ What Greenpeace did right

- It planned the campaign in detail, identifying Nestlé's key vulnerabilities.
- It made excellent use of its creative team and produced high-quality content: the imagery is disturbing and memorable, the message is clear.
- It identified a clear and deliverable behavior change it was requiring of Nestlé.
- It mobilized its extensive network of professional and volunteer campaigners to pressurize Nestlé.

ETHICS BRANDJACK This is a model campaign, and will be a core case study for NGOs and businesses for some time, at least, until someone – probably Greenpeace – surpasses it.

39 Facebook called on to unfriend coal
February 2010 onwards

Facebook is, by its nature, one of the most social media-savvy companies in existence. It must have believed that by choosing to build its new, energy-efficient data center in a depressed part of rural Oregon it was beyond criticism. However, the local power utility generates most of its electricity from coal – and that is controversial.

IT data centers are massive users of electricity, which is required not only to power the servers, but also to cool them. The Pacific northwest of the US, with its relatively equable climate, is a popular location for such data centers. The fairly cool climate means that, for much of the year, cooling can be accomplished using fresh air. The state of Oregon also provides tax breaks for companies locating in rural areas, which are often short of jobs.

Given that energy use is one of the major costs in a data center, it is in the interests of the operator to invest in energy-saving measures, and Facebook consciously did this from the outset, talking loudly about the environmental benefits of this investment. Locals in Oregon praised the decision to place the data center in a depressed area with limited local employment prospects. Facebook's decision to locate in Prineville, Oregon, which was announced in January 2010, was initially popular.

By February 2010, however, Greenpeace and other environmental groups were criticizing Facebook for not taking more note of how its electricity was going to be generated. Pacificorp, the local utility, generates 58 percent of its electricity from coal. Greenpeace has argued that major customers such as Facebook can exert pressure on utility businesses to shift from coal.

Greenpeace's major tactic was to set up a Facebook page criticizing Facebook and urging the company to "unfriend coal." It also used the phrase "the so coal network" to describe Facebook. As of November 2010, supporters claimed that more than 600,000 Facebook members supported the campaign. The campaign is not trivial. Greenpeace claims that the growth in data centers is such that, worldwide, by 2020 they will be using more electricity than France, Germany, Canada, and Brazil combined. By the time the campaign began, Facebook was already committed to contracts for the building of the data center, so backing out or relocating was not really an option. In contrast to the Greenpeace campaign on BP's approach to bituminous deposits (CS 40), Greenpeace had not identified the critical timeline in advance and wasn't really able to influence Facebook's decision making.

Interestingly, Facebook was extremely resistant to the campaign. It hit back at Greenpeace, not only defending its own record in designing in energy efficiency but also pointing out that Greenpeace's own data center in Virginia is largely coal powered. In August 2010, Facebook announced plans to extend the Prineville data center and, perhaps even more provocatively, in November 2010, it committed to a new data center in North Carolina that will also be mostly powered by coal. That Facebook made three announcements about new data center capacity in the same year clearly indicates the speed at which this company was growing. That it felt able to defy Greenpeace campaigns on the issue reflects the company's strength in its social networks.

By October 2011, however, Greenpeace was claiming victory. Facebook announced another data center, outside the US. This one was to be in Sweden, close to the Arctic Circle and making even greater use of fresh air cooling. Furthermore, the center is "close to renewable hydropower in the region." This is not one of Greenpeace's customary victories. Facebook did not invite the

NGO inside to agree to a new policy and get Greenpeace endorsement for the new strategy. Greenpeace picked up the story from tech blogs. It does seem possible that Facebook's decision was linked, in part, to considerations about coal. But this looks very much like a campaign that Greenpeace lost. The later decision to invest in Sweden allowed both sides to save a bit of face.

Learnings

Facebook showed a remarkable resistance to change and a willingness to fight back. It is able to rely on the fact that people have a considerable network utility invested in Facebook. If all your friends are on Facebook, the cost of defecting to a rival social network is considerable. It can also take the Facebook group that Greenpeace established as being not a sample but the totality of its disaffected customers – and it is one-tenth of one percent of the total.

That Facebook decided not only to expand its Oregon facility but to choose a site for a second facility that is also coal powered shows that the organization is not being intimidated by Greenpeace. The tough-minded *tu quoque* (you too) defense may be logically fallacious, but it shows a willingness to take on one of the grandmasters of social media.

As Facebook points out, there isn't a perfect solution to this problem. US utility markets do not, typically, allow customers to choose suppliers, and other factors affect the cost and the carbon footprint of a data center.

Was the subsequent choice of Sweden as the base for a new data center related to the Greenpeace campaign? Who knows, but Greenpeace has decided to claim credit.

✓ What Facebook did right

- It stressed the environmental benefits of choosing a temperate climate and investing in energy-efficiency measures.
- It hit back at Greenpeace's own choices regarding data centers.
- Otherwise, it mostly refused to engage on the issue. If it isn't willing to change its decision, it is better to change the subject.
- It may have adapted its later strategy in line with the criticism.

✗ What Facebook did wrong

- By riding out the storm, and relying on the significant social investments its users have in the network, it comes over as arrogant. If a viable competitor emerges, this may end up hurting the company.

Facebook was put in a situation where its strategic decisions were examined from an environmental perspective.

40 Oil giant faces three crises at once
March–October 2010

From March to October 2010, one of the largest corporations in the world faced an existential crisis focused around a catastrophic oil spill. Almost simultaneously, the company was facing two other challenges in the form of two highly targeted social media campaigns. The first of these – a Greenpeace contest to choose a new logo for BP – had been long in the planning, and just happened to coincide with the Gulf of Mexico disaster.

The BP logo contest shows Greenpeace at its most professional. The organization had estimated, more than a year in advance, that by June 2010, BP would be making a critical decision about whether it was going to exploit Canadian tar (oil) sands. Greenpeace wished to exert pressure on BP that would force the company to abandon its plans. The group's chosen method was to organize a contest to design a new logo and choose a new slogan for BP that would make a mockery of its all-green image and its tagline, "Beyond Petroleum."

As it happened, by the time June 2010 came around, the month when BP was supposed to make its decision about Canadian tar sands, the Deepwater Horizon disaster was making headlines around the world. As a result, Greenpeace recalibrated its campaign to capitalize on the developing PR crisis, but without taking its eye off the main objective of influencing the tar sands decision. Greenpeace takes the view that any exploitation of tar sands carries unacceptable environmental costs, and it is a core objective for the group to oppose any such developments. In the light of the Gulf of Mexico issue, the group widened the campaign to focus on other marginal resources such as deep water fields.

BP had made itself particularly vulnerable to environmental pressure. In the early 2000s, when it first adopted the slogan "Beyond Petroleum" to emphasize its interest in alternative fuels, the company became a target of environmentalists who seriously doubted the company's claim of being a forward-looking, environmentally conscious organization. Although BP had become one of the biggest global investors in renewable energy, environmentalists pointed out that its efforts were dwarfed by ongoing investments in oil. Furthermore, BP's new initiatives in oil exploration were projects that would take decades to complete. Clearly, the company was not looking at moving beyond petroleum any time soon. By trying to be seen as the "greenest" oil company, BP was asking the world to hold it to a standard it must have known, internally, that it couldn't meet.

The Greenpeace campaign was inspired. As had become the Greenpeace way, it integrated traditional media with direct action stunts and a well-targeted social media campaign. The social media element was creative and engaging. Greenpeace invited the public to redesign BP's green floral logo to "something which suits their dirty business." Many of the entries were of a high quality, with images that skillfully blended BP's green floral logo with oil slicks, dead fish, crippled birds, or skulls. In some of the logo proposals, the green and white of the "BP" was overlaid with black or red. One especially creative design recast the flower as a roulette wheel accompanied by the slogan "gambling with your future." The initials "BP" took on a host of new meanings as Greenpeace collected suggestions like "Birds' Pain," "Bent on Profit," "Butcher for Profit," "Britain's Pollution," "Black Poison," "Blame other People," among others.

On April 20, 2010, the semi-submersible Deepwater Horizon rig in the Macondo field of the Gulf of Mexico exploded. Eleven workers were killed in the explosion. The rig burned for 36 hours and then sank. This was the beginning of what was to become one of the worst environmental disasters in American history. From the point of view of BP's relationships with its stakeholders, a major blowout adjacent to the important media market of the US was especially damaging. Burning oil provides excellent TV footage in a way that the slowly developing issue of the oil industry's carbon footprint does not. For weeks, US viewers could see live broadcast images of oil gushing out of a broken pipe on the ocean's floor while the name "BP" was repeated over and over again by commentators.

BP struggled for months with the task of capping the leak. It engaged in an unseemly buck-passing game with its partners, Anadarko and Halliburton, as it tried to pass the blame for the original explosion. It was heavily criticized by President Barack Obama who, to the fury of the British media, called the company "British Petroleum." (The company had intentionally dropped that name many years before when it created the "BP" logo and tagline.) President Obama also joined the chorus accusing the company of buck-passing.

One of the company's biggest weaknesses was the manifest unsuitability of its CEO, Tony Hayward, to the task of engaging with stakeholders. He seemed to regard the process of giving evidence to the US Congress as a waste of his time, although he still found time to go sailing in the clear blue, unpolluted waters off the Isle of Wight. He consistently told Congress that he didn't know the answers to their questions. (In a rapidly developing situation, it is inevitable that you will be asked questions to which you don't know the answer. The appropriate response is to stress that you are actively trying to find out the answers, and you will report back when you do. "I don't know," on its own, can imply that you also don't much care.) Eventually, the BP board removed Hayward from the role of CEO and gave him other tasks. The better performing Bob Dudley, president of BP America, took over the global CEO role. In the circumstances, his American accent was reassuring.

As BP's issues with the Deepwater Horizon developed, Greenpeace somewhat changed the focus of its tar sands campaign to talk about other marginal oil resources such as deep water oil. One of the most effective parallel stunts was to close down BP's gas stations all across London. In part, this was done by tripping, and then removing, the safety switches. The most visual aspect of the campaign, though, was displaying banners reading "Closed: Moving Beyond Petroleum."

In parallel with this, an anonymous Twitter account, @bpglobalpr, began to appear. Initially, there was much speculation as to who might have been responsible, with some people wondering if it might be Greenpeace and others suggesting a BP insider could be behind it. As the issue developed, the author slowly "came out," first under the pseudonym Leroy Stick, and finally revealing himself to be the comedian Josh Simpson. (An anonymous approach was never really in line with the Greenpeace style. The organization likes to heavily brand its protests.)

Beginning in May 2010, the account soon attracted a cult following of more than 180,000 – some twelve times more than the official account @bpamerica. As so often with social media campaigns, it was quality, humor, and authenticity that counted. One of @bpglobalpr's most famous tweets was:

> Safety is our primary concern. Well, profits, then safety. Oh, no—profits, image, then safety, but still—it's right up there.

There were many, many others that struck a nerve. Many people retweeted their favorites, so the satire reached a much larger group than the 180,000 followers. Numerous journalists were among the followers, and it was frequently reported in the print and broadcast media.

A few of Simpson's other "hits" are included below:

> ATTN: Photographers- Breasts and rainbows exist! Quit taking awful pictures of oily animals, you jerks. (http://ow.ly/2auXN)

Here's the truth: we got food poisoning from shrimp one time and said, "Let's make sure that never happens again." (#bpcares)

As long as we can get loaded potato skins at T.G.I.Friday's, seafood can suck it. (http://ow.ly/24XhO #bpcares)

This BP Offshore Oil Strike board game is ridiculous. Oil tycoons don't have to follow any "rules". (http://ow.ly/28qp1)

Funny, the liberal media never talks about sharks we've killed. (#bpcares)

Now that we're done testifying before Congress, it's fairly safe to say the worst part of this is over. (#bpcares)

Obama wants us to start a liability account to pay spill victims. We'd rather not, but thanks for asking! (#bpcares)

BP, more or less, did nothing about Simpson. The company could have asked Twitter to close the account, but Twitter would only have complied if it thought that people were genuinely confused into thinking that @bpglobalpr was the real BP's Twitter account. To suggest that anyone might have been taken in would have been embarrassing in the extreme, given the content of the parody feed. It did ask for the account page to be clarified, stating that it was a parody. It got its own @bpamerica account verified. (The account name had been held by BP since 2008.) But, sensibly, it did not call in its lawyers. If one of the largest corporations in the world had taken legal action against a lone satirist, we can be sure who would have won the PR battle, especially as it was difficult to argue that BP was in the right on the actual issues.

It is obviously difficult to give either Greenpeace or Josh Simpson credit for claiming the scalp of Tony Hayward – given that the US president engaged in a not very subtle call for BP's CEO to be fired. Given Hayward's own performance, his critics didn't need to do much to arrange his downfall, and may even have regretted it, since Bob Dudley is a more credible spokesperson for the multinational.

BP's catastrophic summer would have been dreadful with or without social media and the double brandjacking it faced. This was the largest oil spill in US waters, and it exposed BP's weaknesses in planning for such a scenario, as well as its PR response. But the brandjackings were a significant part of the way the crisis played out. BP's engineering-led culture is based on huge investments and decades-long timescales. The instantaneous deadlines of social media are alien to this way of thinking. BP was not up to the task of responding in real time. Its reaction to the brandjackings reinforced its other PR failings, including the weakness of global CEO, Tony Hayward.

It seems clear that organizations facing real-world crises are going to have to adapt to significant aspects of the mediasphere being driven online by activists bringing brandjacking techniques to the debate.

☒ What BP did wrong

- It failed to recognize that a CEO's job includes managing relations with stakeholders. Engineering skill alone is not enough for the task. BP needed someone who can be a spokesperson for the organization.
- Tony Hayward seemed to regard communicating with the media and Congress as an unwelcome distraction.
- It failed to communicate that it had a plan to get to the bottom of the problem and, crucially, report back. It should have been clear that BP intended to be transparent and share the results of any findings. The unseemly buck-passing with investment partners reflected badly on all concerned. Without this commitment, it lacked a convincing response to the criticisms from Greenpeace and Josh Simpson.
- It seemed to think that it could stay in control of its message. The mediasphere develops too fast for that. Forget "brand management" – that just doesn't work anymore.

☑ What BP did right

- It recognized that lawyers can't help. It did not try to sue Josh Simpson. (It is not clear that there would have been any basis for an action against Greenpeace.)
- It postponed the decision on Canadian tar sands. This was not the time to engage in another costly PR battle on a deeply controversial subject.

⛊ What BP could have done differently

- It could have engaged with its critics, in an authentic, modest, and humble way.
- BP could have begun by recognizing that the problem was serious, and reflected badly on the company. On the ground, BP was helping people in the Gulf who had been damaged by the oil spill, but completely failed to communicate that it understood the seriousness of the situation. Tony Hayward's comment that the quantity of oil was "a drop in the ocean" – whatever its merits in a purely arithmetic sense – was grossly insensitive.

Once more, Greenpeace takes the lead in highlighting the perceived failings of a multinational. It effectively uses a campaign planned for other purposes to expose BP at a vulnerable time.

SELF BRANDJACK The company's environmental planning came in for much criticism, as did the CEO.

IMPERSONATION BRANDJACK Josh Simpson produced excellent copy that was widely shared around the world.

41 Boeing sends a form letter to an eight-year-old child
May 2010

It must be a real problem, running a major engineering company. Random members of the public keep writing in with their fatuous "designs," which they expect you to take seriously. Hardly any of them are worth a second glance. Most ideas have almost certainly been considered by your design department already. And if you do end up adopting one of the ideas, Joe Public will accuse you of stealing it, even though your guys thought of it first. Much better to throw the letters away unread, and write back to say you didn't even look at the ideas it contained.

This must be particularly so for Boeing. After all, these random members of the public are not your customers. Airline CEOs are your customers, and *their* customers generally can't tell your products from an Airbus, and don't need to. This attitude held firm for Boeing, until they met Harry Winsor. I should stress that I am not talking about Harry Windsor, with a "d," the younger son of the Prince of Wales. Boeing might have spotted a problem if it had dispatched a form rejection letter to Prince Harry, who is, in any case, a pilot, and could probably make a direct phone call to Boeing's CEO if he wanted. No, this Harry Winsor had a very different superpower, one we all used to have – he is eight.

The design he sent in is probably not going to revolutionize flying, and was drawn in crayon. An appropriate response might have been an invitation to see Boeing's factory, or at least a few snapshots. Instead, Boeing wrote:

> Like many large companies … we do not accept unsolicited ideas. Experience shows that most ideas had already been considered by our engineers and there can be unintended consequences to simply accepting these ideas. The time, cost and risk involved in processing them, therefore, were not justified by the benefits gained.

So while we appreciate your interest, we regret to inform you that we have disposed of your message and retained no copies. Please understand that this was done on the basis of an established company policy, not on the merit of your idea.[19]

A letter from the head of Boeing *could* have been exciting to an eight-year-old child. But not when it is written like this. I expect Harry was puzzled and upset. His father, John Winsor, is an advertising executive, and he was annoyed, so he posted the letter on his blog, and pretty soon the whole thing went viral.

As the story started to rise up Twitter, Boeing rapidly spotted there was a problem, and it needed to act fast. Pretty soon it posted this response: "The letter Mr. Winsor posted is, as he said, a required response. For kids, we can do better. We'll work on it." They also posted: "@arun4 we're expert at airplanes but novices at social media. We're learning as we go." Both responses show the necessary humility and engagement. Notice that the second is an @reply, posted directly (but publicly) to a Twitteratus who had been critical of the company.

Boeing did a lot more than just reach out on Twitter. One of its engineers sent Harry a long personal letter. The director of communications invited him for a tour of the factory. This being Twitter, a lot of other people jumped on the bandwagon. The Museum of Flight also offered a free tour, and Future of Flight offered to host a "Harry Winsor Design your own Airplane Show."

Learnings

There seems little doubt that Boeing learned well, and quickly, on this one. The company did a rapid about-face, apologized to Harry privately and in public. It did a lot more for him than would have been necessary at the beginning, if it had got it right to start with.

Boeing has realized that it has relationships with consumers, and not just with its customers. This is not marketing. It is not advertising. It is not about simply broadcasting a message, and not much caring if it got through. This is about relationships with your publics, and building a human connection. Before printing off that form letter, take a closer look at the design. If it is in crayon, you might need a different strategy.

☒ What Boeing did wrong

- It forgot that it needs a human face, even though its customers are mostly huge corporations.

- It used a form response without, apparently, any screening process.

✓ What Boeing did right

- It acted immediately to right the wrong, showing humanity and a sense of fun.
- It was remarkably swift, showing an engagement in social media atypical of a company without consumer sales.
- It showed clear humility, confessing to its own inadequacy in social media. *We're learning as we go* is a statement that applies to everyone in the social media space, even Mark Zuckerberg.

SELF BRANDJACK The form letter was, with hindsight, a silly move. The company seemed unaware that its publics go well beyond the people who actually buy airplanes.

42 Pampers faced a customer revolt, and rumors of a recall

May 2010

Pampers – the P&G diaper brand – updated its Cruisers and Swaddlers products with a new technology called "dry max," which it claimed was the biggest breakthrough in diaper technology in decades. There were reports of rashes and "chemical burns" on some children, parents demanded the return of the old product or boycotted the brand, the US Consumer Product Safety Commission (CPSC) launched an investigation, and finally a recall was announced. The recall, however, was not announced by P&G, which continued to insist that complaints about the product were in line with the industry standard. Rumors of a recall were completely false.

Babies, of course, are special. And since babies can't speak, mothers are special by extension. The media are disinclined to question the veracity of mothers who claim that their babies are suffering. But in this case, there does seem to have been a health panic about nothing. And nothing the dermatologists from P&G could say could outweigh hysterical claims of chemical burns and outright false claims that P&G had issued a recall. There was coverage in the media over the announcement that the CPSC was to investigate Pampers. It had to. As the CPSC pointed out, it had to take anything to do with children seriously. There was much less coverage when the CPSC announced that it had found nothing wrong with Pampers.

When you think about it, the whole idea of a recall for a product that is designed for single use is absurd. If the product isn't working for your child, buy a different product. If there is real evidence of harm, then institute a lawsuit. But the company is not going to recall your product the way Toyota did with its cars (see CS 37). If the problem had proved real, P&G would have withdrawn the product, offered refunds, and – in the case of actual medical costs – compensation. It is not going to take the product back and repair it.

The story was short-lived. Nearly all the matches for a Google search show stories published in the first two weeks of May 2010.

P&G's response to the story was to call in a number of mom bloggers to see the products being made and blog about their experience. At first, this tactic was praised by, among others, Social Media Influence. But soon criticisms of the approach began to arise, with claims that it took days or weeks for the blogs to appear, and when they did, they read like corporate press releases rather than authentic blogs.

Learnings

First, Pampers should have realized that some stories simply have a short life cycle. While preparing for a response was sensible, the stories actually dried up before the response was implemented. In these circumstances, it is often best to just move on. Engaging with key influencers in social media is an excellent policy, but it has to be done authentically. If it smells like a set-up, it will do more harm than good. There are some people who will continue to smell conspiracies, no matter how silly, everywhere. Such people will interpret any evidence debunking their theory as evidence of a cover-up.

✓ What P&G did right

- It engaged with mom bloggers, but should have refocused the engagement when the original rumors died down.

✗ What P&G did wrong

- It gave the story new life by continuing with its response strategy after the story had died.
- It engaged in such a way as to raise suspicions about its authenticity.

CUSTOMER REVOLT BRANDJACK Some customers remained attached to the previous product design, and refused to accept assurances that the new one had no safety risks.

There seems to have been a conscious effort to promote the idea that a recall was in progress.

43 A drinks brand is hijacked by a drinking game
June 2010

CNN reports that the game began in the southern US and spread up both coasts.[20] Wherever it started, it become something of a digital phenomenon, with videos and snapshots of victims being "iced" appearing from all parts of the US. It goes like this. Someone surreptitiously passes you a bottle of Smirnoff Ice. As soon as you see it, you are obliged to go down on one knee and drink it. However, you can block an icing if you already have your own bottle in hand. Then the failed icer needs to go down on both knees and drink both bottles.

Speculation abounded that Diageo, British owners of the Smirnoff brand, was involved in creating the game, but the multinational has always denied it, going no further than to say "some people think it's fun," before moving on to the obligatory "Diageo never wants underage Icing."

The New York Times talked of a "mercurial line" between guerrilla marketing and a viral social media meme. There certainly seem to be both risks and opportunities for Diageo. Consuming the drink is presented as a forfeit, which is presumably not the brand value to which Smirnoff aspires. On the other hand, it does mean sales to people who would never otherwise buy the drink. Some participants have made it clear in interviews that they don't like the sugary taste – which rather reinforces both points. However, Smirnoff Ice has always marketed mostly to women, and the game is played mostly by men, so the "forfeit" angle could be thought of as making a man drink a "girly" drink rather than an unpleasant one.

There are risks for the reputation of Smirnoff: serious drunkenness or underage drinking run counter to the responsible drinking theme that drinks companies tend to promote. It is always possible that a serious incident will arise, and be linked to the game.

On the whole, the trend seems to be good for the brand. As the online trends website sosticky.com puts it:

> Icing went viral because it's a game, it's competitive, and it involves alcohol! People are having fun with the product *beyond* its specific function as a beverage. The fact that it's a girly drink just adds to the cache. Marketing ploy or not, Icing made Smirnoff cool again.[21]

Learnings

Diageo seems to be handling the situation well – more or less keeping out of it, while stressing that it is aware of the risks regarding things such as underage drinking. A meme is spreading, which promotes purchases, but which is not linked to the company. The product is reaching consumers who would otherwise never purchase it.

✓ What Diageo did right

- It has maintained a cool distance from the game. Something that promotes the product outwith the normal restraints with which drinks companies comply is good for Diageo, but carries risks, of which it seems to be aware.

CHEEKY BRANDJACK Game makes drink a game forfeit.

44 A nightclub hijacks an expensive sponsorship
August 2010

Barclays is one of the major retail banks in the UK, with a strong presence throughout the country. Its brand building has involved major investments in sponsorship, including the national soccer league. Since 2010, it has been principal sponsor of the mayor of London's bike hire scheme. The bank's familiar light blue logo is on every one of the hire bikes, and docking stations use the logo of the London Underground, but in Barclays' blue, not Transport for London's bright red.

Despite the expensive, multi-year sponsorship from Barclays, everyone refers to the bikes as "Boris bikes," after Boris Johnson, the mayor of London. A similar scheme introduced in New York a few years later has been successfully branded as "Citi Bikes", named after the sponsors Citibank, but attempts to rename them as "Mike's Bikes" in honour of Mayor Mike Bloomberg didn't catch on.

Barfly is a trendy music outlet, and someone must have noticed that the two names begin with the same letters. With carefully designed stickers, the nightclub (or someone else) overwrote the "Barclays" branding with "Barfly." There may not have been many of these, indeed, it is possible that there was only one, but the photograph shared on Twitpic caught the attention of bloggers, including this author.

☑ What Barfly did right

- It took a visual image and hijacked it to its own purpose.

 IMPERSONATION BRANDJACK Attempt to subvert another company's sponsorship.

CHEEKY BRANDJACK Fun way of riding someone else's budget.

45 A JetBlue flight attendant redefines "air rage"
August 2010

JetBlue (see also CS 12) likes to cultivate a quirky, friendly image and encourages staff to be pleasant and friendly to customers. At some point, for reasons which were disputed, Steven Slater, JetBlue flight attendant, found it impossible to remain friendly. The incident took place on a flight from Pittsburgh that had just landed in New York.

Slater's account of the initiating incident is that he told a passenger who was struggling with a bag in the overhead bin to sit down because the seat belt light was still on. The passenger swore at him, the bag struck Slater in the head, and the passenger refused to apologize. According to Wikipedia, Slater's account is disputed by several passengers who were present. Slater subsequently agreed to a plea bargain and was sentenced to a year's probation.

There is less dispute about what followed. Slater seems to have sworn at a passenger over the public address system, announced that "after 20 years in the airline industry I'm done," grabbed at least one beer, deployed the slide, and exited the plane.[22] Neighbors of Slater's family in California suggest that he had spent some time caring for his dying mother, a former flight attendant, and he had also cared for his father, a former pilot.

For obvious reasons, the incident generated considerable online and MSM interest, with some people describing it as "the best way to resign, ever." Most people have encountered tense situations on aircraft, and Slater's reaction is, in its own way, rather entertaining. Media coverage inevitably focused on his spectacular mode of exit from the plane. Nearly everyone has heard about the slides that can be deployed from aircraft but, since most flights pass off without incident, hardly anyone has ever seen them used. That one should be used just so a flight attendant could make a dramatic exit is, inevitably, newsworthy.

JetBlue was not at all pleased about this focus. According to Fox News, Rob Maruster, JetBlue's COO, sent a memo to staff in which he criticized the way the media glossed over the significance of Slater deploying the slide:

> Slides deploy extremely quickly, with enough force to kill a person … Slides can be as dangerous as a gun, and that's the reason we have intensive initial and recurrent training. It is an insult to all aviation professionals to have this particular element of the story treated without the seriousness it deserves.[23]

Far from treating this seriously, social media, like the MSM, treated it all as a bit of fun. Months after the event, the Facebook page I Support Steven Slater had over 6,000 fans and Free Steven Slater had over 34,000. JetBlue's messages about taking safety, including the safety of its staff, seriously were not getting through.

Learnings

Some stories have a life of their own. It is hard to fight the viral success of memes, such as those that cast Steven Slater as a folk hero, with a dramatic reaction to a bad day at work.

There are always difficulties for a company caught in the situation of commenting on issues that are, in part, sub judice. The facts may not be clear, and no one wants to deny a defendant a fair trial. A natural tendency towards restraint in such a situation can make it difficult for a company to get its side of the story heard.

This is a company that prides itself on its high level of customer engagement and, since the February 2007 problems at JFK (CS 12), has invested heavily in social media. It carries its focus on personal engagement into the digital space. Its response to the Slater incident was written up in the company blog, although the item is no longer available.

It is difficult to see that JetBlue could have handled this any better. The drama of the story was always going to predominate. Continuing to get its broader social media engagement about right and waiting for this story to blow over seems the most sensible strategy. Even upping its engagement by, for example, putting the CEO on Digg Dialogg runs the risk of keeping the story alive, and maybe even leading Digg to invite Steven Slater on.

☑ **What JetBlue did right**

- Rob Maruster wrote a memo to staff letting them know the company's position.
- It maintained a relatively low profile, condemning Slater's actions, but making it clear that many details had yet to be clarified.
- It maintained its strong, positive engagement in social media.

STAFF BRANDJACK   A clear case of staff misconduct reflecting badly on the brand. Unlike Comcast (CS 7), it did not reinforce existing negative impressions of customer service.

46 McDonald's: heart disease campaign
September 2010

McDonald's became the unsurprising target of the campaign group Physicians Committee for Responsible Medicine (PCRM), which advocated for a vegan diet and against the use of animals in experiments. The hard-hitting ad Consequences shows an overweight middle-aged man lying dead in a morgue, clutching a half-eaten Big Mac while his widow sobs over his body. The camera pans round to his feet and the McDonald's golden arches appear with the slogan "I was lovin' it." The ad then suggests going vegetarian for the night.

The ad was run in Washington DC during *The Daily Show*, after PCRM's research showed that DC had more McDonald's, Burger Kings, and KFCs than comparable cities. PCRM said it was considering running the ad in other major markets such as Chicago and Detroit. The ad became something of a hit on YouTube, with over 1 million views in the first two months.

McDonald's was not exactly pleased, saying:

> This commercial is outrageous, misleading and unfair to all consumers. McDonald's trusts our customers to put such outlandish propaganda in perspective, and to make food and lifestyle choices that are right for them.[24]

By "unfair", I suppose we can assume the corporation means that eating half of a Big Mac can't, on its own, cause heart disease, since no one suggests that eating a fatty, high calorie diet over many years can't contribute to heart disease. If that is its definition of "fair," then no ad is fair, and it is not what we expect of them. A single Big Mac can't cause a customer to have a happy life, either. Nor can a single Coke cause you to start hanging around with young beautiful people.

McDonald's – or rather the franchise owners of the New York tri-state area – hit back with an effective campaign. Working with the PR agency MWW, it established the McDonald's Nutrition Network (MNN), designed to reach out to the mom bloggers. Mom bloggers have become an influential segment of the blogosphere and outreach has proved a complex, but potentially rewarding, task. MNN hired a dietician to tell the story and get the word out to mom bloggers. This included organizing meetings in which local bloggers would be invited to a presentation from the dietician. The experiential aspect of the campaign proved far more effective than outreach organized purely online. MNN also provides seed money for local initiatives based on providing information about nutrition or healthy eating choices. The applications for these grants totalled almost 600 percent of target, and the launch of the initiative had almost 100 media hits.

The social media element of the campaign, which included using Facebook and Twitter to promote the various other initiatives, won PR Daily's Social Media Award for 2012.[25]

Learnings

One of the fascinating lessons from this campaign is the multiplier effect that can be achieved by bringing bloggers together. Blogging is a somewhat isolated experience. Although bloggers certainly interact, conducting one-to-one and many-to-many conversations through their blogs and traffic-driving sites such as Twitter, bringing them together changes the level of interaction. It encourages them to cooperate with each other and they are likely to stay in touch afterwards. It puts to the forefront of their interaction with each other the inciting incident that brought them together – the very message that McDonald's was trying to communicate.

☒ What McDonald's did wrong

- The immediate reaction to the PCRM initiative was difficult to justify.

☑ What McDonald's did right

- McDonald's – or rather its tri-state area franchisees – took the issues seriously and engaged with influential bloggers.
- The blogger meeting greatly enhanced the effectiveness of the engagement both between McDonald's and the bloggers and between the bloggers.
- It invested in third-party messaging about nutrition.

NGO links fast-food chain with heart disease, but franchisees hit back with powerful social media campaign.

47 Greenpeace strikes again: Burger King caves in over palm oil
September 2010

By September 2010, Greenpeace had developed what amounted to a formula for its palm oil campaign. By now, the focus was expressly and publicly to persuade major companies to stop buying from Sinar Mas Group, an Indonesian conglomerate with a subsidiary PT Smart, which produces palm oil for export.

The formula includes producing a parody of some element of the branding – putting "Killer" in the red font of Kit Kat, for example, or rechristening Burger King as "Cutter King." The second stage is to mobilize support in social media and mob the Facebook pages and Twitter feeds of the target company. Facebook has now become such an important tool for business-to-consumer (B2C) businesses that a mass campaign on the Facebook page can be effective.

The owner of a Facebook page can delete any content from it, but if enough people have been mobilized, it is difficult to keep pace with the new comments being posted. Closing your Facebook page to external contributors undermines the purpose of communicating via social media. Facebook opens terrific opportunities for businesses, but also makes them accountable to their publics.

Sinar Mas commissioned Control Union Certification and BSI Group to produce an audit of its operations which, it claimed, showed that it was conducting a sustainable operation. Greenpeace slated the report as greenwash, and claimed it was only looking at a small proportion of the production cycle. Burger King reviewed the audit and concluded that it raised sufficient concerns for it to end its relationship with Sinar Mas. It decided that continuing to source palm oil from Sinar Mas would be in conflict with its CSR policy.[26]

Learnings

Facebook is both a key asset and a key vulnerability for B2C businesses. B2B brands are, as yet, less impacted by Facebook, and LinkedIn may yet prove a more relevant platform, both in terms of opportunities and threats.

Greenpeace is not unbeatable, but when its focus is as specific as a sourcing decision, it is rarely worth having the battle. Greenpeace can mobilize tremendous assets in terms of resources and professionalism, which few corporations can match. The palm oil campaign is now so effective that the time has probably come for customers of Sinar Mas to anticipate that they will become a future target and act preemptively.

✓ What Greenpeace did right

- It identified a key vulnerability in Burger King's sourcing strategy.
- It brought its typical creativity to the process.

✓ What Burger King did right

- It quickly surrendered on the key issue rather than engage in a fruitless fight, while presenting the issue as a decision it made in line with its CSR policy.

ETHICS BRANDJACK NGO puts environmental issues at the heart of sourcing strategy.

48 Website aggregates hostility to airline, but also reinforces the airline's message

September 2010

Ryanair is the most aggressive low-cost airline in Europe. The business model is to pack as many people into the cabin as possible, and charge for all extras, including snack food and checked luggage. It is the second largest airline in Europe as measured by passenger numbers, and the largest in the world measured by international passenger numbers. Critics, including the I Hate Ryanair website, suggest it is the world's most hated airline. This might even be true, but does not seem to be incompatible with rapid growth and large passenger demand.

The MSM stories about Ryanair are legion. The airline charges disabled passengers for the use of collapsible wheelchairs to assist them in getting to the flight. (In reality, it turns out, the airline passes on the charges that the airport charges it.) It charges passengers for peanuts and drinks. It is notoriously rigid about the size and weight of carry-on luggage. Its airports are often not conveniently located, and frequently nowhere near the cities whose name they bear. It has been reported that staff are made to pay for their uniforms and banned from charging cell phones at work. When things go wrong, it is poor at making alternative travel arrangements or paying compensation. It makes you wonder why the airline is so successful. But the answer is simple. It is cheap. It is very, very cheap.

This being the business model, it is not surprising that it is relatively easy to find stories of dissatisfied passengers and staff. Ryanair is not offering a luxury service, or pretending to do so. But most people don't travel in order to have fun on the flight. The flight is something you have to put up with to get to where you are going. And there are large numbers of people who will choose their carrier based on price. This is Ryanair's market, and it is good at giving that market what it wants.

The I Hate Ryanair website is targeted at people who have had a bad experience flying – or, perhaps, not flying – with Ryanair. They form a small proportion of Ryanair's customers, but the overall numbers are still large. The website has an associated Facebook page and Twitter feed. It keeps banging home the message that there is a cost to Ryanair's low fares, and that the actual price you pay, when taxes and additional charges are added in, will be higher than you expect. Yet, people keep choosing Ryanair.

What Ryanair's critics don't seem to understand is the basic point that Ryanair has a clear business model and a clear marketing message. Michael O'Leary, the company's flamboyant and aggressive CEO, *wants* people to know that he keeps costs low, because that is how he keeps fares low. Ryanair loves it when the newspapers report – accurately or not – that the company has fired an employee for stealing electricity by charging a cell phone. Everyone who reads the story thinks "gosh, that's a bit mean," and then a little voice in the back of their mind says "no wonder they are so cheap." Publicity that any other company would regard as highly damaging reinforces Ryanair's market position.

As it happens, Ryanair has a modern fleet. The business model is based on filling every seat, every time – and the seats are close together. In terms of carbon footprint per passenger mile, Ryanair outperforms every other short-haul airline in Europe and outperforms its nearest competitor by a large margin. Does Michael O'Leary ever say that his is the carbon-friendly airline? Of course not. It would dilute the message. He doesn't want his customers thinking that anything distracts him from keeping his costs as low as possible.

The airline occasionally even courts bad publicity. A story that it was planning to charge passengers for using the toilet was untrue, but actively leaked from within Ryanair to distract attention from another story. At the time, the airline was cutting back on check-in staff – a more serious loss of customer service, but not as newsworthy as speculation that cabin crew would have to ask passengers if it was a number one or a number two.

Sure, it flies to airports that are rather inconveniently located. Being closer would cost a premium, and Ryanair doesn't pay premiums. It is targeting customers who don't pay premiums. As the BBC's *Panorama* documentary on the airline put it, people want Michael O'Leary to be a hard-nosed bastard when he is negotiating landing slots at airports, so they put up with it when they are his customers.

The I Hate Ryanair website is doing Ryanair's job. It is reinforcing the only brand value that Ryanair wants to see reinforced – low cost. The site hit the headlines when Ryanair went to court. The website was accepting advertising that, the court concluded, meant it was "passing off" – benefitting from the Ryanair brand. The owner of the site was forced to surrender the domain name ihateryanair.com and relocated to ihateryanair.org, where he doesn't take advertising. But, note, it was Ryanair's decision to take legal action that got the website into the papers. Are you seeing a pattern here?

Learnings

Ryanair has an extremely focused brand strategy built around one message. Other potentially positive messages that would distract from this are ignored. Bad publicity that reinforces the brand message is actively sought. I can't help suspecting that Michael O'Leary loves the fact ihateryanair is delivering his branding message for free, and he knew that bringing the legal action would not close the website down and would put it all over the media.

In other case studies, I have suggested that reaching for your lawyers is usually a bad thing. In this case, we should add a caveat. Don't bring a legal action unless bad publicity was what you wanted.

☒ What I Hate Ryanair did wrong

- It reinforces Ryanair's key message and builds its reputation.

☑ What Ryanair did right

- It took the website to court, raising the profile of a minor website to widespread coverage.

SELF BRANDJACK Company lets critics accuse it of stinginess while loving the association with cheap fares.

49 A graffiti artist satirizes a major multinational
October 2010

Banksy is the pseudonym of one of Britain's most famous "guerilla artists", a political activist and graffiti artist whose art and installations attract national attention. BP, the target of much brandjacking during 2010, was in the firing line again when Banksy decided to decorate a child's fairground ride. The picture, showing a dolphin surrounded by pollution and a barrel bearing BP's logo, and an associated video, showing a child on the ride, spread widely across the Internet, further highlighting BP's considerable woes.

> ☑ **What Banksy did right**
>
> • He created a strong visual and a powerful associated film with a clear message.

ETHICS **BRANDJACK**	Artist creatively keeps environmental critique of company at the top of the agenda.

50 Wedding celebrant insults the happy couple
October 2010

The Republic of the Maldives is an island chain in the Indian Ocean, consisting of 26 atolls. Until the 1970s, its economy was dependent mostly on fishing but today tourism is the main industry. For wealthy European tourists, Indian Ocean atolls are approximately as close as the Caribbean, at 4–5,000 miles each. These are expensive vacations aimed at two principal markets: the wealthy, and the more moderately successful who are splashing out on a once-in-a-lifetime vacation. Weddings and honeymoons are, unsurprisingly, an important part of the latter market.

In October 2010, a wedding video, in which an unwitting couple were victims of a cruel prank, went viral on YouTube. The celebrant explains in English that he is about to perform a ceremony, but then shifts into an obscene and insulting tirade, delivered entirely in the local Dhivehi language. He maintains the tone and chanting style of a wedding, but tells the couple their marriage is unlawful and calls them "swine" and "infidels."

Among other things, the celebrant says:

> Your marriage is not a valid one. You are not the kind of people who can have a valid marriage. One of you is an infidel. The other, too, is an

infidel – and we have reason to believe – an atheist, who does not even believe in an infidel religion.

And:

> You fornicate and make a lot of children. You drink and you eat pork. Most of the children that you have are marked with spots and blemishes. These children that you have are bastards.

On other occasions, the celebrant seems to be making lewd remarks about the bride's breasts.

Once the subtitled version of the wedding hit YouTube, waves in the MSM were huge. The government of the Maldives and the tourist resort went into immediate crisis mode. Ismail Yasir, deputy tourism minister of the Maldives, told the BBC that the whole country was furious about the incident. He vehemently denied that it was symptomatic of bad feeling between locals and tourists:

> I am sure almost all Maldivians are aware that tourism is the main industry in the Maldives and is very important.

> We don't want for such incidents to be characterised as normal in the Maldives and I am sure it is not so.[27]

The Vilu Reef hotel, which charges $1,300 for the ceremony, was also extremely apologetic, but, in a statement to the AFP news agency, came up with the unfortunate line: "The man had used filthy language. Otherwise the ceremony was OK."[28]

Other than the unfortunate incident, Mrs. Lincoln, how did you enjoy the play?

This was far from the end of the matter. The police launched an investigation into the incident, which led to two hotel employees being arrested. President Nasheed raised the matter in his weekly radio address to the nation, calling the incident "absolutely disgraceful" and continuing: "bad behaviour, such as that depicted in the YouTube video, can cause enormous damage to the country's tourism industry."[29] He also announced new rules that all hotels will be obliged to obey in conducting wedding or recommitment ceremonies.

Learnings

The Maldives government seemed to handle the issue rather well, with the hotel making an unfortunate blunder. It should be noted, however, that absent from the analysis is any mention of how the couple themselves were treated by either the government or the hotel. The couple have not even been identified, with early media reports seeming to assume they were British (perhaps because the initial instructions to guests at the ceremony were delivered in English), a tourism ministry official identifying them as French, and a foreign ministry official suggesting they were Swiss.

The couple have not spoken out. This could, of course, mean that they were hastily offered generous compensation they considered sufficient, although it may just mean that they would rather forget the incident.

The Maldives government was quick to apologize, and slowly escalated the issue as it stayed in the news, from initially reacting via the tourism ministry and embassies to the president himself making a statement. They were clear that the individuals responsible were being held accountable with immediate police investigations and prompt arrests. The president announced new regulations to prevent similar incidents occurring in the future.

The official website of the Maldives tourism board did not seem to be engaged in social media, although some private resorts in the country were. Given the high end product offering, including the business conference market, this looks to have been a blunder, especially given the social media disaster that unfolded. Almost three years later, this has been partially rectified. Maldives Tourism has a Twitter feed – but tweets infrequently and has fewer than 1,000 followers. The Facebook page is better supported, with over 10,000 likes. This compares with the Bahamas (with a similar population), which has over 11,000 followers for @VisitTheBahamas and 380,000 likes for Travel Bahamas on Facebook.

✓ What the Maldives government did right

- It instantly apologized and demonstrated an understanding of the seriousness of the issue.
- As the story continued, it escalated the response from the tourism ministry up to the president.
- It demonstrated a commitment to ensuring no recurrence by introducing new regulations and guidelines.

▶ What the Maldives government should do

- It should carefully build investment in social media.

☒ What the Vilu Reef did wrong

- It seemed to minimize the significance of the problem.

STAFF **BRANDJACK**	One member of staff's misconduct hits the reputation not only of an exclusive hotel but the entire country.

51 NPR fires Juan Williams
October 2010

NPR is an American public service broadcaster, producing speech-based radio distinct from talk radio, which consists mostly of phone-in programs with opinionated hosts. NPR is funded by a mixture of government grants and donations. It is obliged to be politically neutral, but has been the subject of consistent allegations of liberal bias and more occasional allegations of conservative bias. Again, this contrasts with talk radio, which is generally not only expressly opinionated, but also appeals directly to a conservative audience.

Juan Williams was a contributor to both NPR and Fox News, the conservatives' answer to perceived liberal bias in the three US terrestrial networks – ABC, CBS, and NBC – as well as CNN, MSNBC, and NPR. Although the terrestrial networks keep up a show of impartiality, Fox, CNN, and MSNBC have more or less stopped pretending. As Charles Krauthammer has said, with Fox, Rupert Murdoch found "a niche market that contained 50 percent of the population." Williams, however, was always seen as an expressly liberal voice on an expressly conservative show. He was the foil to Bill O'Reilly on *The O'Reilly Factor*. This made NPR somewhat uncomfortable, and it asked for him not to be identified as an employee of NPR when appearing on Fox. Whether it was his liberal views or his appearance on a conservative show that made NPR uncomfortable was less than clear.

The tensions between Williams' two jobs reached breaking point when he expressed the view that seeing airline passengers "in Muslim garb" worried him. As part of the same segment, he was at pains to make it clear that it was quite wrong to label all Muslims as extremists or terrorists. NPR dismissed Williams.

There was an immediate reaction from conservative bloggers and commentators. Among the points raised was that Williams had been contributing to Fox in an opinionated way for years, and NPR had long accepted this, albeit with some measure of discomfort. Williams was only fired when he stepped outside liberal orthodoxy. NPR seemed to interpret the public espousal of liberal views to be compatible with his role at NPR (as a senior news analyst), but a single deviation from liberal views was a sacking offense. Plainly, such an analysis is not the whole story. Williams was being accused of racial and religious stereotyping, something he strongly denied.

The controversy was difficult for NPR. Although it does not have a strong conservative listenership, it does receive taxpayer funding, and any implication of bias was a threat to that. John Boehner, then house minority (Republican) leader, was one of those questioning federal funding for NPR as a result of the controversy and, to make matters worse, the following month the Republicans made sweeping gains in congressional elections, making Boehner speaker.

NPR's own ombudsman concluded that the firing of Williams had not been handled well.[30] In January, the month Boehner became speaker, NPR published a report in which external legal counsel declared the firing had been "entirely legal." In any such social media controversy, the assurance that your actions have been "entirely legal" is the minimum requirement, but it falls far short of a ringing endorsement of your behavior. At the same time as the report was published, Ellen Weiss, senior VP of news, resigned. The board expressed confidence in the ongoing leadership of CEO Vivian Schiller.

Learnings

Increasingly, journalists have multimedia and multiplatform careers. Nor is it especially unusual for journalists to cross the divide between reporters, analysts, and commentators. As an organization that is not only in the public eye but in receipt of taxpayer funding, NPR needs to be clear that it is impartial, but also fair.

☒ What NPR did wrong

- It acted too fast, firing Williams without appearing to investigate fully first.
- It had confused messages, being unclear whether expressing opinions on another platform is generally acceptable or not.
- The CEO suggested that Williams should have kept his feelings about Muslims "between himself and his psychiatrist."

☑ What NPR did right

- It apologized for not speaking to Williams in person before announcing the dismissal and not preparing staff internally for the announcement.

- It apologized for not preparing its messaging properly.
- It organized a full investigation of the events and publicly announced the results.
- It apologized for the psychiatrist remark.

| **SELF BRANDJACK** | Internal procedures were simply not adequate in this situation. |

52 Amazon tries to defend *The Pedophile's Guide to Love & Pleasure*
November 2010

Amazon must have anticipated that a book with the title *The Pedophile's Guide to Love & Pleasure* would be controversial. The reaction, two groups talking past each other, one about protecting children and the other about freedom of speech, was equally predictable. So why did the most social media-savvy organization of them all appear to get caught unawares?

Everything about the book was controversial. One key debate was the question of what the content of the book actually was. Some said it was a "how to" guide, giving pedophiles advice on how to attract children and avoid being caught. Others argued that – in accordance with the subtitle, *A Child Lover's Code of Conduct* – the book was advocating good, or perhaps less bad, conduct by people sexually drawn to children. The book's author advocates the view that "penetration is out," and argues that people who follow his guidelines can expect to receive liter (sic) sentences.

This author is not in a position to settle the arguments as to whether the book ever advocated illegal behavior, or provided people with information on how to get away with criminal and exploitative acts. I haven't read the book; it is no longer available; and, frankly, I would not be willing to read it for you, even to settle this point in the spirit of academic enquiry. What does seem to be clear is that the book offered advice, such as using pets to approach children, which, while not criminal or harmful in itself, could certainly be used by people with criminal and harmful intent.

Amazon can hardly have failed to realize that the content and the title would be hugely contentious. Management had a standard freedom of speech argument prepared to defend publishing the book. Amazon argued that it would be censorship to decline to sell a book on the grounds that it and others found it offensive. It also expressed support for the right of its customers to make their own purchasing decisions. Well, er, maybe. The controversy was apparently good for sales, as the book made it onto the bestsellers list before being withdrawn, amid widespread calls for boycotts of Amazon.

Amazon, despite being named for warrior women, was both hesitant and inconsistent in its attitude. According to the *San Francisco Chronicle:* "The timeline on its removal is odd: Amazon defended the book, then removed it, then reinstated it, and then removed it *again.*"[31] This hardly implies that Amazon was fully prepared for the wholly predictable outcry. Its attitude can have left no one on any side of the debate happy.

It is worth asking what led Amazon to change its mind. In asking the question, I don't mean to query why the company reached the conclusion it ultimately did. There are many fine and obvious reasons for doing that. But, given that the reasons are *so* obvious, why did it initially adopt one position and then shift to another – apparently more than once?

In principle, shifting your position during a developing crisis is not bad, and sometimes it is essential, but it needs to be done with care, if you are to avoid offending all sides of the debate. So why did Amazon's position change? Sometimes, an organization will change its mind because critics raise an argument it had not previously considered. In this case, the principal arguments seemed to be that pedophilia is wrong, harmful to children, and illegal. It is inconceivable that Amazon had not considered all these points.

Sometimes, an organization will change its mind because the strength of reaction is greater than it had imagined. Perhaps more people criticize an organization's attitude than it believed would, or the reaction is so emotive that it is hard to get a counterargument heard. Again, it is difficult to see how these points could possibly apply when considering pedophilia. The third most certainly applied, but was also wholly predictable. Just how contentious did Amazon imagine the subject was?

It seems that Amazon was completely unprepared for a widespread and highly emotive response, which should have been completely predictable. Amazon was into social media before any other organization. While it is not a platform for conducting an ordinary social or business life the way Facebook and LinkedIn are, it *is* a community. Its book review process is collaborative. It makes recommendations based on past spending patterns and what people who make purchasing decisions such as yours also tend to like. Intuitively, and encoded into its DNA, Amazon *gets* social media. So its inability to see this blindingly obvious pitfall is simply staggering.

Learnings

In the publishing business, you will always find yourself in controversial areas. Wherever you choose to draw the line on acceptable and unacceptable content, someone will think you should have drawn it somewhere else. This is inevitable. You therefore need to be prepared for the issue, in a way in which Amazon conspicuously was not.

First, you need a clear and consistent definition of free expression, and why you support it. In the US, people sometimes fall back on the First Amendment, but this is inadequate. It restrains the government from censorship. It does not oblige publishers to publish anything that anyone asks them to, or bookstores to carry every book that is available. These are judgment calls, which every publisher and bookstore must make individually. If it is not your position that you will publish anything of appropriate quality that is legal in your jurisdiction – and this is not Amazon's position: it had already withdrawn other controversial books and games – you must be prepared to make a case for free expression, but also why you chose to draw the line in the way you did.

Feel free to discuss these matters with your community. Involve your publics in sharing the burden of making such decisions. This should not devolve into a simple vote, as minority opinions are worth defending, but if you are unsure how your community will react, engage with them. There are 122 pages of discussions on this book still up on Amazon.com, so the discussions are certainly happening.

☒ What Amazon did wrong

- It reacted as though it had been taken by surprise, when none of the reactions were at all surprising.
- It shifted its position three times without really explaining why.
- It alienated both sides of the debate.
- It failed to involve its community in an open discussion about the issues.
- It left people thinking their concerns had not really been heard.

▥▶ What Amazon could have done differently

- It could have engaged in a lengthy burden-sharing discussion about appropriate guidelines for acceptable content: let its community discuss things, feel involved, and even bound in to the decision.

Some surprising misjudgments here, compounded by a refusal to engage.

 In this most controversial of issues, the company seems surprised by a focus on the morality of its decision.

53 "Alaska Airlines hates families"
November 2010

Airlines expect passengers to at the gate 30 or more minutes before takeoff. Some passengers cut this close, and then when something goes wrong, end up being a little late. How the airline handles this situation is critical to its standing with its customers.

In this instance, Alaska Airlines decided to give a ticket to a standby passenger, although the delayed family claims to have been at the gate 20 minutes before takeoff. The Blais family was delayed by a diaper emergency. As a result, the family had to make other arrangements to get home to Edmonton at a cost of over $1,000. As compensation, the airline had offered $800 of flight vouchers and to fly them standby. The problem was that their luggage had already flown and the standby might have taken days.

Dan Blais wrote this up in his blog under the headline "Alaska Airlines hates families," which is, obviously, putting it a bit strongly. The story was then picked up by the Edmonton Journal. Reactions on the paper's website varied, from some supportive of the Blais family, to others pointing out that if they had been earlier, there would not have been an issue. This point was then heatedly debated by supporters of the Blais family. The facts, as revealed in the story, are not 100 percent clear on the point, but it looks as though the family did not arrive at the gate until too late. If they had arrived at the gate and then had to step away, things would probably have been different, and this difference goes to the heart of the question as to whether the family had any realistic control over the situation as it arose.

In the arguments on the Edmonton Journal website, the antagonists seem almost ideological on the matter. Some suggest that non-parents don't understand about diaper emergencies. This seems unlikely to me. I suspect the ideologies are people who arrive in plenty of time – who are not sympathetic to the Blais family – versus those who like to arrive with only a minute or two to spare, and expect others to accommodate them if they are delayed. Umm, you might have picked up my own leaning on this ideological scale.

The airline should, however, have identified that this was going to be a problem. Airlines deal with these issues all the time, for all sorts of reasons. Sometimes passengers are late, sometimes the airline has overbooked, sometimes a flight has been canceled for weather or technical reasons, and passengers from that flight have to be accommodated on other flights. When passengers are delayed overnight, airlines often do discriminate against families, putting single travelers at the top of the list, followed by couples, and families last: this is not only because single travelers are easier to slot into a crowded flight, but also because a family of four can be accommodated in one room, whereas four single people need four rooms at much greater cost to the airline.

Because airlines have to deal with fraught passengers who have been bumped from flights – because of the airline's failing and the passengers' – all the time, they know that tempers can get frayed. They also know that there are a lot of people out there who will sympathize with the plight of the passengers, having been in similar situations themselves. This being so, airlines that wish to maintain a good relationship with their passengers need to empower their staff to act with discretion. If the Blais family was really there with 20 minutes to spare, it would have been perfectly possible to accommodate them. Bouncing them for a standby passenger was unnecessary, and the airline should have done rather more than just offer flight vouchers once it had happened.

This is the situation into which it was forced. As the story gathered momentum on Twitter, Alaska Airlines stepped in and reimbursed the Blais family for the full cost of traveling by a different route.

Learnings

Speed kills. In the social media world, stories can quickly gather pace. It is much better if your customers walk away satisfied than if you have to rectify the situation later. Even the $800 in flight vouchers originally offered to Dan Blais and his wife might have done more good if they had been offered to the standby passengers who had been boarded instead, in exchange for returning to standby.

Alaska was, however, able to fall back on some existing relationships. It is notable that among those speaking up for the airline are not only those critical of the Blais family, but also people supportive of Alaska Airlines in particular. One commentator pointed out that it is the most on-time airline in North America.

X	**What Alaska Airlines did wrong**

- It acted overzealously in bumping the Blais family.
- When there was still the opportunity to control the situation, staff were not sufficiently flexible in their approach.
- It tried to defend a situation when it knew that there would be much support and sympathy for the family.

✓	**What Alaska Airlines did right**

- It eventually made a settlement with the Blais family.
- It seems to have some strength of support within its community, which it can cultivate to help see it through future problems.

 Company should have anticipated negative reaction by customer.

54 When a department store and the Dogs Trust clash
November 2010

The John Lewis Partnership – a major chain of department stores in the UK – regularly produces an iconic Christmas advertising campaign, and often sets the theme for Christmas shopping. It is almost as iconic as the regular campaign by the Dogs Trust: a dog is for life, not just for Christmas.

John Lewis likes to be thought of as an especially ethical and family-friendly company. Its employees are "partners" and share in the profits. It has long been the only major store that allows people to bring dogs (other than guide dogs) into its stores. It did not expect its Christmas 2010 ad campaign to be on the wrong end of a Facebook campaign, and complaints from the Dogs Trust.

The theme of the campaign was "For those who care about showing they care" and showed a montage of stories in which people were hiding presents for other people. The whole thing played with Elton John's "Your song" (performed by Ellie Goulding) as the theme song. The final image showed a dog in an outside kennel in the snow and a boy hanging a stocking on the kennel before going back into the warm.

Beverley Cuddy, editor of *Dogs Today*, commented that her first reaction on seeing the ad was one of disappointment.[32] The image with the dog is meant to heart-warming, as the rest of the ad is, but portrays a rather old-fashioned image of a dog outside in a wooden shed-style kennel, not inside with the family. The image reminds the author of Spike, the dog that was always chained up in the *Tom and Jerry* cartoons. Cuddy associated it with the 1950s. A little depressed, she tweeted about it, and found that others felt the same. The more they talked and thought about it, the more they realized this was not a representation of dogs that they thought was appropriate to 2010.

When one of the Twitterati set up a Facebook page complaining about the ad, hundreds, then thousands, signed up. But what angered Cuddy the most was that some people defended the practice of keeping dogs outside, even in the snow. Some argued that dogs have fur, and can therefore stand the cold. Leading animal charities, such as the Dogs Trust, spoke out strongly against the ad. John Lewis initially reassured everyone that the ad was shot in July and the snow was fake. The actual dog shown was in no way mistreated, and the dog's owner had been completely happy with the representation. That, however, was not the point that people were complaining about. It was that the ad seemed to be legitimizing a way of keeping dogs that is almost extinct.

Cuddy concedes that not all dogs are the same. The actual dog shown is a deerhound, a hunting dog, much better able to stand the cold than many other breeds, although deerhound owners were among those condemning the image. Anyone capable of recognizing the dog's breed from a few seconds of footage is probably already well informed on how to care for a dog. According to Cuddy, the campaign objected as much to the isolation of the dog as the cold: "Dogs are pack animals, and are never happy alone."

The campaign gathered momentum, when, during snowfalls in late November that year, a dog in Luton died from being kept outside at night. By this time, John Lewis's own Facebook page was a warzone between people slamming the ad and others speaking out in favor of it. The fact that people defended the practice of keeping dogs outside in sheds is the thing that most upset Cuddy. She felt the ad gave people "confidence to express views they would previously have been ashamed of."

When the story was picked up the BBC and the leading broadsheet paper, the *Daily Telegraph,* John Lewis put out a statement saying the ad had been edited and it would now be running a shorter version, which did not include the dog image. At the same time, however, the advertising magazine *Campaign* ran a story suggesting that the full-length, 60-second ad would still be used in some primetime slots, with the 30-second version running more frequently.[33] This inconsistent messaging suggests the chain did not really own up to its mistakes.

Cuddy, however, is certain that the 60-second version was dropped. The store initially planned to run it up to December 18 (the Saturday before Christmas), but it was not actually running it that late. She is also convinced that the store was trying to spin different lines to different audiences, telling some that the full-length version had been dropped, while implying to industry sources that this had been the plan all along.

Learnings

There is not the slightest suggestion that John Lewis intended to "glamorize," as critics put it, animal cruelty. Cuddy is intuitively certain that the campaign was conceived by people who were not well informed about modern practices for keeping dogs. They thought the image was touching and heart-warming, and simply did not realize that dogs are almost never kept in those conditions today, so the little boy's dash outside to see to the dog would not be necessary.

The company was understandably reluctant to back away from the campaign, which would have been expensive to commission. But the instant discomfort and slow-building anger that dog lovers felt for the ad could have been uncovered by more extensive focus groups or consulting with dog charities.

In social media, you don't control your critics, but you don't control your supporters either. Like "Janet," the pro-ExxonMobil Twitterata (see CS 22), supporters of the department store were pursuing lines of defense that the store itself would have been most uncomfortable advocating, such as the view that keeping dogs in sheds is acceptable.

☒ What John Lewis did wrong

- It failed to take remedial action, such as promising to consult animal charities before using animals in future campaigns.
- It gave mixed messages on the question of whether the longer version of the ad had been dropped or not.

SELF BRANDJACK	A serious misjudgment, never properly acknowledged, which hit the store in the important family market.
ETHICS BRANDJACK	Animal welfare issues anger campaigners more than almost any other.
AGGREGATION BRANDJACK	Grumbling on Twitter turned to anger, and people decided to launch a campaign. Offline protests would have been impractical before the ad had run its course.

Notes

1   RAN: understory.ran.org/2008/01/23/ran-supporters-shut-down-gm-greenwashing-site, accessed 01/20/2014.

2   *The New York Times*: www.nytimes.com/2008/01/28/business/media/28target.html, accessed 01/20/2014.

3   Sheila Marikar, writing on ABC News: abcnews.go.com/Entertainment/BeautySecrets/story?id=4839919, accessed 01/20/2014.

4   Business Insider: www.businessinsider.com/2008/6/j-c-penney-thanks-youtube-ad-agency-for-massive-free-ad-campaign, accessed 01/20/2014.

5   Business Insider: www.businessinsider.com/2008/6/ad-agency-jc-penney, accessed 01/20/2014.

6   Racked: racked.com/tags/augmented-reality, accessed 01/20/2014.

7   Twitterati is the accepted plural noun. The singular would be Twitteratus for a male. In the female form, Twitterata would be the singular and the plural Twitteratae. Latin had no plural form designed specifically for a group that contained both male and female, and the male plural was used in this case.

8   Jeremiah Owyang: www.web-strategist.com/blog/2008/07/29/when-brands-under-fire-step-into-the-fracas-exxon-joins-twitter, accessed 01/20/2014.

9   Jeremiah Owyang: www.web-strategist.com/blog/2008/08/01/how-janet-fooled-the-twittersphere-shes-the-voice-of-exxon-mobil, accessed 01/20/2014.

10 BBC News Online: news.bbc.co.uk/1/hi/7703129.stm, accessed 01/20/2014.

11 *The Independent*: www.independent.co.uk/news/uk/home-news/virgin-atlantic-sacks-13-staff-for-calling-its-flyers-chavs-982192.html, accessed 01/20/2014.

12 *The Guardian*: www.theguardian.com/commentisfree/2009/feb/22/wikipedia-internet, accessed 01/20/2014.

13 Jarvis, J. (2009) *What Would Google Do?* New York: Collins Business.

14 One person provided commentary, while the other sneezed on a pizza, picked his nose and put the snot into a garlic bread, put pieces of cheese and pepper up his nose, and dropped his pants to wipe a sponge in the crack before using it to scrub a pan.

15 Dooce: dooce.com/2009/08/28/containing-a-capital-letter-or-two, accessed 01/20/2014.

16 SmartBlog: smartblogs.com/social-media/2010/09/09/andys-answers-how-whirlpool-creates-a-consistent-brand-voice-in-social-media, accessed 01/20/2014.

17 Jezebel: jezebel.com/5379070/pepsi-releases-iphone-app-to-help-men-score-with-women-and-brag-about-it-on-twitter, accessed 01/20/2014.

18 *Daily Telegraph*, February 11, 2010, accessed 01/20/2014.

19 John Winsor's blog: www.johnwinsor.com/my_weblog/2010/04/is-your-customer-service-ready-for-the-new-world-of-openness.html, accessed 01/20/2014.

20 Online link now dead, but still cited in Wikipedia, accessed 01/20/2014.

21 Jackie Prince: jackieprince.wordpress.com/category/sticky/page/4, accessed 01/20/2014.

22 *The Mirror*: www.mirror.co.uk/news/uk-news/air-stewards-amazing-tantrum-over-240878, accessed 01/20/2014.

23 Fox News: www.foxnews.com/us/2010/08/12/lawyer-jetblue-flight-attendant-infamous-meltdown-wants-return-flying, accessed 01/20/2014.

24 Google News: www.google.com/hostednews/afp/article/ALeqM5iGHHcnnjtq4kx72h6kpuWmVAbqow, accessed 01/20/2014.

25 PR Daily: www.prdaily.com/awards/specialedition/71.aspx, accessed 01/20/2014.

26   Greenpeace: www.greenpeace.org/usa/en/media-center/news-releases/Burger-King-cancels-palm-oil-contract-with-rainforest-destroyer-Sinar-Mas, accessed 01/20/2014.

27   BBC News Online: www.bbc.co.uk/news/world-south-asia-11644328, accessed 01/20/2014.

28   Ibid.

29   BBC News Online: www.bbc.co.uk/news/world-south-asia-11652040, accessed 01/20/2014.

30   NPR: www.npr.org/blogs/ombudsman/2010/10/21/130713285/npr-terminates-contract-with-juan-williams, accessed 01/20/2014.

31   Business Insider: www.businessinsider.com/amazon-caves-pedophile-guide-pulled-from-the-kindle-store-2010-11, accessed 01/20/2014.

32   Interviewed by the author.

33   *Campaign*: www.campaignlive.co.uk/news/1042025, accessed 01/20/2014.

The case studies: 2011

55 Zine al-Abidine Ben Ali and the Dignity Revolution
December 2010–January 2011

When the Arab Spring began, it did not begin in the most repressive country in the region, where people might be thought to have the most reason to rebel, nor did it start in the most liberal country, where the anticipated reaction from the state might have been less severe. It began in Tunisia, a politically authoritarian country with a moderate foreign policy, a recent decline in fairly robust growth, and a successful tourist industry. Perhaps tourism – which brings with it foreign languages, Internet cafés, and exposure to the outside world – was the critical factor. Certainly, Egypt, another major tourist destination, came next.

Zine al-Abidine Ben Ali had been in power since 1987 when, as prime minister, he had organized a coup against the president. Since then, he had been regularly "re-elected" with 90–100 percent of the vote on 90 percent plus turnouts. The successful tourist industry had depended on the expectation that Tunisia would remain a fairly stable country. This, combined with its fairly convenient location, a short flight from Italy, France, or Switzerland, had proved crucial to the country's economic development.

In retrospect, media coverage of the events that led to Ben Ali's fall was light at first. The media inside Tunisia was government controlled and the international media did not, initially, see the wider significance of what was to become the "Arab Spring." Some saw political machinations at work, with Jillian York, blogger and activist, contrasting Western neglect of Tunisia with the widespread coverage of the "green" protests in Iran in 2009–10. It is worth noting in this context that Iran is not only a much larger energy exporter than Tunisia, it also has a population of almost 80 million, compared to just over 10 million in Tunisia.

Although Zied El Hani, Tunisian journalist and blogger, called the events in Tunisia the "Facebook revolution" (the term "Jasmine Revolution" was used in the West, but not in Tunisia, which referred to it as the Dignity Revolution),[1] it is not entirely clear how much of the unrest began in social media. It *did* start with younger people – as most political unrest does. But the inciting incident, the self-immolation of Mohamed Bouazizi, was an individual protest. It took place less than an hour after Bouazizi's attempt to resolve a harassment issue at the governor's office and was not filmed. Bouazizi's suicide had huge consequences for the Arab world, but it seems he did not plan or anticipate that. Imagine how much more powerful its impact would have been if it had been filmed and uploaded to YouTube.

News of Bouazizi's self-immolation spread around Tunisia. It is estimated that some 5,000 people attended his funeral and President Ben Ali visited him when he was dying in hospital. He was not a celebrity in life – he was a street vendor whose merchandise had been stolen by corrupt police officers.

It seems clear that Ben Ali believed in 20th-century technologies. He believed that his control of the mass media gave him control of society. He could simply assert that he was popular, and had been elected by huge popular margins, and people would believe this. Social media took him completely by surprise.

On January 14, less than a month after the first protests, which had started the day after Bouazizi's self-immolation, Ben Ali fled Tunisia. His initial destination was France, but if he ever had permission to land there, it was rescinded before he arrived and he fled instead to Saudi Arabia.

Learnings

The mass media are less than a century old. One hundred years ago people had films – silent and black and white – and newspapers that were mostly local. Radio and TV were in the future. The notion of centrally controlling the media occurred to governments almost immediately, with communism and national socialism built on it. But those days are gone. Some governments have not got the message yet. Aside from the obvious – running a corrupt and oppressive government – the main thing that Ben Ali did wrong was failing to realize how much times had changed.

As for Mohamed Bouazizi, it is difficult to criticize the tactics of the man who sparked the Arab Spring and posthumously won the Sakharov Prize for Freedom of Thought, but if sparking a revolution was his intention, he would have been wise to make sure someone had been on hand with a camera phone.

ETHICS BRANDJACK A corrupt government brought down by its victims.

AGGREGATION BRANDJACK Critics who had previously been isolated from the means of communication were able to unite online.

56 The Red Cross: social media outreach and Twitter gaffe
January–February 2011

The Red Cross has been praised for its use of social media in crisis situations and its research into such use. In January 2011, the charity published the results of a survey showing that almost 70 percent want emergency services to monitor social media, and many would use social media as a backup if directly calling the emergency phone number was not possible. Of course, in most circumstances where people have access to social media, they also have access to a phone. Around half of those questioned by the Red Cross suggested that if caught up in a crisis, they would use social media to alert friends and families that they were okay. This is a use that ties directly into the main strengths of social media. Such a message reaches a person's direct network and can be reassuring.

As a known crisis develops, social media can be a tremendous source of information from the ground. The public put social media fourth – behind TV, radio, and online news sites – as a source of information, but at the granular level required by rescue services, it has considerable potential.

Against the background of seeking to set disaster and crisis relief standards for the use of social media, it was slightly embarrassing for the Red Cross to be caught up in its own brandjack. Fortunately, it reacted swiftly to deal with the issue. In February 2011, the official American Red Cross account tweeted: "Ryan found two more 4 bottle packs of Dogfish Head's Midas Touch beer … when we drink we do it right #gettngslizzerd." As you might imagine, the tweet was intended for a personal account. The Red Cross reacted quickly with an official tweet: "We've deleted the rogue tweet but rest assured the Red Cross is sober and we've confiscated the keys."

The Red Cross also took the issue up in its blog, where it reported that the fumble had inspired some people to give blood. Dogfish, the beer brand, also used its Twitter feed to encourage blood donations.

Learnings

React fast and react with humor. The fact that the Red Cross was the victim of an error, and an understandable one that might affect any organization, helped with the good-humored way in which people responded. The Red Cross was tapping into a deep reservoir of goodwill. Unlike Vodafone (CS 34), there was nothing inherently offensive about the content of the tweet and, unlike Comcast (CS 7), there was nothing that was resonant of wider customer service failings.

✓ What the Red Cross did right

- It reacted fast.
- It acknowledged the error in a light-hearted way.

STAFF BRANDJACK A minor slip by a member of staff exposes the brand to ridicule.

57 Hosni Mubarak: "first, kill the Internet"
January 2011

Hosni Mubarak was president of Egypt for almost 30 years from the assassination of Anwar Sadat until his resignation in January 2011. Throughout that time, he was continually "re-elected" by unlikely margins in elections with no other candidates, although with the option of voting against. Elections to the Egyptian Parliament were similarly criticized by outside observers for their unreliability. Opposition parties, such as the Muslim Brotherhood, were banned, although candidates linked to the Brotherhood were occasionally allowed to contest elections and occasionally declared the winner of those elections.

Mubarak had risen to power through the ranks of the military and maintained strong links there, which conferred two political advantages at home. The military – in contrast to the police and internal security services – remained fairly popular with many Egyptians and, in a crisis, he would need the military to maintain control.

To maintain the support – or at least the acceptance – of Western governments, Mubarak pursued a three-pronged strategy. By allowing small numbers of Islamists to be elected to the Egyptian Parliament, he persuaded liberal critics at home and abroad that any democratically elected government would probably be worse. He maintained a moderate pro-Western stance in foreign affairs, trying to clamp down on al-Qaeda-linked terrorists. He affiliated his National Democratic Party – the principal successor to the Arab Socialist Union – to the Socialist International. This meant that many foreign leaders, including François Mitterrand, Tony Blair, and Gerhard Schröder, dealt with Mubarak as leader of a sister political party.

Nonetheless, dissatisfaction with Mubarak's rule was high by 2011, among Islamists, liberals, and other critics of his regime. In addition to the arbitrary arrests, repression of speech, stolen elections, and rampant corruption, people were enduring severe economic issues, including high inflation and unemployment.

Following the revolution in Tunisia, opposition activists began to plan a national day of protest for January 25. Internet activists Asmaa Mahfouz and Wael Ghonim have been particularly highlighted for their contributions. Mahfouz created a video blog (vlog), which went viral in the days leading up to January 25. A Facebook page promoting the protest had more 80,000 followers. Ghonim was the administrator of another Facebook page – We Are All Khaled Said – highlighting the fate of an Egyptian who had been tortured and killed by security forces in Alexandria. Ghonim was regional sales and marketing manager for Google at the time of his own secret arrest and interrogation by security forces.

While Shakespeare urged revolutionaries to "first, kill all the lawyers," Mubarak's instinct was to, first, kill the Internet. The day after the national day of protest, the government clamped down on Internet service providers and cell phone operators. If this was designed to confuse or frustrate the street demonstrations, it failed, and probably backfired. This failure was predictable; indeed, it was predicted on this author's blog, among many other places. People who have relied on the Internet for information about opposition to the government are unlikely to interpret its sudden silence as a display of strength by the government, but as an obvious sign of vulnerability. Far from encouraging people to stay at home, the street protests began to gather strength.

As the protests continued, the army increasingly refused to support the police. Small nods to political reform were insufficient to satisfy the demonstrators. First, Mubarak promised that neither he nor his son would contest the next presidential election, while remaining determined to stay in office until then. Then he handed many powers to his deputy. Finally, he quit altogether and fled to Sharm el-Sheikh, the tourist resort on the Red Sea. Now, he and his family face trial on charges of corruption and political repression. Mubarak was moved from prison to hospital in late 2012. He was convicted in 2012 of damaging the economy by shutting down the Internet, but the conviction was overturned in 2013. Some reports suggest he slipped into a coma in July 2013. He has been released from custody and is presently (January 2014) in a military hospital.

Learnings

Mubarak came to power without an election as the result of an assassination. He had a blank slate in front of him and could have pursued any policies he chose. That he stayed in power for 30 years has to be a testimony to something more than just brutality and corruption. He must have had considerable political skills as well. But when it came to 2011, the world had changed too fast for him to keep up. With hindsight, he could have pushed democratic reforms somewhat earlier, and still left office as something of a hero. The things he conceded in desperation in January 2011 would have been taken as massive steps towards liberalization just a year – perhaps even a few months – earlier.

☒ What Mubarak did wrong

- He believed that he could close down digital channels of communication, and that, if he did so, it would leave the opposition leaderless and confused.
- He made concessions only when forced to, when they were inevitably too late to save his own career.

☑ .What the revolutionaries did right

- They ceded the leadership of the cause to a wide, diverse, tech-savvy generation, while the scarier Muslim Brotherhood stayed in the background.

SELF BRANDJACK The personal and policy failings of Mubarak, his cronies, and his family came under scrutiny as a result of the transparency that digital channels bring.

ETHICS BRANDJACK Outsiders such as Mahfouz and Ghonim were able to highlight the repression of the Mubarak regime by skilled use of social media.

58 The US Department of State: WikiLeaks
January 2011

In 2011, WikiLeaks, the well-established website, together with a number of global media partners, including *The Guardian* and *Der Spiegel*, released material from US Department of State cables. From the beginning, material was redacted to prevent risking lives. WikiLeaks and its media partners worked hard to identify materials that might cause serious risks to identifiable individuals. Part of the criticism of the project was that it would never be possible to fully identify such information, as they would not know what additional information was already in the hands of repressive security services and/or terrorists.

Since the objective of WikiLeaks is to massively increase the data that is in the public domain, it marks a dramatic shift towards decentralization of power. WikiLeaks uses the power of digital channels to undermine the powerful. In that sense, the website is a brandjacker at heart. It undermines secrecy to shine a searchlight in such a way as to uncover corruption and abuse. In the WikiLeaks world, it is harder than ever for a government (or any other organization) to maintain an unjustified reputation. Information is harder to hide.

Within the State Department cables were many examples of unsurprising inanities. For example, we learned that Hillary Clinton likes to be briefed in some detail before visiting a country on behalf of the US. The embarrassing revelations often consisted of putting into writing something the State Department would have preferred not to confirm publicly. It was stated that Angela Merkel was boring and Nicolas Sarkozy was arrogant. It is not likely to have been news to either of those individuals that many people had formed that view of them, but they would most certainly have preferred it not to have been recorded in official Department of State cables. (This author commented on Brandjack News at the time that the same could have been said of almost all German and French leaders since 1945.)

Ultimately, the power of WikiLeaks is not in what was revealed but in its potential to drive change in governments around the world. The US government is already one of the most open on the planet. Corruption and repression in the US are extremely low by global standards. Information from within the Chinese government on anything like the same scale would have astonishing consequences. This is why China tried to block access to WikiLeaks.

WikiLeaks has had some reputation issues of its own since the State Department cables were published. It engaged in a slanging match with *The Guardian* over which of them was responsible for publishing the full, that is, unredacted, version of the cables in an unencrypted file. Julian Assange, the site's founder, is wanted in Sweden on charges of attempted rape. Assange denies the charges and alleges a political conspiracy against him. He is currently living in the Ecuadorian Embassy in London, UK, subject of a European Arrest Warrant.

Learnings

WikiLeaks stands as an example of how hard it is for governments to maintain secrecy and confidentiality in the WikiLeaks world.

Similarly, businesses are exposed to greater pressures; fraud can be exposed, as can deceptive practices that fall short of criminal fraud.

| **SELF BRANDJACK** | The US Department of State was caught out with its own words. |
| **STAFF BRANDJACK** | Information leaked from within the department was the source of the scandal. |

59 Ali Abdullah Saleh
February 2011–February 2012

Yemen differs considerably from Egypt and Tunisia. It is neither a major tourist destination nor – like Egypt – a political powerhouse. Egypt is much the largest country in the Arab world, with a powerful military. Nor was Yemen ever a consistent friend and ally of the West, far from it. Yemen, under Saleh, was close to Saddam Hussein and the Islamic Republic of Iran.

Saleh's background involved rising through the ranks of the military in what was then North Yemen (officially, the Yemen Arab Republic), a somewhat pro-Western, or at least anti-communist, state. South Yemen (The People's Democratic Republic of Yemen) was a Soviet satellite. Saleh was president of North Yemen from 1978 until the state's merger with South Yemen in 1990. He was then president of the merged country, generally just called Yemen (but officially, the Republic of Yemen), until 2012.

During the Bush and Obama administrations, Yemen became important in the global war on terror, as it is a reluctant host to a number of al-Qaeda operations. While not exactly friendly to Western interests, Saleh was a co-enemy of al-Qaeda. He met George W. Bush and Dick Cheney during this period, and later senior members of the Obama administration.

With poorer infrastructure than either Tunisia or Egypt, the evidence for large-scale Internet activism in Yemen's anti-Saleh protests is thin. Satellite broadcasts covering the success of the Arab Spring in other countries undoubtedly influenced the progress of demonstrations against the Saleh regime. The clearest involvement of Internet hacktivism in the ultimately successful pressure for Saleh to step down was when Wikileaks obtained cables from the US Department of State, reporting that Hamid al-Ahmar, a leader in Yemen's largest tribal confederation, was planning to stage demonstrations with the aim of bringing Saleh down.

Ultimately, Saleh was able to stay in office – although not fully in power – for a year, despite the demonstrations. He handed some power to his vice-president, was seriously injured in an assassination attempt, and returned to office after his hospitalization, before finally stepping down in February 2012.

Learnings

Like all the dictators caught up in the Arab Spring, Saleh failed to realize how much the world had changed. He had successfully manipulated the constitution for years, claiming votes of 96 percent in his re-elections and extending his term of office after winning one of the rigged elections. By 2011, even in an underdeveloped country, it was no longer possible to dominate the flow of information the way he had been doing for more than three decades.

☒ What Saleh did wrong

- He stuck to the old model, and tried to control the population through the media.

⯈ What Saleh could have done differently

- He could have moved further and faster to promote real reform.

SELF BRANDJACK A dictator was brought down by his own failings and his collapsing ability to manipulate and dominate the media.

60 John Galliano: anti-Semitic rant
February 2011

John Galliano was one of the most high-profile fashion designers in the world. As head of the Dior range in Paris, he had close relationships with supermodels, some of whom were said to waive their fees in order to appear at his launches. His private design clients had included some of the most famous women in the world, including the late Princess Diana. He reproduced some of Dior's period range for Madonna in the film *Evita*. He was also a well-known fixture in the bars and cafés of the Marais district of Paris, which is the gay and the Jewish district of the French capital.

On February 25, 2011, Galliano was suspended by Dior after having been briefly arrested during a fracas at a bar in the Marais, where he had been accused of launching an anti-Semitic tirade against fellow customers. It is not atypical of a crisis that once a story hits the media, other people come forward to reinforce the story. On the same day that Dior announced Galliano's suspension, the French citizen journalism website, Citizenside, received footage of a previous Galliano tirade in December 2010. In this footage, Galliano had yelled at a group of Italians "I love Hitler ... People like you would be dead. Your mothers, your forefathers would all be f***ing gassed."[2] Just a few days later, on March 1, Dior issued proceedings to have Galliano sacked.

Some of Galliano's celebrity friends came to his defense, arguing that what he said should not be taken too seriously because he was plainly drunk. Patricia Field, fellow fashion designer, even compared Galliano's rant to the song "Springtime for Hitler" in the Mel Brooks comedy, *The Producers.* Others were highly outspoken in their criticism of him. Natalie Portman, a Jewish American actress and a descendant of Holocaust victims, described herself as "deeply shocked and disgusted."[3] No one seems to have commented that Galliano, as a gay man, would himself have been sent to the gas chambers by the man he professed to love.

Later that year, it was announced that Galliano was in rehabilitation – presumably for alcohol problems rather than anti-Semitism. In September 2011, he was convicted of making anti-Semitic remarks. He has also apologized "unreservedly" over the incident.

Learnings

Attempting to mobilize celebrity support is a legitimate tactic. In this case the support was viral, with Field sending an email to some 500 friends, contacts, and media representatives. She condemned the way Galliano's friends had deserted him. Her problem was the seriousness of the incident and the potency of the evidence against him. Celebrities no longer have private lives in public, if they ever did. Twenty years ago, Galliano would have faced the risk that someone at a neighboring table was a journalist. In the days of citizen journalism and video cameras built in to cell phones, that risk is one in one. Trying to shift the narrative to Galliano's alcohol problems was never going to work in such a circumstance.

SELF BRANDJACK Galliano lost control while drunk and said things that were utterly indefensible.

61 **Muammar Gaddafi**

March–October 2011

Libya's maverick leader from 1969 until (officially) 1977 or (in practice) 2011 was always difficult to classify. It was clear what he was against: Israel, the US, the West in general, Libya's Berber minority, and the Shia branch of Islam. It was less clear what he favored. Sometimes it was pan-Arab nationalism. Sometimes it was pan-Africanism. At different times, he offered to merge Libya with Tunisia, Morocco, and Egypt. He was often friendly to the Soviet Union, and bought much of his military supplies from the USSR before its collapse, but he rejected both communism and atheism, advocating "Islamic socialism." He supported militant groups against Israel as well as Western countries, including long-term sponsorship of the Red Army Faction (West Germany) and the IRA (Northern Ireland). He sent money to Western political groups, including the Workers' Revolutionary Party. He consistently denied involvement in the bombing of Pan Am 103 over Lockerbie, Scotland. He sent troops to support Idi Amin, the insane Ugandan dictator, against a combination of Ugandan dissidents and the army of Tanzania.

After 1977, he held no official position in Libya and the country continued to have two official power structures – the state and the revolution – but few doubted that Gaddafi and his family remained in absolute power. One of the more bizarre stories surrounding him followed the US bombing of Tripoli in 1986. Gaddafi always claimed that his adopted daughter was killed in the raid. In 2011, it emerged that many Libyans believed she had survived and was working as a nurse in Tripoli, unacknowledged by her father as part of his propaganda campaign against the US.

After 2003, when coalition forces removed Saddam Hussein from power in Iraq, and Saddam himself was captured by US troops and convicted of crimes against humanity, Gaddafi largely abandoned his sponsorship of terrorism along with his weapons of mass destruction program, although his policies of terror and repression at home continued.

During the 2011 Arab Spring, Gaddafi consistently blamed foreigners, the media, spies, and "rodents" for the uprising, which saw Libya's second city, Benghazi, quickly fall to the rebels. After Western intervention to prevent the use of air power against the rebels, there were fairly rapid advances across the country to Tripoli and, eventually, Sirte, Gaddafi's home town. International media coverage, especially by Sky News, of the fall of Tripoli and by Al Jazeera of the discovery of Gaddafi's body were global events. Around the world, ordinary citizens stood vigil outside Libyan embassies.

The one thing it was impossible for Gaddafi to concede was that the people of Libya – whom he claimed to represent through the "revolutionary" structures of the country – had been liberated by technology from his iron control over the media. Attempts to close down cell phone services, satellite broadcasts, and Internet service providers – as in Egypt – only served to convince people that the government was weak and desperate, and that acting against it would therefore be successful. Putting control of the media in the hands of citizens is a one-way process. Once the worms are out of the can, the only way to put them back is to use a much larger can.

Learnings

It seems likely that Gaddafi was genuinely delusional. He probably believed that he was popular and that attempts to have him removed must have been external in origin. However, it seems clear that the uprising was overwhelmingly internal and organic. Where Gaddafi's erratic behavior and support for militant organizations around the world came back to haunt him was in his complete lack of support in other countries. Not only were Western countries against him, he had no backing from the Arab League or African Union. Only Venezuela was seen as a possible bolt-hole for him and his family.

☒ Where Gaddafi went wrong

- He tried – like Ben Ali and Mubarak – to isolate his people from alternative points of view. He ended up isolating himself from reality. He believed his own propaganda, and failed to recognize that his regime was in danger.

SELF BRANDJACK | Corrupt dictator brought down through his own self-belief.

62 NPR: fundraising chief calls Tea Party "racist"
March 2011

Just a few months after the Juan Williams controversy (see CS 51), NPR again found itself in a public difficulty. Fundraising chief Ron Schiller was caught out in a sting operation by Breitbart.com, a multimedia web-based news platform and blog. Andrew Breitbart had long been a critic of "big media" and its alleged liberal bias. NPR is often at the forefront of conservative criticism of the media. Breitbart.com has a substantial reputation in sting operations against liberal organizations, including the media.

In this case, the target was Ron Schiller, VP of fundraising at NPR. Since the network is funded in considerable measure by donations, Schiller's position was a key one. By the time of the sting operation, he was already due to leave NPR. Ron Schiller should not be confused with Vivian Schiller, NPR's CEO at the time, to whom he is not related. The main focus of this sting was to offer money to NPR on behalf of a fictitious Muslim group affiliated with the Muslim Brotherhood. The money was offered with no strings attached, but the people making the offer made controversial comments about Israel. According to NPR, Schiller repeatedly declined the money.[4]

Schiller made a number of controversial comments himself, which came at a difficult time for NPR. Following not only the Juan William controversy but a change of control in Congress, the subject of NPR's federal subsidy was being debated in Congress. Schiller not only made derogatory remarks about Republicans and the Tea Party, but also said that, in the long-term, NPR would be better off without taxpayer funding, a view very much contrary to NPR's own funding strategy.

Schiller argued that Republicans are generally less educated than Democrats – a widely held view, although exit polls of voters suggest the reverse.[5] He stated that Republicans and the Tea Party in particular are obsessed with people's personal lives. In fact, while necessarily having some overlap with the wider conservative movement, the Tea Party is primarily focused on economic policy – TEA stands for Taxed Enough Already – and arose in response to President Obama's reorganization of American healthcare. He also said that the Tea Party is "deeply, deeply, racist," although he provided no examples, and media attempts to make this case have generally come up short.

Ron Schiller was already leaving NPR when the sting happened, but he brought his resignation forward and left immediately. Vivian Schiller also resigned her role as CEO after this incident, following so closely on the Juan Williams controversy (see CS 51).

Learnings

NPR already had a difficult relationship with the incoming Congress, which had not been helped by the Juan Williams controversy. The strongly held view by many Republicans that the network is biased was reinforced by Schiller's candid comments at the very time

Congress was considering cutting the network's funding. Worse, Schiller made it clear he did not think NPR even needed the funding.

✓ What NPR did right

- Ron Schiller's departure was brought forward and Vivian Schiller also left the company.
- It apologized, and made it clear that Schiller's remarks did not reflect NPR's values.

 Senior executive reveals his real beliefs while posing as impartial.

63 Asma al-Assad: *Vogue's* "rose in the desert"
March 2011

What is the responsibility of a journalist for a specialist publication with regard to the wider context of the subjects being covered? *Vogue* is a fashion magazine. It covers glamorous, fashionable celebrities. Asma al-Assad, wife of Syrian dictator, Bashar Assad, is slim, attractive, and highly educated. As journalist Joan Juliet Buck put it to NPR: "I think that *Vogue* is always on the lookout for good-looking first ladies because they're a combination of power and beauty and elegance." But, there are ethical differences between a flattering write-up of the Duchess of Cambridge and one about Asma al-Assad.

Vogue was heavily criticized for what amounted to a puff piece about the wife of a dictator who was then – and still is – conducting a brutal war against the people of his country. The Syrian regime was paying an American PR company a retainer to secure exactly this sort of coverage about Asma. Surely *Vogue* should have realized it was dancing to the tune of the Syrian state? But where should the line be drawn? To some degree, a glamorous, British first lady in an Arab country is inherently newsworthy. And if journalists can't write about her clothes, can they write about her charitable activities? If she were a noted research scientist, would peer-reviewed journals turn down her work because of her marriage to a dictator?

Articles in fashion magazines are long planned. The interview at the heart of the feature was conducted in December 2010, before the Arab Spring, but published in March 2011 when the uprising against the Ba'athist regime was already underway. Even before the uprising, Syria was on the US State Department's list of state sponsors of terrorism.

Vogue encountered a storm of protest and removed the article from its digital edition, although for some time afterwards, the article was still available on

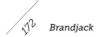

the Syrian government's website. Eventually, Anna Wintour, the editor, made a statement condemning Mrs. Assad. But the controversy raged on.

Buck, who wrote the article, later became a staunch critic of the Syrian regime and *Vogue*'s coverage. Buck did not choose the infamous "rose in the desert" headline. She also claims that the children photographed in *Vogue* were not the ones she saw when she conducted the interview. Did the Assads bring in more attractive children as props for the photoshoot? It is all eerily reminiscent of the story that Gaddafi faked the death of his daughter in the US bombing of Tripoli in 1986 and she grew up estranged from her father so that he could blame the US for her "death."

Learnings

As the media become more integrated by technology and globalization, it becomes harder for them to remain segregated by theme. Fashion magazines – long accustomed to campaigns on fur, animal testing, and working conditions in the developing world – will increasingly find themselves in the firing line over human rights issues.

☒ What *Vogue* did wrong

- It seems to have ignored the obvious moral and ethical questions around a puff piece for a dictator's family. This was in the middle of a civil war and regular media reports about the bombing of civilians. If not then, when?

☑ What *Vogue* did right

- It reacted to the protest, but did not seem to take up genuine news issues around the incident.

SELF BRANDJACK Fashion magazine allows its obsessions to obscure its view of human rights and decency.

64 Chrysler f-bomb tweet

March 2011

Accidentally tweeting from the wrong account is a perennial risk for people who work in social media and have access to a corporate Twitter account for an employer or client.

The Red Cross incident in January 2011 was bad enough, but what if the embarrassing tweet not only includes the f-word but also touches on the client's core business. This was the case when @chryslerautos sent the following: "I find it ironic that Detroit is known as the #motorcity and yet no one here knows how to f**king drive." For one of the big three motor manufacturers to simultaneously insult its customers and the city in which it is based is not something to be laughed off the way a Red Cross employee "#gettingslizzerd" can.

At the time, @chryslerautos had 7,500 followers. The tweet was retweeted everywhere and attracted the immediate attention of digital media – such as Mashable – and MSM. Chrysler issued an immediate apology: "Our apologies – our account was compromised earlier today. We are taking steps to resolve it." Almost immediately, speculation was rife that the error came from Chrysler's social media consultancy, not the in-house team. This was later confirmed, as Chrysler announced that the tweet had been sent by an employee of New Media Strategies who, the blog post claimed, had since been fired.[6] Mashable reported a few days later that Chrysler's corporate Twitter account had gained followers in the days after the controversy and the mass retweeting of the rogue tweet. The day after the tweet, *Advertising Age* reported that Chrysler had decided not to renew with the agency.[7]

Learnings

It cannot be said too many times. If you manage more than one social media account, you need to be *very* careful about keeping them separate. Putting out a personal tweet on a corporate account is embarrassing enough. It could be potentially even worse to put out a corporate tweet on behalf of the wrong client. This one, however, is an outstanding example in which a personal comment impinged directly on the client's core business. It is not the sort of thing that someone working for Chrysler (directly or indirectly) should have been saying on a personal account either. At some point, all the disclaimers in the world about tweet's being your own views are going to be insufficient.

☑ What Chrysler did right

- It apologized immediately, promising that action was being taken.
- It expanded on this in a blog, giving more details as to how it came about (employee of an agency, not Chrysler) and what had been done (employee fired).

 Consultant makes a simple, but devastating, error.

65 Mark Zuckerberg: kill what you eat
May 2011

On May 4, 2011, Mark Zuckerberg put out an update on Facebook – where else would the billionaire founder of the platform announce something? – that he had just killed a chicken, a goat, and a pig. Reactions were predictable, ranging from those who thought the comment odd to those who found it disgusting.

But this was just the first stage in the campaign. This was the teaser to get people interested. He later explained in an email to *Fortune* magazine that this was part of a personal challenge: from now on he would only eat animals he had personally killed. He mentioned that he planned to take up hunting and had been eating a great deal of vegetarian food, including every time he ate out. Given Zuckerberg's Jewish heritage, the inclusion of a pig in the list of animals he has killed needs the clarification that he is an atheist.

This position is an unusual one, which produced some mockery. What would happen, one social media commentator asked, if people only used social media platforms they had coded themselves? But from different sides of the political and culture war divides, Zuckerberg's position has mostly been welcomed. On Field and Stream, comments reflect a generally positive view of Zuckerberg's prospective hunting.[8] Environmentalists welcomed his commitment to a sustainable diet. Zuckerberg's challenge includes an awareness that every time he eats meat, an animal has had to die.

This is not to say that there has not been ongoing criticism. In addition to the mockery – based on a not unreasonable point about division of labor – there is anger in some quarters. A popular YouTube video mocks Zuckerberg for allegedly taking pleasure in killing animals. Some commentators argue that people are obliged to eat meat because "we have dominion over animals." The "dominion" comment is presumably based on the Bible. But doesn't dominion incorporate the concept that people can choose not to eat meat? Commentators also make the self-evidently false claim that meat is "essential" to the human diet.

Learnings

Zuckerberg was stepping onto dangerous ground here. People feel strongly about animals and their diet. People get especially offended if they think that someone else is claiming moral superiority over them by virtue of a particular diet. Such a claim grates with people. Zuckerberg was adopting a stance with the potential to offend meat eaters and vegetarians, while stepping into a debate in which he has no particular expertise. Wisely, he has avoided debating the matter. He has talked about his own decision as a personal challenge. He has adopted no position on what other people should or should not eat. His business operates in countries where vegetarianism is common and in others where it is virtually unheard of. He has attracted a little anger, as well as some mockery, for his stance.

☑ What Zuckerberg did right

- The initial teaser comment on Facebook was risky. It had the potential to upset animal lovers, most of whom would never dream of personally killing an animal, even if they are happy to eat meat. But, by rapidly clarifying an intelligent, if slightly oddball position, he deflected nearly all criticism.

SELF BRANDJACK	High-profile CEO steps into a debate well outside his area of expertise, but neatly sidesteps most anger.

66 Dove accused of using a racist ad
May 2011

Dove, the Unilever soap brand previously singled out by Greenpeace as the focus of its campaign against Sinar Mas (CS 20), found itself in a Twitterstorm over an allegedly racist ad. The ad showed before and after close-ups of skin using its product. Unfortunately, the three models standing underneath seem to be arranged progressively from before to after as black, Latina, and white. The ad was heavily criticized online, with the feminist blogger Jezebel calling it "unintentionally racist" and commenting: "Bye-bye black skin, hello white skin! (Scrub hard!)."[9]

After the matter was taken up by the gossip site Gawker.com and the blog The Huffington Post, it made its way into the MSM, with the UK's *Daily Mail*, one of the most widely read online news sources in the US, picking it up. Dove rapidly issued a statement, which several sites credit to Gawker:[10]

> We believe that real beauty comes in many shapes, sizes, colors and ages and are committed to featuring realistic and attainable images of beauty in all our advertising. We are also dedicated to educating and encouraging all women and girls to build a positive relationship with beauty, to help raise self-esteem and to enable them to realize their full potential.

The ad is intended to illustrate the benefits of using Dove VisibleCare Body Wash, by making skin visibly more beautiful in just one week. All three women are intended to demonstrate the "after" product benefit. We do not condone any activity or imagery that intentionally insults any audience.

Most media were prepared to give Dove the benefit of the doubt. Only 23 percent of those voting in an online poll at the liberal Huffington Post thought the ad was intentionally racist, and the black news site The Root (owned by the *Washington Post*) argued that it would be bizarre to think that the brand was actively trying to communicate that black people could become whiter by washing with Dove.[11]

Learnings

It's never about what you say. It is always about what people hear. It may be that only a minority of people found the ad offensive, but if one in four of your customers, shareholders, or suppliers find your ad campaign offensive, you are in big trouble. Online, people who are offended by your ads don't need to persuade an editor that the offense is intended. They can dive into their own blog or Twitter account and spread the meme.

As ever, this means two things:
- Try to anticipate possible offense. If all three women were meant to illustrate the "after" phase, the white woman could have been on the left. It is the apparent progression from darker to lighter, with the black woman standing on the "before" side, that enables people to see a hidden message.
- You can't anticipate all possible blunders, so be ready to apologize quickly.

 Poor choice of imagery leads to an unnecessary controversy.

67 David H. Koch Theater
May 2011

David H. Koch is billionaire entrepreneur, philanthropist, and political activist. He has given multimillion dollar donations to a wide variety of causes, especially in medical research and the arts. In 2008, Gary Weiss described him as "one of the most generous but low-key philanthropists in America."[12] Despite his relatively low profile in these causes, there are some eponymous recipients of his generosity, including the David H. Koch Chair of the Prostate Cancer Foundation, the David H. Koch Institute for Integrative Cancer Research at MIT (Koch's alma mater), the David H. Koch Cancer Research Building at Johns Hopkins, and New York City Ballet's David H. Koch Theater. All of this is relatively uncontentious.

Koch's political activities are much more contentious. Until 1984, he was a member of the Libertarian Party and was its candidate for vice-president of the US in 1980. The Libertarians scored 1.6 percent, which was their highest percentage up to that point, but slipped from third to fourth place due to the independent candidacy of former Republican congressman, John Anderson. Since 1984, Koch has been a Republican. Although he has not run for office, he has given large donations to political causes, including Americans for Prosperity and the libertarian think tanks Cato Institute and Reason Foundation. Koch is known to support a wide variety of causes, including lower taxes, free-market capitalism, gay marriage, and ending drug prohibition. He opposed President Obama's Affordable Care Act and has been skeptical of anthropogenic global warming.[13]

His views, which are still broadly libertarian, are outside the mainstream of both major parties in the US. On economic questions, his views are clearly different from the majority of those in the arts and education communities, whom he has generously sponsored. Both these communities are tech-savvy and heavily engaged in social media, so it is no surprise that he has come under fire in these forums.

The liberal blog, The Other 98%, attacked the Koch brothers. (Charles, David's elder brother, is co-owner of Koch Industries, but takes an even lower profile in his donations to political and charitable causes.) The blog claimed they are "the kind of guys that try to derail health care reform because they've concluded that it will cut into their profit margins." No evidence was offered for the claim about motives, or for similar claims about the reasons for supporting research by global warming skeptics. The blog was key in promoting social media activism in support of a publicity stunt at the David H. Koch Theater, in which images were projected onto the side of the theatre with think bubbles rising out of Koch's name or images of him. The phrases attributed to Koch included "I'm the Tea Party's wallet" and "I bought this theater to hide my evil deeds."[14]

For the record, Koch says he has never been to a Tea Party event and no one from the Tea Party has ever even approached him.[15]

Learnings
As with the criticism of John Mackey of Whole Foods Market (another libertarian; see CS 15), activists wanted to assume that people who shared their values, this time in terms of supporting the arts, would share their political values too. They found this was not the case and assumed that Koch was a bad person and only supporting the arts to provide cover for his inherent badness.

☒ What Koch did wrong
• He tried to straddle the line between public and private figure. If he wants to publicize his philanthropy – and put his name on buildings – he must accept that this makes him a public figure and that people will criticize him. • If he is going to be a public figure, he needs to engage in social media to influence public perceptions of him and his philanthropic activities.

ETHICS BRANDJACK Philanthropist attacked for not sharing all the values of the communities he sponsors.

68 FIFA corruption allegations
May–June 2011

If there is one field where you can reasonably expect motivated fans to become involved in both creating and engaging in the news, it is sport, perhaps especially Association Football, with its worldwide following. Bloggers and, in the pre-digital age, fanzines have been at the heart of covering football for decades. There are also whole teams of professional journalists on the case, so demands for transparency in the relatively closed world of professional football are intense.

In the summer of 2011, the sport's governing body, Fédération Internationale de Football Association (FIFA), came under huge media scrutiny, in social media and the MSM, over a disputed election to the FIFA presidency and allegations of corruption against President Sepp Blatter and two vice-presidents, Mohamed bin Hammam and Jack Warner. All three have denied the allegations.

Despite considerable criticism in social media for his comments on women footballers (they should wear tighter shorts, to attract the interest of men), gay fans (they should stay away from Qatar, hosts of the 2022 World Cup, or refrain from sexual activity while there), and goal line technology (for years he opposed it), Blatter was eventually re-elected to a fourth term as FIFA president when his only opponent, bin Hammam, withdrew from the contest.

Mohamed bin Hammam had been widely accused of offering bribes to secure the 2022 World Cup for Qatar. Blatter himself had been accused of offering a $100,000 bribe to secure support for his first re-election bid in 2002. Given that over 200 countries are affiliated to FIFA, a bribe of this magnitude for a single vote would be out of all proportion to Blatter's expected legal earnings from the job over the five-year term. It might be expected that if he were offering bribes of this sort more widely, more such allegations would have emerged.

Also accused of corruption was Jack Warner, the president of CONCACAF, the football federation for the Caribbean, and a FIFA vice-president. For the MSM and social media, Warner is the gift that keeps on giving. Blogs, including PR Daily and Brandjack News, could never resist the opportunity to republish and push out virally his very individual way of providing "no comment" to a BBC journalist at Zurich airport, in which he threatened to spit on the journalist, and made pejorative remarks about the man's mother, suggesting that he could "go find her" when the journalist said that his mother was dead. Warner had previously told the same journalist to "go f**k yourself."

Such YouTube footage – although beginning with the BBC's *Panorama* rather than in the social sphere – is very much the basis of viral reputation in the social age. It is exactly the sort of thing that the Twitterati and Facebookers love to share. It is no surprise, therefore, that the pressure on Warner became unbearable, and he quit the FIFA executive in June 2011. FIFA then abandoned its investigation into Warner, declaring that the presumption of innocence was still intact, and apparently not considering that the organization's own reputation was on the line along with Warner's.

In May 2012, the director of public prosecutions in Trinidad and Tobago, where Warner (an elected MP) remained in the Cabinet until 2013, announced that Warner would not be prosecuted over corruption allegations, which Warner blames on "Sepp Blatter and his minions." *The Guardian* – although based in the UK, with its notoriously strict libel laws – felt able to use the some- what loaded headline "Jack Warner to escape prosecution over alleged Fifa bribery scandal."

Learnings

FIFA has been beset by allegations and counterallegations of corruption for years. Mixed with an undoubted degree of sore losership from countries that have failed in bids to host the World Cup and some extreme missteps by senior executives, controversies are sure to continue. Yet FIFA runs the most popular team sport in the world, by a staggering margin. It should be possible to engage that fanbase in discussions, both about the rules – the goal line technology controversy – and about decision making. What are, and what should be, the criteria for assessing and awarding the right to hold the World Cup? Media in the UK were furious at England losing its bid for the 2018 World Cup, complaining that the English bid was technically the best. But if the criteria are concerned with legacy – reaching countries that have not hosted the tournament before or where there is little existing fanbase – then England's bid was always a waste of time and money. Should the criteria not be openly discussed by transparent engagement with fans?

☒ What FIFA did wrong

- It needs a thoroughgoing external investigation of the corruption allegations, which should not have been dropped when Warner resigned.
- Future plans for hosting the World Cup need to arise from open and transparent engagement with fans.

ETHICS BRANDJACK	An unwillingness to engage transparently can only heighten suspicions of corruption.
SELF BRANDJACK	Internal bickering put the issue of corruption into the global public domain.

69 TSA #diapergate fiasco
June 2011

America's Transportation Security Administration (TSA) is not the most popular organization. Some say that TSA is an abbreviation for Thousands Standing Around. It is one of many organizations that has attracted a fake Twitter feed.

The story began with reports in the media that TSA agents had made a 95-year-old disabled woman remove her adult diaper before she could board a plane. With this story raging in social media and the MSM, with comments from the fake Twitter account, the TSA's real Twitter feed was silent for a day. Jean Weber, the passenger's daughter who had put the story into the public domain, was described by the media as "one of the most sought-after women in America."

The day following the first media storm – a Sunday – the TSA issued a statement to CNN:[16]

> While every person and item must be screened before entering the
> secure boarding area, TSA works with passengers to resolve security
> alarms in a respectful and sensitive manner. We have reviewed the
> circumstances involving this screening and determined that our officers
> acted professionally, according to proper procedure and did not require
> this passenger to remove an adult diaper.

Effectively, the TSA denied the story. But Jean Weber stood by her story. Her mother had been forced to remove her diaper in the face of being denied access to the plane. Social media, including the fake TSA Twitter feed, would not let the story drop, but it was another two days before the TSA issued any further statement, this time on its blog:[17]

> Various options to proceed through the checkpoint were presented to
> the passenger and her daughter during private screening to resolve an
> anomaly discovered during a pat down. Although TSA did not request it,
> the daughter ultimately chose to remove the adult diaper in a bathroom
> and return to the checkpoint.

According to Jean Weber, the only "options" presented to her were remove the diaper or be denied access to the plane. Technically, I suppose, it is true that the TSA did not *require* the diaper's removal, the word used in the original TSA statement, but the other option was rather restrictive.

Learnings

The truth is hard to establish here with any certainty. But Jean Weber's account is reconcilable with the TSA's statements. If everything Weber says was true, then the TSA's statements are, technically, true as well. They did not "require" the diaper's removal, there were "options" presented, and Weber "ultimately chose" to remove the diaper. But if that is the basis of the TSA's stand, it was one based on legalisms and not on ordinary conversational speech. Technically, the highwayman who points a gun at you and says "your money or your life" is giving you an option. In Weber's account, there were not "options" to "proceed through the checkpoint" – just the option of proceed or not.

Notice also the use of phrases like "the daughter," and not "Ms. Weber" or "the passenger's own daughter" as someone might say in conversation. Social media are conversational. The people who speak in human language are the ones who get their messages heard.

[X] What the TSA did wrong

- It ignored the growing storm in social and mainstream media for far too long before making its first statement and for even longer before clarifying.
- It does not seem to have offered a spokesperson, just carefully crafted and overly lawyered statements.
- If Weber is to be believed, the TSA's statements, while technically true, are so close to the edge of being untrue that they are likely to have deceived people.

SELF BRANDJACK	Public sector is too slow and too lawyerly in its response to burgeoning criticism.

70 #SeriouslyMcDonalds
June 2011

The #SeriouslyMcDonalds hoax was one the most malicious fake brandjacks. The picture at its heart had been around since 2010 but, for some reason, suddenly went viral in June 2011. People tweeted the pic – presumably either believing it was real, or because they found it amusing.

It is probably a measure of both the general level of naiveté in the world and the low regard in which McDonald's is held in some quarters that this meme received the attention it did. It suggests that with a sufficiently disliked target – and this does not necessarily mean disliked by a majority, just by a significant group of people – you can make up more or less anything you like and at least some people will believe it. The insane conspiracy theories to which the last three presidents of the USA have been subject demonstrate this.

McDonald's responded quickly, but with a light touch. It immediately tweeted that the photograph was a hoax, but sent personal messages to only two of those retweeting the pic. Perhaps it concluded that to respond to everyone – as Vodafone did with its rogue tweet (CS 34) – would give the issue more attention than it deserved. If that was the strategy, it was probably a mistake. For several days, the #SeriouslyMcDonalds hashtag was trending on Twitter.

Learnings

Social media always put a premium on a quick response and an authentic, unlawyered response, but the question of how much response is appropriate must be assessed on a case-by-case basis. Responding to every individual runs the risk of raising the profile of a negative issue. Responding too lightly has risks of its own and, this time, it seems as though McDonald's erred on the side of caution. The issue kept growing after McDonald's had firmly responded that it was a hoax. While most people should have seen this immediately, especially if they tried phoning the number on the notice, which is a KFC helpline, some didn't.

The next stage of a response is to develop a strong base in social media with your fans. McDonald's did start working on this, and launched a powerful and engaging campaign called #MeetTheFarmers a few months later.

✓ What McDonald's did right

- It responded quickly and firmly.

✗ What McDonald's did wrong

- It responded impersonally and with insufficient vigor.

FAKE BRANDJACK | Multinational falls victim to a malicious hoax.

71 Ken breaks up with Barbie
June 2011

The longstanding campaign by Greenpeace against Sinar Mas and its subsidiary Asia Pulp and Paper (APP) took a new turn as the NGO turned its fire on Mattel. Previous campaigns, including Dove, Kit Kat, and Burger King, have focused on palm oil, but with Mattel it was APP that was the focus of the campaign, specifically as a supplier of packaging using wood pulp allegedly derived from clear-cutting Indonesia's rainforests and destroying the habitats of endangered animals. The campaign began with a well-plotted video in which a journalist interviews Ken about his life in the Barbie dreamhouse. Ken is shocked to discover that the "shoot" Barbie is on in the rainforests is to kill orangutans and tigers. He storms off set, yelling "it's over."

As with other videos from Greenpeace, it quickly went viral. At the time of writing (two years after the Barbie campaign), the main Greenpeace Twitter account had almost 1 million followers. There are many other Greenpeace accounts on a country-by-country basis, plus Facebook, YouTube, and many other social media outlets. The main Facebook page has 1.3 million likes. The sophisticated campaigning and significant budgets of Greenpeace are augmented by these off-budget resources, which we could conservatively estimate as including 50,000 volunteers. In the social media age, Greenpeace does not need its volunteers to join marches or deliver leaflets. A quick click is all that is required, and the numbers willing to do this are vastly greater than the numbers for climbing buildings or occupying offices.

That does not mean the old Greenpeace has gone. The group also climbed onto the roof of Mattel's headquarters and hung a banner there, creating video footage and still shots for the MSM. Greenpeace campaigns are always multimedia these days. While "Ken" was hanging his banner, telling Barbie it was over, a Greenpeace "Barbie" turned up in a pink bulldozer asking "as long as I look good, who cares about tigers in some distant rainforest?" The breakup between the lovers got nastier, with the two engaged in a constant war of words on Twitter and Facebook.

The campaign began on June 8 and by June 25 Mattel had frozen its contracts with APP. At that point, things stalled for a while. Ken was less vocal on Twitter, with occasional tweets to thank celebrities for their support. (Leonardo DiCaprio was one. Will he play Ken in the movie?) Then, after another five days of silence, Ken was venting his anger again. Suspending the contracts and announcing a review of its suppliers was not enough. Greenpeace wanted specific pledges from Mattel about a new sourcing strategy.

Eventually, Greenpeace claimed victory and Mattel surrendered in October.[18] Why would it not? The opportunity to market the dreamhouse as ecofriendly weighed against an ongoing battle with Greenpeace? A no-brainer.

Learnings

Greenpeace continues to set the standard. The videos now bear the legend "Mattel has now agreed to drop deforestation. Tell Barnes & Noble to do the same." It leaves this author wondering why anyone would want to fight Greenpeace on this issue. Surely high-profile customers of Sinar Mas and APP don't want to wait for Greenpeace to pick on them but are, instead, reviewing their supply chains without waiting.

☑ **What Greenpeace did right**

- A textbook campaign based in social media and MSM. The plot-line worked. And the stunt of getting Barbie arrested was brilliant.
- The innovative idea of two Twitter accounts in which the protagonists battled it out, both scripted by Greenpeace, is going to run and run.

☑ **What Mattel did right**

- It surrendered.

☒ **What Mattel did wrong**

- It hesitated, surrendered, and hesitated again.

ETHICS BRANDJACK | Beautifully choreographed assault on a major brand by the guys in green.

72 U pay tax 2?
June 2011

One of the particular strengths of social media is the ability to organize offline stunts or flashmobs to parallel online protests. This can be done in a largely leaderless way or mobilized by well-known activist groups such as Greenpeace, best known for hiring boats or scaling buildings, despite its truly awesome online campaigning skills.

This combination of the offline stunt and the social media campaign has been taken up strongly by UK Uncut, which campaigns against cuts in government spending and tax avoidance by wealthy and/or prominent people. This was especially apparent in the campaign against the rock group, U2, and Bono, the band's high-profile frontman. U2 has been successful since the 1980s. Bono is well known for his campaigns on behalf of Africa, both raising money and influencing the policy agenda, calling for different terms of trade and increased aid. He shared the Person of the Year award from *Time* magazine in 2006 with Bill and Melinda Gates as examples of humanitarians. He has met leading political figures from around the world to advance the policy agenda he supports.

When U2 relocated its business from Ireland (the band's members, including Bono, are Irish) to the Netherlands for tax purposes, this attracted criticism. After all, by advocating more government expenditure on aid, Bono is advocating more taxes, many of which would presumably fall on people who earn much less money than he does, especially if U2 is engaged in aggressively minimizing its tax liability. The decision was also made at a time when the Irish economy, having boomed for many years and been christened the "Celtic tiger," was suffering the aftermath of the 2008 banking crisis, with the government taking on private sector debts on top of its own considerable debts.

When U2 headlined at the Glastonbury Festival, UK – long a hotbed of political activism as well as music – Art Uncut, an offshoot of UK Uncut, was there to stage a welcome, waving a banner bearing the legend "U pay tax 2?" and filming the event for YouTube. Within minutes, the inflatable banner was removed by security staff with – according to protestors – unnecessary violence. One of the protestors got her finger broken.[19]

As of August 2012, Art Uncut had only 2,500 followers on Twitter, but UK Uncut had 45,000. Twelve months on, the Art Uncut account seems to have vanished, but UK Uncut has risen to almost 70,000.

Learnings

The Glastonbury Festival is a core market for U2's music and there is significant overlap with the constituency both for Bono's political activism and that of Art Uncut. To stage – and then publicize through social media – a protest at this forum goes to the heart of the hypocrisy charge against Bono, and implies that he has become detached from his political and musical roots by swanning around with George W. Bush, Gordon Brown, and Barack Obama.

☑ What Art Uncut did right

- A visual protest at Glastonbury produced decent footage for the social media protest, and knock-on coverage in the MSM.
- Targeting Bono's core constituencies – both political and musical – hit his reputation hard.

☒ What Bono and U2 did wrong

- The action was hard to defend for celebrities trying to take the moral high ground on an important issue, and there was not much attempt at doing so.

ETHICS BRANDJACK High-profile humanitarian invites, and receives, charges of hypocrisy.

73 Starbucks homophobic rant
June 2011

Starbucks is a progressive chain, headquartered in the liberal city of Seattle, Washington, on America's west coast. It has a strong tradition of CSR and a commitment to fair trade. It has a young, and often progressive, customer base, and has been rather good at connecting with its customers in novel uses of social media, including the http://mystarbucksidea.force.com website. For such a company to be accused of practicing, or even tolerating, homophobia is a major crisis. It puts the company out of line with the values of a significant section of its customer base, in the US and Europe.

This story began with a blog publishing a letter of complaint from a customer to Starbucks, and rapidly went viral in social media and the MSM. The letter describes the author as a loyal Starbucks customer of many years' standing. She apparently overheard part of a conversation in which a Starbucks manager in Long Island, New York was firing an employee called Jeffery. While this author is unable to verify the contents of the letter, it reads as an attempt at a fair summary of what the customer heard. She concedes that she did not hear the whole conversation and did not know the background. The manager was, apparently, unhappy that Jeffery had been sharing inappropriate personal details with his colleagues at work. The implication was that these personal details were considered inappropriate, in part because Jeffery was gay.

If true, the story raises a number of key issues concerning the manager's judgment. Even on the best reading of it, there are a number of difficult issues for the company. Let us assume, for the sake of argument, that Jeffery's behavior was in some way inappropriate. Sharing details about your sex life with work colleagues certainly *can* cross such a line. That doesn't necessarily make it a firing offense. People can – and probably should – be warned first, and only fired if they continue to behave inappropriately. Even then, there are certain standards of professional practice that would be expected of a manager:

1 If at all possible, the whole conversation should be held in private, and not where customers can hear. This is especially important, given the sensitive nature of the allegations against Jeffery.
2 If the conversation has to be in public, it needs to be especially sensitively handled. The precise nature of the allegations against him should not be made clear to a casual outsider. If Jeffery has been warned about inappropriate conversations before (as he should have been), then it should be possible to allude to these in a way that makes things clear to Jeffery, but not to a customer.

3 It should not have been implied that the gayness of his conversations was a factor in rendering them inappropriate. His sexuality should not have been alluded to at all in any way that was audible and comprehensible to customers, as this violates his privacy. If he had raised the issue, it should have been stressed that this was *not* a factor in his dismissal.

Within 30 hours, the blog and associated social media activities had reached such a pitch that Starbucks contacted the blogger directly. The company promised that it was investigating. The gay couple at the heart of the blog took the corporation at its word and stopped promoting the blog and cut back on their media interviews. They were also contacted by Jeffery who thanked them and the social media community for support.

But then came a third update. This time the bloggers claimed they had been lied to. The Starbucks investigation had concluded that they must have misunderstood the situation. The bloggers claimed this was not really possible. For this reason, they reject Starbucks' claim to have taken the issue seriously as a "lie."[20]

It was true that they may only have had a partial picture, but they had clearly learned that Jeffery was being fired and that he was gay. None of this should have been apparent to a customer in the store. While it does not necessarily follow that Jeffrey had been the victim of discrimination, it does seem to be the case that his dismissal was badly handled.

Learnings

Starbucks has not stated that the events described in the letter are true and that action has been taken. The community would probably have understood if the company had stood its ground on privacy and refused to divulge *what* action had been taken. Nor has it said that, after an investigation, it concluded that the letter is simply false. According to the blog, two weeks after promising a thorough investigation, Starbucks still had not contacted Jeffery.

Even if the investigation was inconclusive, it should be possible to draft a decent statement, along the lines of: "After a thorough investigation, we are unable to confirm that the events described in the letter transpired in the way described. However, we have reinforced to all our staff, and managers especially, the values that Starbucks supports. We would never allow discrimination against an employee for being gay and value and protect the privacy of all our employees." How hard is that?

The original response on the Starbucks blog does stress the company's support for lesbian, gay, bisexual, and transgender (LGBT) people and that it is proud of its record and the awards it has won in this area. Much as the blogger seems to think that Starbucks has been acting to protect its reputation at the expense of its staff, it seems to this commentator that it has done the exact opposite. Its reluctance to conclude that a manager transgressed its policies – even if only procedurally – has done great damage to the company's reputation.

This analysis is necessarily vague as Starbucks ignored several requests for a comment.

The bloggers appealed for people to forego a coffee at Starbucks for one day and instead donate $5 to The Trevor Project, an organization providing intervention and suicide prevention services to LGBTQ young people.

☒ What Starbucks did wrong

- On the best reading of the facts – unless the bloggers are fabricating things – Jeffery's dismissal was badly handled and, even if it was justified, his privacy was violated.
- It promised a "thorough" investigation and does not seem to have lived up to that promise.

ETHICS BRANDJACK	Company seems to be out of line with the prevailing values of its customers.
STAFF BRANDJACK	Apparent misconduct by a manager tarnishes the entire reputation of the company.

74 Chesapeake Energy hits back at *NY Times* story
June 2011

The New York Times published a 2,500-word article[21] on the possible overstating of gas reserves open to recovery by the controversial technique of hydraulic fracturing, or fracking. Although the article was about the industry as a whole, the first industry executive quoted was from Chesapeake Energy. The company proved remarkably adept in hitting back at the *NY Times* in social media.

The same day as the article, which was published on a Sunday, Chesapeake CEO Aubrey McClendon sent an email to all staff refuting the article, which he described as "misleading" and motivated by an anti-industry agenda.[22]

The *NY Times* article was based on memos and emails in the public domain, which, the paper claimed, cast doubt on industry claims about the extent of natural gas reserves in the US. In this context, the word "reserves" refers not to the geological measure of the total gas extant, it means gas that is commercially extractable. That's a figure that varies constantly with the price of gas. If prices are high, more marginal reserves can be profitably extracted. The paper concedes that major discoveries are often subject to downward revisions, because the discovery itself brings the price down. It is also worth noting that the market for natural gas – unlike that for oil – is often governed more by local than by global factors. Gas can only be transported if there is an infrastructure, such as a pipeline network, meaning that higher reserves in the US will lead to falling local prices, even while prices remain strong in other markets. This means there is always going to be a debate about the extent and viability of reserves. There's no doubt that the article reveals, as it claims, *doubts* about the extent of the reserves. However, to this (reasonably informed) lay observer, it also reads as though journalists have selected contributions to one side of an active debate and used them as the source for the article.

McClendon produced a hard-hitting response to the article, and Chesapeake actively promoted it in social media. The group purchased "promotion" of Chesapeake tweets to people searching for the hashtag #NaturalGas but also, more innovatively, to those searching for @NYTimes. The company actively responded to anyone tweeting about the *NY Times* article with a message referring them to McClendon's letter, which it had posted on its Facebook page. The Facebook page then became the venue for the debate about the subject, with critics and supporters of the article chiming in. Months later, McClendon's letter and the comments were still available.

Learnings

Chesapeake certainly took a risk by being the first energy company to look over the parapet and hit back against the Gray Lady (the nickname for *The New York Times*). Whatever the merits of the case, Chesapeake seems to have been pretty effective and been widely praised for its proactive approach. The company was at least fairly successful in building a case against the paper, claiming that it had been irresponsible and biased in its reporting.

☑ What Chesapeake did right

- It promptly issued a strong and aggressive response.
- It wrote to its staff first.

- It posted in a managed forum, but allowed debate.
- It aggressively promoted its response in Twitter.

ETHICS **BRANDJACK**	Company took the charges of ethical breaches and threw them back at the paper.

75 BART: shooting and scripted "loyal riders"
July–September 2011

BART (Bay Area Rapid Transit) in San Francisco had an excellent case to make, but threw it away by being inauthentic. Like many municipal transit systems, BART has its own police force. When the BART police shot a homeless man, apparently fleeing the scene when he was challenged in a fare enforcement operation, this raised considerable controversy and led to a mass protest.

Local political activist, Chris Jackson, told CBS local:

> This is something that only happens in communities of color. When we don't pay our fare we get chased and shot by the cops. This is an unacceptable outcome.[23]

There were community protests about the shooting, with flowers laid at the scene, and calls for the BART police to be disbanded.

Kenneth Harding Jr, the dead man, is an unlikely martyr, despite the racial angle, the fact that the operation began as fare enforcement, and the apparently genuine community anger. Even if we doubt police claims that Harding fired first, it later turned out that he was wanted in connection with a murder in Seattle and was a convicted child rapist. The fact that he was being sought by police in another state makes sense of the otherwise inexplicable. Just as it is hard to believe police would shoot a man over fare evasion, it is hard to believe that a fare evader, unless mentally unbalanced, would shoot at police. But Harding knew he was wanted in connection with murder. This makes it much more believable that he would shoot at police to facilitate his own escape. As this further information emerged about the dead man, one might intuitively expect that BART now had the ability to regain control of the story. Unfortunately, BART's attempt to move the story on in August backfired.

One of the great strengths of social media is that you can use it to let your customers tell their own story. BART has many loyal riders. One weakness may be that the choice to use BART is often a functional one. Some riders may use the service daily, without necessarily feeling any particular loyalty to it. It is not a service chosen in a fully competitive market. Many users of mass transit systems are perennial complainers. Nonetheless, identifying loyal riders should not be an impossible task. San Francisco is liberal (in the American, leftwing, sense of the word). There are certainly many people who are proud of their city's commitment to mass transit.

BART's response was to recruit these loyal riders to tell their story. It is a sound tactic for the social media world. On August 11, as protests against the shooting of Harding (and the more sympathetic Charles Hill, shot and killed a few weeks earlier) continued, BART held a press conference, with loyal riders making statements on its behalf. However, in a spectacular misjudgment worthy of a fascist dictator, BART also shut down cell phone services on the system the same day, citing public safety concerns.

Social media also put a huge premium on transparency and authenticity. BART's decision to use "loyal riders" and then provide them with a script emerged in early September and provoked a strong backlash. Who were these people? Were they "loyal riders" or actors? Suggesting edits to someone's script or even discussing ideas – "some of our riders have suggested X is the thing they most like about BART" – might well be okay, but providing scripts, even if they are based on interviews with the riders, crosses the line from customer endorsement to scripting actors.

Learnings

BART has a pretty good case here. Hill was a drug user who was armed with a knife and threw a bottle at police.[24] Demonstrators plainly made an error, jumping to unwarranted conclusions about Harding, who turned out to be someone with whom it is hard to sympathize. But BART threw these advantages away by seeking to disrupt protests by shutting down the wireless service and then making use of inauthentic "loyal riders."

☒ What BART did wrong

- It tried to disrupt protests in a dictatorial style. Much better to argue against the protesters, while stressing a commitment to transparency and engagement. Even make the point that the protests were organized using BART's own wireless system.
- Scripting the "loyal riders" might well have been the norm for ads or in-house videos only a few years ago, but at a press conference and for use on YouTube, the standard is different. Social

media users prize authenticity. Using scripted spokespeople while presenting them as genuine customer ambassadors will have been seen by people as a betrayal and a deception.

SELF BRANDJACK	BART throws away some strong advantages by misunderstanding its customers and the new rules of social media.

76 Gmail Man: Microsoft hit ad
July 2011

The Gmail Man ad seems to have begun at a Microsoft sales conference. Microsoft refused to comment to ZDNet as to whether Microsoft was responsible for the ad, but it was later posted on YouTube (a Google service) by what appears to be the official Microsoft account. The ad is a hit piece on Gmail, and describes what it is about to show as "the opposite experience of Office 365."

The ad shows a mailman – Gmail Man – delivering letters, but also reading through them to pick out key words. He talks to one woman in her office about an embarrassing *burning … sensation* and *cat … dander* while offering a cream to help. She replies that she had been scared of *burning* a *lasagne*, which her husband thought was *sensation-al* and had a *cat* called *Dandy*.

This author can certainly confirm that ad targeting is not always as neat as it should be. When reading a *Wall Street Journal* column by Peggy Noonan, an ad popped up for information on Noonan syndrome, a type of dwarfism unconnected with the columnist. Google has always been upfront about Gmail scanning people's mail and using the information to target ads. The service is provided at no cost and if people want a greater degree of privacy, they can always use a paid-for service. Personally, this author is relaxed about ad targeting and would prefer it if the targeting were more precise. The only thing worse than a well-targeted ad is a badly targeted one. How many women have received spam mail offering to increase the size of their penises?

Highlighting to users the disadvantages of Gmail does not seem offensive in itself, but it does bring home how easy it is for anyone to put up an ad – even one attacking a Google service on a Google platform. Unlike Greenpeace, Microsoft does not claim to speak with any particular moral authority, but it is highlighting an ethical issue: a Google practice which, while not secret, is also not one that Google has any interest in stressing and which some users may not be aware of, or had not fully thought through.

Learnings

Google is good at social media. Although its Google+ platform has not – or not yet – seriously challenged Facebook, LinkedIn, or Twitter, YouTube remains the breakthrough technology of the social age.

Google rightly ignored the Gmail Man ad. It still sits on YouTube. The community there comments both for and against it, and Google does not interfere in the discussion or remove the video. Google *does*, however, remove videos on request that violate intellectual property rights. It is possible that it would have removed a similar ad targeting Microsoft, if it had been asked to do so.

In one sense, the ad hits a nerve. Google cannot deny the basic charges, which are its business model for Gmail, and for other platforms too. In general, Google does not charge for its services, but does target ads based on its ever growing mountain of data. Neither challenging the messages in the ad nor banning it from Google platforms would have been effective.

☑ What Microsoft did right

- It made true charges that will concern some people in a light-hearted and humorous way.

☑ What Google did right

- It ignored the whole thing, neither challenging the messages nor getting heavy-handed about the use of Google platforms to promote an anti-Google message.

ETHICS BRANDJACK Multinational makes true charges about the business model of a competitor.

77 Airbnb #ransackgate

July 2011

Airbnb is a service that links people who want to rent out their homes, or parts thereof, on a cheap and short-term basis with customers for the same service. It is certainly not a service for everyone. As Keith Trivitt put it on PR Daily: "Think about how absurd that concept sounds." At the very least, you would think that a customer going into this would realize that there are some risks involved in participating with the service.

The complaint that went viral on Twitter under the hashtag #ransackgate was by a customer who blogs as EJ. She describes a horrendous experience of returning to find her home robbed and vandalized. Her passport, credit cards, and much else had been stolen. In upsetting and "creepy" ways, things had been senselessly moved to other locations in her apartment. Something – she wasn't sure what, but possibly her missing bed linen – had been burned in the fireplace, even though it was the height of a California summer, with the flue closed so that ash was all over the place.[25]

The customer's experience – if true, and some people have implied that it might not be – is plainly a severe one. Airbnb claims that 97 percent of the people using its service are completely reliable, but as EJ herself concedes, someone is always going to get the 3 percent.

Despite a shaky start – Airbnb did not have a 24-hour helpline – EJ was mostly complimentary about the service she received. Customer support teams were helpful and cooperated fully with the San Francisco Police Department (SFPD). There was no insurance or other coverage for the customer, but there had never been any representation that there would be.

But her blog also goes on to challenge the whole premise of Airbnb's business model. EJ had apparently previously arranged a short-term let of her apartment through Craigslist, which is free. So what, exactly, was Airbnb doing to earn its $20 fee? Craigslist is full of warnings about due diligence. Both companies merely facilitate people getting together and do not vet participants in any way. But by keeping contact details of the parties confidential until the deal has been struck, Airbnb makes it harder for the parties to engage in due diligence. Far from warning people to research the other person themselves, it prevents such research from happening. EJ also suggests that, by charging a fee, the company *implies* that it has engaged in at least some vetting.

EJ went silent on the issue for some weeks after her first blog. This probably fed speculation that the story was bogus and that she possibly didn't even exist. However, Airbnb, after a shaky start, did go public, saying that it had set up a 24-hour helpline, as EJ had requested in her blog, and a $50,000 insurance policy for hosts. Trivitt speculates that this was in response to criticism of the initial, slow PR response.

After a month of silence, EJ blogged again. She recognized that her silence may have contributed to rumors that the story was not true, but explained that she had been frightened because the criminals who trashed her apartment were still out there, she did not want to jeopardize the criminal investigation, and she had, initially, had concerns about Airbnb's reaction if she kept blogging on the subject. In a thoughtful and analytical blog, she picked apart comments from Airbnb's CEO, who, sensibly, was now the lead spokesperson on the ongoing crisis.

EJ claimed that Airbnb's claim to have been helpful was not fully true, the company had stopped being supportive, and the customer support team had not been in contact at all, since the day she published her blog. A carefully worded statement from Airbnb could have implied that the company played some role in securing EJ's safety. She clarified that this was not true. Airbnb claimed that, due to the company's cooperation, a suspect was in custody. She said she had no knowledge either way regarding the company's cooperation with the authorities, but she had not been informed that anyone was in custody regarding her issue. One person had been arrested, but passed to another jurisdiction in connection with another offense. And, in any case, she believed that multiple offenders were involved with the theft and vandalism at her property. EJ also claimed that in the one contact she had had from Airbnb since her blog had been published, the company had complained that the coverage was damaging its business and implied it wanted her to shut the blog down.

The lengthy blogs were clear and well written. They told a good story. People remember stories, especially when told in the first person by a sympathetic narrator. The stories may or may not have been true, but they were believable, and the victim will always seem more sympathetic than the corporation.

Learnings

Social media users are always initially sympathetic to the individual rather than the corporation. It is easier to believe a person than a company. Social media always react badly to any attempt at silencing bloggers or critics. There is a *huge* premium on authentic and rapid human engagement.

There was no attempt to bring EJ inside or use her personal experience as a way of humanizing the changes to the business model. Asking for sympathy, as a start-up engaged in a new funding round, is one thing – although not advised, given the sympathy much more obviously due to the victim – but trying to get her to stop blogging on the issue was a major mistake.

Businesses sometimes worry that to pay compensation, when there was no insurance as part of their contract with EJ, might set a precedent. But to use EJ as an example of how and why it is reengineering in response to a difficult situation is a different thing.

Both Dell and United Airlines used critics (Jeff Jarvis and Dave Carroll, CS 4, CS 32) in this way and, in her first blog, EJ wasn't even really a critic, mostly praising the support she had received from Airbnb.

☒ What Airbnb did wrong

- It was slow to react. It took time to develop a coherent line or appoint a single spokesperson. It didn't, initially, do anything to actually fix the problem.
- It may have pressured EJ into shutting down her blog. Certainly, she claims that as one reason for her month of silence after the first blog.
- It may have tried to claim undue credit for securing EJ's safety and the SFPD's investigation.

☑ What Airbnb did right

- After a shaky start, it put forward its CEO as a human face. Since EJ remained anonymous, this at least gave the corporation something of an edge.
- After some hesitation, it *did* fix the problem, at least for future hosts, with a 24-hour helpline and an insurance policy.
- At this point, it also agreed "We have really screwed things up."[26]

CUSTOMER REVOLT BRANDJACK	A customer's bad experience goes viral and the company initially mishandles the fallout.

78 Wenzhou train crash
July 2011

On July 23, 2011, two high-speed trains crashed in Wenzhou, China. They were traveling over a viaduct at the time and since both trains were derailed, several carriages fell off the viaduct. Although the trains were not traveling at high speeds (around 60 mph), there were considerable casualties. At least 40 people were killed and almost 200 injured, with a dozen serious injuries.

This is China, and the reaction was typical of the Chinese Communist Party. Once initial rescues had been completed, officials ordered that the story should be buried. Literally. The railway carriages were to be buried on the spot. Future historians may regard the Wenzhou train crash as one of the most important turning points of 2011, and possibly the 21st century. What happens when the government orders a cover-up, and the people say "no"?

The government response came in two phases, and was straight out of the textbook. But the two phases came from different textbooks. The first was one of media control. There was no attempt to prevent *any* reporting of the crash, but authorities issued specific instructions about *how* the story was to be covered. Media were not supposed to send journalists to the scene. There was to be no linking of the story to the fact that the trains were high speed. (In fairness, as noted above, the trains were not actually traveling at high speed.) Reports were to be infrequent. The "suggested" theme for reporting was the triumph of love in the face of tragedy.

Until this point, media control had been fairly effective. Although there are many independent media, and have been since the 1980s, strict government guidelines cover the reporting of all sorts of sensitive issues. Many media only relay news without actually gathering any of their own, and state-owned agencies such as Xinhua are influential over what is reported and how it is reported.

But the rise of the Internet in the years since 2000 has changed things. Increasingly, young people look to online sources for news, just as they do in the West. The "Great Firewall of China" is supposed to prevent people from accessing international news sources, and Western Internet giants have been heavily criticized for cooperating with the Chinese government in blocking access to international media. China has its own Internet. An Internet with Chinese characteristics, if you like. But it still has all the decentralized features that make it hard to control.

According to McKinsey, China had 513 million Internet users in 2012, more than twice as many as the US, and social media in China date back to online communities in 1994. The most commonly used social media sites are Renren and Sina Weibo. Renren is similar to Facebook and Sina Weibo to Twitter. Both were full of content criticizing the government and its reaction to the crash. Wang Yongping, the Ministry of Railways spokesperson, was widely ridiculed and became the punchline of numerous jokes.

A Chinese student told me some years ago that on Chinese social media sites, there are certain banned phrases, such as "Tibet independence," "Taiwan independence" or "Tiananmen Square." If you type these characters, they simply do not appear on the screen. But computers are stupid. Computers do what you say, not what you mean. If you insert a small spelling error (the English example the student gave was "Tiibet independence"), everyone knows what you mean.

So the story was not suppressed. Even state-owned media began to report the story in unapproved ways. Xinhua itself issued – and then retracted – an investigation into the causes of the crash. The government strategy changed.

A major review of rail safety was launched, with the promise that the results would be publicly reported. Construction of a new high-speed rail was suspended while the enquiry was conducted.

This is another textbook response, but this time the textbook is the one for crisis response in the West.

Learnings

In a crisis, you should first proffer help and sympathy to the victims. Second, you promise to investigate and publish the findings. These are the golden rules, and it seems they have arrived in China. The Chinese government – having seen Mubarak fall and Gaddafi killed earlier in the year – seems to have accepted that the old ways of controlling the media no longer function, at least not in a crisis.

It would be far too early to say that we know what lessons the government has drawn from this. But it is not difficult to imagine that these lessons could be far-reaching. China is not unstable in the way that most Arab countries are. China does not have a youth population bulge – and it is young people who mostly demonstrate and riot. And Chinese people are not facing the economic dissatisfaction that afflicts most Arab countries. Chinese people don't have time to riot. They have jobs. But this should not be read as meaning they are happy with their government. We could well be on the point of major change. Let us hope it is evolutionary and not violent.

☒ What the Chinese government did wrong

- It tried to organize the traditional cover-up.

☑ What the Chinese government did right

- It quickly recognized that this would not work, and ordered an open public enquiry instead.

SELF BRANDJACK An attempt to literally bury a story backfires, and possibly changes the world.

---

79 IE users "less intelligent" hoax
August 2011

PC World, the *Daily Telegraph*, and numerous other online and offline media reported that Aptiquant, a psychometric testing firm, had invited Internet users to undertake IQ tests.[27] The firm then cross-tabulated the scores with the browser the person was using and found a statistically significant correlation. Users of Microsoft's Internet Explorer (IE) were found to be slightly less intelligent than average, while users of Chrome, Firefox, and Safari were slightly more intelligent. People using Camino, Opera, or Internet Explorer with Google Chrome Frame scored "exceptionally high." The study claimed to be based on tests administered to 100,000 users. (As a matter of full disclosure, this author is a former IE user, and Netscape before that, but had shifted to Chrome some time before this study was published.)

Several experts were quoted as offering explanations for this result. Matt Rossoff of *Business Insider* was one of those to suggest that, since IE is usually the default browser, anyone who lacked the skills to download another browser would, of necessity, be an IE user.[28]

After the story broke, Aptiquant kept it going by claiming that it had been threatened with a lawsuit by IE users. Although widely reported in the media, the study turned out to be a hoax. *The Telegraph*, to its credit, still has the story up on its website, with a note that the story is a hoax and a link to the follow-up. Although taken in by the hoaxers, the paper has chosen not to wipe the story away.

The story ran for several days in a number of MSM publications and was widely promoted in social media. According to the *Daily Telegraph,* it was readers of the BBC website who first suggested it was a hoax. Aptiquant had an extensive website, but a little digging showed it had only been live for a month, despite claims that the company had been in business since 2006. The photographs and detailed biographies of staff had been lifted from the website of a French company. When the *Daily Telegraph* contacted "Aptiquant," it was told the study was a hoax and the hoaxers were surprised that it had taken several days to unravel.

Learnings

Hoaxes work well when they play into an image that people – or at least a significant body of people – already believe. The most actively engaged Internet users are the ones most likely to have a strong view on the merits of different browsers. For the reasons cited by Matt Rossoff, default users are IE users. These are likely to include those less interested in online applications and infrequent users of the Internet. As such, dedicated followers of Chrome, Safari, and other browsers often look down on IE users. A hoax study claiming that IE users were smarter than average would probably have been denounced as a hoax more quickly.

The purported basis of the study – IQ tests correlated against browser information – would have been easy to do. Which browser someone is using can easily be read by a website, so it is not a question people would have to answer. People doing the test would not have been alerted to possible cross-tabulation as, for instance, if people performing the test were asked, apropos of nothing, what their political leaning was.

One other thing we learn from this is how journalists check stories these days. They look at corporate websites, which are what companies, even fake companies, say about themselves. They don't check publicly available data such as the annual accounts of businesses, which have to be lodged with the authorities for any limited liability company.

✓ What the hoaxers did right

- They described a practical research project that could easily have been real.
- Their fake results were in line with the inbuilt prejudices of a significant proportion of Internet-savvy people.
- The fake website was extensive, and established weeks in advance of the press release announcing the study.

| FAKE BRANDJACK | Strong hoax, well planned and faultlessly executed. |

80 The "Facebook riots"
August 2011

The looting, disorder, and protest that hit several English cities in August 2011 had a variety of features, which is why the language surrounding it becomes contentious. Were these "riots" – disorder arising from political protest? Was it a matter of looting – people trying to get the latest flat screen TV or Nike trainers? Where would the vandalism – the burning of shops and vehicles – fit into either scenario? What was the role of peaceful political protest in the early stages of the disorder?

A timeline seems to suggest that it began with peaceful protest, almost immediately descended into violence, with the violence becoming looting.

The term "riot" is a flattering one for the large numbers of people whose only interest was looting, which is why some commentators derisively used the term "shopping riots."

One key inciting event was the death of Mark Duggan, who was shot dead by police on 4 August. Early reports suggested he may have been armed and may have fired first. A police radio had a bullet embedded in it. It turned out that the bullet embedded in the radio was police issue. However, an illegal gun was recovered from the scene (although, it seems, not from Duggan's body) and CCTV seemed to show Duggan purchasing a gun earlier. A man has subsequently been convicted of selling him a gun and Duggan's fingerprints were on the box that appears to have contained the gun. There is no physical evidence to confirm police accounts that he fired the gun at them. Eyewitness accounts are contradictory, with some media reporting saying the police challenged Duggan to "put it down" before shooting him and others that Duggan was pinned down at the time.[29]

On 7 August, before much of the above evidence had emerged, people in Tottenham held a protest against the killing of Mark Duggan. At that time, the only evidence available was contradictory accounts from the police and the family. Police have been accused of reacting to this demonstration in a heavy-handed way.[30] Riots followed the breaking up of this demonstration.

This was followed by several more nights of disturbances, which were not limited to the Tottenham area in which the Duggan family lived. These took place in other parts of London, including noted shopping districts such as Oxford Street. On subsequent days, there were disturbances in other major cities, possibly triggered by public announcements that police from those cities were being drafted in to London.

There was considerable use of social media, including Facebook, Twitter, and BlackBerry Messenger (BBM) in gathering and coordinating people for participation in riots and looting. Facebook has a "real names" policy, so Twitter and BBM were generally considered more secure. Communities hit back, also using social media. People filmed the looting and posted pictures on Facebook pages calling for witnesses to come forward and people to identify those filmed in the act.

In January 2014, the inquest into Mark Duggan's death concluded that he had been shot lawfully.[31]

Learnings

This author has no particular expertise in policing tactics and will not comment on allegations of heavy-handed responses to the initial demonstration. However, the social media angles are fascinating. While some media blamed Facebook and other social media for the disorder, this seems bizarre. Crimes plotted by phone are not "phone crimes" and those plotted in pubs are not "beer crimes." The role of social media – combined with CCTV and crowdsourced gathering of evidence – seems to have huge implications for the future. As digital facial recognition improves, it may become harder and harder for people with a social media profile to be involved in crime at all.

FAKE BRANDJACK Facebook, Twitter, and BlackBerry were dismissive of attempts to link their platforms to the crimes, but did not overreact to allegations that lacked basic credibility in the first place.

81 Nivea's "re-civilize yourself" ad
August 2011

Nivea's "re-civilize yourself" ad was controversial from the beginning, with people immediately citing racism or racial insensitivity. Judge for yourselves as the image is easy to find online.[32] The ad was heavily criticized in social media and, to a lesser extent, in the MSM, before being withdrawn. Most blog and digital media platforms allowed people to debate the issue, and the fact that people were piling into the discussion on both sides almost certainly prolonged the debate.

Among the issues drawn out in the debate were the fact that both images in the ad are of a black man (probably the same man). This is not suggesting that the black man becomes white; however, it is showing someone moving from an Afro haircut to a neatly trimmed Barack Obama cut. The word "civilize" was parsed to death by commentators. Was not this the mission of colonialists and imperialists, to bring the "benefits" of "civilization" to the black man? Of course, this ad says *recivilize* yourself, suggesting the person had been civilized, became uncivilized, and should become civilized again. Would the ad have been offensive if it had shown a white person? Probably not, but that is hardly definitive, given past use of the word "civilize" in a specifically racial context. While some people defended the ad, it certainly seems like bad judgment, and Nivea itself came to share that view.[33]

Unless, as some commentators suggested, the whole controversy was one Nivea had deliberately courted to generate publicity. The ads appeared in media everywhere, without Nivea having to buy the space. While overtly racist ads that generated such controversy would most certainly have damaged the company's reputation, something more marginal that it could back away from later may not have done. Nivea has unequivocally stated "It was never our intention to offend anyone," so we can assume that the company denies it deliberately courted controversy.

Designing ads mostly for the controversy factor and subsequent earned media coverage is common in politics. The abiding image of the 1992 UK general election, in which the Conservatives campaigned with the slogan "Labour's double whammy," was a poster that appeared in only a handful of places but was widely reported in the media. By 2005, posters did not have to appear anywhere. A crowdsourced suggestion for the Labour Party, which showed Michael Howard, opposition leader, and Oliver Letwin, shadow chancellor, as flying pigs, was criticized as potentially anti-Semitic (Howard and Letwin are both Jewish). The controversy raged in the media for some time and the "poster" received a great deal of coverage. But there was never any actual poster. It was never displayed anywhere. It was just an idea discussed on a Labour Party website.

Learnings

If this had been a deliberate attempt to court controversy, it would have been a risky one. Some people were certainly angry. Nonetheless, there were probably more people defending the ad, or suggesting it was a bad judgment with no bad intent, than there were people who were offended.

[X] What Nivea did wrong

- Deliberately or not, the company allowed a dubious ad to go to press. It gave the impression that managers did not properly research their ads or consider the implications.

[✓] What Nivea did right

- It allowed the debate to run for a while, then apologized.

SELF BRANDJACK Poor judgment by the company created an unnecessary controversy in a sensitive area.

82 Indiana University Health: State Fair stage collapse
August 2011

Hospitals can often get caught up in international or crisis news stories that are not of their own making. Whether it is treating celebrities or victims of a high-profile tragedy, hospitals can be at the center of the story. In the US, hospitals are covered by strict legislation designed to protect the privacy of patients.

The stage collapse at the Indiana State Fair was a classic example of the way in which stories break in the social media world. Even people at the fair – including, ironically, the director of emarketing for Indiana University Health (IUH) – often heard about the story first from Twitter. The actual stage collapse was filmed on cell phones and rapidly uploaded to YouTube. As with any tragedy of this scale – six people were killed and scores of people injured – a range of people are interested parties and become embroiled in the media debate. The state governor was visibly emotional at a press conference. Families of those killed and injured were making statements.

On the whole, IUH was well prepared. It had recently reordered its crisis and disaster procedures to take account of social media. The president and CEO of the group was soon blogging on the issue, with fairly bland statements wishing people well and thanking first responders. The group issued a tweet with "thoughts and prayers" for the victims almost immediately. There were regular updates to the media about the scale of the emergency response.

However, IUH made one understandable, but unfortunate error. No one turned off the system designed to send preprogramed tweets at set intervals throughout the fair. The day after the stage collapse, when the fair was closed, IUH sent a tweet urging people attending the fair to call in on the IUH booth. The tweet got an almost immediate response, with another Twitter user calling for it to be deleted. It was, and an apology – and explanation – was soon issued.

Learnings

A good response by IUH expressing sympathy for the victims and providing information to the media was marred by a single, careless error.

X	What IUH did wrong

- It forgot that preprogramed tweets would continue during the crisis, unless the system was proactively disabled.

SELF BRANDJACK   A careless error undoes months of planning.

83 Anders Breivik, Lacoste
September 2011

In July 2011, Anders Breivik carried out two mass murders, one in Oslo and one on the Norwegian island of Utøya. In these attacks he killed 77 people, most of them teenagers. His motive was political. He targeted government buildings in Oslo and a youth camp on Utøya organized by the Workers' Youth League, the youth wing of the Labour Party.

In September, he was sent to trial for these attacks. The photograph of him sitting in the police car on the way to court showed him wearing a red Lacoste sweater. Lacoste had several options at this point, and chose the wrong one. It contacted the Norwegian authorities and asked if Breivik could be prevented from wearing its brand. Ignoring the issue would have been the wise choice.

A prisoner facing trial but who has not actually been convicted would normally make his own judgments about what to wear to court. It would be prejudicial for a defendant to appear in prison clothing, although that is common in some countries. It is unlikely, therefore, that the Norwegian authorities had any way of preventing Breivik from wearing Lacoste. Nor is it clear why they would wish to cooperate with the French clothing brand. What would be in it for the Norwegian police or judiciary to take action against someone legally wearing a particular clothing line, just because this didn't suit the reputation of the manufacturer?

Of course, the Internet started digging. Breivik is, to say the least, an opinionated man. Whether he is legally insane is a matter for the Norwegian courts, which ruled in 2012 that he was not. But Breivik's websites are forthcoming on his opinions. According to Hawkblocker.com, Breivik was vocal in his "manifesto" in favor of the Lacoste brand.

This issue arose for Lacoste not long after Abercrombie & Fitch had asked the makers of the US reality TV series *Jersey Shore* to stop the show's stars wearing Abercrombie & Fitch clothing. This divided commentators. Was the brand seeking to publicize its connection with the hit show, or was it concerned to prevent its image being tarnished by association with the tacky antics of the show's participants. Certainly, the *effect* was to raise the connection in public awareness.

Despite some conspiracy theorists – including Hawkblocker.com[34] – this cannot have been the intention of Lacoste. *Jersey Shore* may be tacky, but at least it has a cult following. No brand is going to want to be associated with a mass killer like Breivik. The tiny group for whom he is a hero is outnumbered 100 to 1 by those who revile him.

Learnings

Sometimes, it is better to just shut up. If someone else had noticed the connection – and hardly anyone had prior to Lacoste bringing it to public attention – some anodyne comment about how the company hates everything Breivik stands for, but cannot stop anyone from wearing its clothing, would have sufficed. The fact that Breivik was wearing Lacoste, and, presumably, clothing made by other manufacturers too, was not newsworthy. Lacoste trying to stop him wearing the brand was. This is probably an example of people falling into a fairly typical trap. People who do their job for eight hours a day become obsessed with that which they do for a living. People who live and breathe the Lacoste brand looked at Breivik and saw the green crocodile on his chest. Everyone else saw a mass murderer on the way to court.

☒ What Lacoste did wrong

- It turned a nothing of an issue into major international news and linked the brand with a mass murdering terrorist.

SELF BRANDJACK An issue no one would have noticed goes viral through mishandling.

84 Bank of America debit card fee
September 2011

Following the 2010 Dodd-Frank banking legislation in the US, especially the Durbin amendment that capped the fees that banks could charge for card transactions, Bank of America decided to introduce a monthly $5 charge to its debit card users. The timing was, in part, dictated by legislation, which had cost the bank $1.9 billion in revenue. But maybe someone should have thought about the climate of opinion that led to the legislation. Banks were not exactly popular around the world in 2011, and the announcement came at the beginning of the Occupy Wall Street movement.

The details of the proposed charges – which were to start from January 2012 – seemed almost calculated to provoke a hostile reaction. The charges were waived in the case of customers who had mortgages with the bank. Other premium customers, such as those with substantial deposits at the bank, were also to have the fee waived. This structure was never going to play well, as it seemed to hit poorer customers harder than richer ones. It would have been relatively easy for the bank to have structured its discounts for multiple accounts differently, so that other charges, relating to the mortgage and savings accounts, were waived for customers with active debit cards rather than giving the discount on the controversial new charge.

President Obama got in on the act, criticizing the bank, saying: "You don't have some inherent right just to, you know, get a certain amount of profit."[35] Adding: "you have to treat [your customers] fairly and transparently." One thing that can be said in favor of the bank's proposed fee structure is that it *was* transparent. Instead of charging the retailer – and therefore embedding its charges into higher retail prices – it was charging the customer, transparently, for services it was providing.

Customers, however, did not feel that they had been engaged in the process. Molly Katchpole, a 22-year-old recent graduate working part time on political causes in Washington DC, launched an online petition against the bank's new charges. Within weeks, she had more than 300,000 signatures. By October, the bank had withdrawn the plan.

Learnings

This was not thought through. The difficult financial climate the bank faced after the Dodd-Frank Act came about because of public hostility. This was not a time to be launching new charges. The proposed structure was sure to be seen by customers as unfair. The flat fee was a higher proportional charge on low users. Perhaps that could be justified on grounds of simplicity and transparency, if it wasn't for fee waivers for favored, premium customers. This plan played right into the prejudices of the Occupy crowd and popular disenchantment with bankers.

X	What Bank of America did wrong

- It failed to engage in adequate consultation to get a good grasp on the views of its customers.
- It created a structure of charges that seemed to favor rich customers over poor ones.

SELF **BRANDJACK**	A poorly planned policy proved impossible to implement.
CUSTOMER **REVOLT** **BRANDJACK**	Motivated customers rebelled.
AGGREGATION **BRANDJACK**	Digital channels were used to bring together a group of customers to organize opposition to the bank.

85 Celebrities support Ramzan Kadyrov's birthday party
October 2011

Ramzan Kadyrov is president of the Chechen Republic, an autonomous region of Russia. As a teenager, he fought alongside his father, an Islamic imam, for Chechen independence in the First Chechen War. The Kadyrovs, however, fought on Moscow's side in the Second Chechen War, after which Ramzan's father became president of the republic. Ramzan did not directly succeed his father as president, but took the post in 2007, as soon as he passed 30, the minimum constitutional age. Since he became president, Kadyrov has been widely criticized for human rights abuses and his implementation of Islam's Sharia law.

On October 5, 2011, there was a period of major festivities in Grozny, the Chechen capital, around the time of Ramzan Kadyrov's 35th birthday. Kadyrov denied it was to celebrate his birthday, but was to celebrate the success of the Chechen Republic. An eclectic group of performance artists from around the world were invited to join in the fun. There is not much record of who declined these invitations, although Shakira, the Colombian singer, indicated an acceptance that she later withdrew, having researched Kadyrov's human rights record.

Four stars who did attend came in for considerable criticism: Hillary Swank, Jean-Claude Van Damme, Seal, and Vanessa-Mae. How this cast of stars was selected is unknown, although Kadyrov has a strong interest in boxing, and Hillary Swank won an Oscar for playing a boxer in *Million Dollar Baby*, while Van Damme is well known for his roles in martial arts films. Vanessa-Mae – the Chinese-British techno violinist – may be the least internationally well known of the four, but has cult followings in several countries and has since become an Olympic athlete, competing for China in the Sochi Winter Olympics. Seal is a British singer-songwriter of Nigerian descent who has won numerous awards and is a coach on *The Voice* in Australia.

Today's celebrities are often sensitive to their image in social media. Vanessa-Mae's Facebook page has over 116,000 likes, although she has little personal presence on Twitter. Van Damme has 2.5 million fans of his Facebook page, but is also more talked about than talking on Twitter. Hilary Swank does not seem to prioritize presence on either Facebook or Twitter. Seal is more strongly engaged, with a fairly active Twitter account with 160,000 followers and more than 75,000 likes on Facebook. For performance stars, YouTube may be the most important social medium. Whether or not they participate, people will constantly be posting footage from films and music videos. It becomes a key place for fans to organize.

Of the stars originally invited, Shakira is by far the most plugged into social media. She has a verified Twitter account with over 21 million followers. She regularly engages bilingually, dividing her tweets between talking about her music career and her humanitarian work for the UN and the charity she founded promoting education in rural Colombia. She has 73 million likes on Facebook. While she is certainly an international star, the scale of her social media following when compared with Van Damme, Seal, and Swank undoubtedly reflects her engagement with these media.

Did her social engagement make her more sensitive to the reputational risk of appearing in Grozny? Probably, although it is also clear that she has prioritized humanitarian causes to a much greater extent than many other stars. Her causes are closely linked to the brand values she presents to her fans and, I think we should assume, are matters of genuine passion for her.

Learnings

It should be no surprise that the star who deliberately cultivates a social media following was the one most sensitive to the human rights issues at stake in appearing in Grozny. Congratulations to Shakira, who handled the whole situation almost faultlessly. Even her initial acceptance probably worked to her advantage, as it put her principled stance of, ultimately, turning down the substantial cash advantages of sucking up to Kadyrov into the public domain.

Hilary Swank is a highly respected actress. In her thirties, she has already won two Oscars and has been working as an executive producer since she was 29. She is known for much more serious films than Van Damme. She was probably more vulnerable than he to alienating audiences and Hollywood power brokers. She reacted well to the situation and by the end of October had fired her management team. She also publicly apologized for appearing in Grozny and announced that she was donating her fee to charitable causes. A spokesperson said "Hilary values her liberal credentials"[36] and claimed she was unaware of the human rights allegations against Kadyrov, although it should be noted that these would not be hard to discover. Has she never heard of Google or Wikipedia? The others did not indicate any plans to donate their fees to charity, and Seal publicly refused to apologize, tweeting "leave me out of your politics."[37]

Stars like Seal, Vanessa-Mae, and Van Damme are going to need to accept that if their brand is available for hire to the highest bidder, then it is not going to confer any moral authority. That may be fine with them. Perhaps they see themselves as purely entertainment industry brands, but it becomes harder for autocrats to claim that the, no pun intended, seal of approval has been conferred by such Western stars appearing at their events. Stars who cultivate their moral brand values do not sell them to the highest bidder. Anyone whose word is for sale has a word that is worth nothing.

Shakira publicly repudiated any association with Kadyrov from the beginning. Swank failed to perform her due diligence but publicly apologized and, by giving away her six-figure fee and sacking her manager, communicated that she understood the seriousness of the situation. By comparison, the others seem, to this author, to be morally bankrupt.

| **SELF BRANDJACK** | Stars take the check without checking out the guy who signed it. |
| **ETHICS BRANDJACK** | Social media hold people accountable for the implications of their decisions. |

86 Chapstick's sexist ad: "censorship" on Facebook page
October 2011

Chapstick's launch of an ad that was in dubious taste and provoked a storm of protest was bad enough. Inviting people to comment, and then deleting the predictable protests, offended the social media community still further. The ad shows a model searching for a missing Chapstick down a sofa with her butt stuck provocatively in the air. "Be heard," Chapstick said. But only, apparently, if your comments are not critical of the company's judgment in producing the ad. According to blogger Margot Magowan, even tasteless comments along the predictable lines of "I know where I want to hide my Chapstick" were apparently left up on the brand's Facebook page, while reasoned complaints about the ad were removed.[38]

It did not take the company long, however, to recognize that it had caused offense and to issue an apology:[39]

> We see that not everyone likes our new ad, and please know that we certainly didn't mean to offend anyone! Our fans and their voices are at the heart of our new advertising campaign, but we know we don't always get it right. We've removed the image and will share a newer ad with our fans soon!

> We apologize that fans have felt like their posts are being deleted and while we never intend to pull anyone's comments off our wall, we do comply with Facebook guidelines and remove posts that use foul language, have repetitive messaging, those that are considered spam-like (multiple posts from a person within a short period of time) and are menacing to fans and employees.

The first part is fine, but the second paragraph deflects from the main point. Fans "felt like their posts are being deleted." Well, were you deleting posts? If so, was it *only* on grounds of profanity or other breaches of Facebook policy, or was it, as critics suggested, because you did not like the content of the posts? The apology does not actually answer that question with any clarity. Note that single entendre sexual remarks *were* apparently being left in place.

Learnings

The concept of getting customers to engage with a discussion about losing Chapsticks is a perfectly sound one. Engagement is at the heart of social media success. No doubt the company was hoping that people would join in with funny stories about places they had mislaid, or found, their Chapsticks. It may seem an unlikely form of engagement, but it is probably a better hope than encouraging conversation about using the product, which is, after all, functional rather than fun.

Given the choice of photograph, two reactions were predictable: people would claim the ad was sexist and others would make sexual remarks about Chapstick and the model. Did Chapstick fail to anticipate either reaction? Did it not have a coherent plan in place to deal with these reactions? Or was it operating on the failed old canard that all publicity is good publicity? Did it really think that deliberately stoking controversy would be a good idea?

✓ What Chapstick did right

- It tried to engage fans in a discussion and invited storytelling.

✗ What Chapstick did wrong

- It either failed to anticipate the controversy or underestimated its scale.

AGGREGATION **BRANDJACK**	Discontented customers are provided with a place to organize by the brand.
UNANTICIPATED **RESPONSE** **BRANDJACK**	Suggestive photo sparks anger and innuendo.

87 Chris Huhne tweets a direct message
October 2011

Managing even one Twitter account from several platforms can get confusing. For example, if someone tweets both from a laptop or tablet and a smartphone, the different operational modes can take one by surprise. To make matters worse, some people have Twitter set to send mentions or direct messages (DMs) by email. The email then includes a "reply" button. That is how this author got caught out, assuming that a reply to a DM would go as a DM, and not as a public tweet. My tweet was not embarrassing. Chris Huhne's was: "@ChrisHuhne: From someone else fine but I do not want my fingerprints on the story. C."

On the scale of things, it could have been worse. In the US, congressman Anthony Weiner accidentally tweeted a picture of his penis, a scandal that would have excited the media immensely, even if it hadn't been for his embarrassing name.

At the time, Huhne was the energy and climate change secretary in the UK's Conservative–Liberal Democrat coalition government. He had twice been a candidate for the leadership of the Liberal Democrats. This author's blog speculated that, while the message could have been entirely innocent, it probably wasn't. An innocent explanation might have been planting a story about climate change, which he did not want associated with the nanny state. Planting a story about an opposition politician would not have been career ending unless the story was highly personal and/or known to be untrue. But Brandjack News wondered if the story was a hit piece on a Conservative or Lib Dem colleague? That is exactly what it turned out to be.

After initially denying things, Huhne eventually confessed that the story in question was aimed at Theresa May, home secretary in the coalition government. He announced that he had apologized to her, although the blogger Guido Fawkes reported that he had not spoken to her, merely leaving a message on her voicemail.[40]

In one respect, social media operatives are very like their colleagues in the MSM. When they get the scent of blood, they do not let go. For Huhne, this story blew up when he was already facing another difficulty: the issue that eventually drove him to resign from the Cabinet. He was in the public eye because of his ongoing divorce. His wife had initiated proceedings because of his admitted adultery. At this time, a story began to circulate on blogs, and then in the *Sunday Times*, that, some years earlier, he had persuaded his wife to cooperate in a lie to the police, claiming that she, not he, had been driving their car when it was photographed speeding. This was important because he had already accumulated points from previous offenses, and this latest offense would have cost him his license. The story went that, due to the divorce, his estranged wife, Vicky Pryce, would no longer stand by this story. When he was formally charged with perverting the course of justice, he resigned from the Cabinet. In 2013, Huhne pled guilty and his former wife's plea of marital coercion was rejected. Both were sentenced to prison.[41]

Learnings

Sending a DM as a tweet is an easy mistake to make, and can be serious. There is a reason you wanted to send it privately, after all. In my case, the identity of the intended recipient was missed out, which was enough to alleviate all embarrassment, since it was her blushes I was saving. In Huhne's case, it was obvious that he was up to something slightly devious from the content of the message.

Huhne was a substantive politician, and would not have been easy for his prime minister or party leader to squeeze him out without good reason. This was not enough, but it is possible that they let it go, in part, because they knew the issue of criminal charges was in the offing and would produce a clearer case for demanding his resignation.

X	**What Chris Huhne did wrong**

- It was a simple, but devastating blunder.
- While popular with his party's grassroots for his blunt manner, Huhne was not well liked by colleagues in either coalition party. The goodwill on which he could rely was limited.

SELF BRANDJACK	Politician's deviousness was not sufficiently disguised, as he was caught in the act of disguising it.

88 Beyoncé Knowles copyright theft allegations
October 2011

Beyoncé Knowles – generally known only by her first name – is one of the most commercially successful performance artists in the world at present. Anne Terese de Keersmaeker was described by Lyn Gardner, on *The Guardian's* theatre blog, as an "avant garde Belgian choreographer,"[42] and is perhaps the closest one can get to answering the notorious question about naming a famous Belgian. In October 2011, Beyoncé was accused of stealing choreography from de Keersmaeker. The MSM were understandably hesitant about taking sides. After all, Beyoncé has access to considerable legal resources. Nonetheless, *The Guardian* ran several pieces on the subject, and reported that Beyoncé had declined to comment. Social media are not so restrained. YouTube gives bloggers the opportunity to demonstrate their point with great simplicity.

There are two main videos on YouTube published to make the point about Beyoncé. One shows Beyoncé's video alongside extracts from two short films by de Keersmaeker. The similarities are striking, not just in terms of the dance moves but also the set and costume designs. Of course, the extracts from de Keersmaeker's work were selected precisely to make this point, and may not be fully representative of the whole.

Perhaps the more devastating presentation is the one that shows Beyoncé's redacted video alongside the original. Beyoncé produced a new version of her "Countdown" video, without the controversial material. The redacted video has more than 40 percent of the original removed, including two sections each more than 25 seconds in length. While there is no specific guidance on how many dance movements in a row constitute plagiarism or copyright theft, in music, one widely followed guideline is seven consecutive notes (although it is a bit of a myth that this guideline has any status in law). While there is much variation, seven notes would often be under seven seconds. Perhaps most striking is the fact that in place of the redacted material, there is little actual dance, with substantial footage of Beyoncé's face instead. Beyoncé has never apologized or offered de Keersmaeker any payment for the "borrowed" choreography. Indeed, I am not able to trace any comment from her at all.

Beyoncé has a great many fans, many of whom rushed to her defense, pointing out that she has teams of choreographers and would not necessarily know if the moves had been stolen. That is almost certainly true, but any business takes responsibility for its employees. If Beyoncé's employees commit an ethical or legal infringement, she bears responsibility.

Beyoncé is not especially engaged in social media, particularly when compared to stars like Shakira. She (at the time of this case study) had almost 10 million followers on Twitter, but was only following 8 people (down from 14 last year) and had not tweeted for six weeks. She is much more strongly involved in Facebook, where she had 49 million likes, but tends to broadcast messages rather than engage.

Lyn Gardner suggested that de Keersmaeker had not lost out through the controversy, becoming much more high profile. As a writer, Gardner should know better. If a famous writer appropriated Gardner's work, it might make her more famous, but she would still deserve royalties for the plagiarized material. It has also been argued that choreographers are often more interested in preserving the artistic integrity of their material than in securing maximum financial return.

In particular, the disparity of income between Beyoncé and de Keersmaeker heightened the opprobrium. Beyoncé could easily afford to be generous, financially and in terms of giving credit. A tiny slice of her income would transform the life of an obscure Belgian choreographer.

Learnings

Beyoncé needs to show a generosity of spirit. At every awards show, when people are praised for their work, the first thing they do is respond along the lines of "I couldn't have done it without ... ." While this is always true, when the influence or inspiration cuts so close to plagiarism, the acknowledgement needs to go much further. Where she has acknowledged inspiration in the past – in particular the work of Bob Fosse – the heightened profile for Fosse's choreography has been enormous.

✓ **What Beyoncé did right**

- She redacted the controversial material.

▶ **What she should have done**

- She should have apologized.
- She should have thanked de Keersmaeker for the influence.
- She should have paid her royalties.

SELF BRANDJACK   The organization (although not necessarily Beyoncé herself) behaved badly, and did not respond well to the social media backlash.

89 Herman Cain: sexual harassment allegations
October–November 2011

Few people live and die in the media to a greater extent than politicians and celebrities. Herman Cain was a US politician and celebrity wannabe whose presidential campaign imploded amid allegations of sexual harassment and somewhat buffoonish responses to "gotcha" questions from journalists.

Cain was always an unlikely candidate for president. A successful businessman with no background in politics, his personable style and clarity of expression briefly left him as frontrunner in a crowded Republican field. But reaching frontrunner status is a mixed blessing. It brings forward critics as well as fans. Cain was – and remains – a savvy social media operator. He has a strong following on Twitter and, since his campaign, has launched his own web-based TV station. His 9-9-9 tax plan (9 percent corporate, income, and sales taxes) offered a simple soundbite approach to almost any economic problem.

Cain's background included not only running a major restaurant chain but also running the highly political trade body for the restaurant business. It was his time at the trade body that produced the ghosts that would prove fatal to Cain's campaign. This author is not in a position to assess the credibility of the sexual harassment allegations, but one thing *is* clear, they may have only reached national attention because of his presidential campaign, but they were *not* initiated at that time. The allegations were originally made during his time at the trade body, and it seems that some payoffs were made by Cain's employer at that time.[43]

At the same time as these serious, but hard-to-assess claims were being reported in social and mainstream media, Cain was asked how he would answer "gotcha" questions like "who is the president of Ubekistan [sic]?" His response was to deliberately (further) mangle the name of the country, saying he didn't know the president of "Ubeki-beki-beki-beki-stan-stan." (NB: most text-based journalists cleaned up the journalist's original mangling of Uzbekistan's name but left Cain's further mangling in place. He could easily have gotchaed the journalist by pointing out there is no such place as Ubekistan.)

Brief video clips are ideal for promoting or mocking politicians or celebrities online. It is easy for a blogger to take a brief clip and circulate it widely on social media. Cain was a victim of this new method of political accountability.

Learnings

Cain is continuing to use social media effectively: at least, if his aim is to be a celebrity commentator and not an elected politician. He maintains a devoted band of fans, and feeds them regular material through caintv.com. Many have speculated that this celebrity status was always the purpose of his presidential campaign, rather than a serious hope of becoming president. Of course, the two aspirations are not contradictory. He might have entered the race recognizing that the White House was never more than a slim possibility but that a sufficiently diverting campaign would always give him a media career to fall back on.

ETHICS BRANDJACK	Old allegations resurface to scuttle political ambitions.
SELF BRANDJACK	Ridiculous response to silly question leaves the candidate looking like a buffoon.

90 Johnson & Johnson accused of poisoning babies
November 2011

The blogger Jezebel (part of Gawker Media) wrote a thoughtful if somewhat alarmist piece about Johnson & Johnson's baby shampoo and the presence of chemicals that are possible carcinogens.[44] While there seems to be little to no evidence that the chemicals – at least in the concentrations involved – pose any detectable risk, Jezebel points out that J&J's call for time to remove the chemicals is open to criticism. The product is already sold without some of the contentious chemicals in some markets, and not only in markets where those chemicals are illegal. In these circumstances, even conceding that there *might* be a risk opens the company to the fairly obvious question: why not remove them, just to be safe?

In the social media world, transparency is no longer an option, it is a basic requirement of business, and transparency means having a clear statement about apparent inconsistencies in your approach. Standing on the law – a J&J statement refers to products being "approved by regulators in the U.S., EU, and China" – is entirely insufficient. It is true that these approvals arise from clinical trials designed to measure long-term effects. But the J&J statement evades the key question of why different standards are being applied in different markets.

The J&J Facebook page is fairly sophisticated, although it had only 34,000 "likes" at the time of this controversy. This probably reflects the transactional nature of the relationship people have with fairly functional products.

One clear mistake was made by J&J: the statement about this controversy was posted on the Facebook page by Jay Kominsky, VP of worldwide communication and public affairs, and not by Susan Nettesheim, VP of product stewardship and toxicology, who wrote the letter to the Campaign for Safe Cosmetics. One powerful line of argument used in the letter, but neglected in the social media side of the campaign, is that an entire bottle of shampoo contains less of the controversial chemicals than a single apple or pear, where the chemical occurs naturally.

Learnings

On the crucial product safety question, J&J is almost certainly in the right. The quantities of these chemicals are tiny, even over a lifetime's exposure. The apple or pear comparison is potent, as most people seem to agree that fruit, even consumed daily, is actively good for a person. Few people consume a bottle of shampoo a day. On the PR side, however, the company is in a difficult situation and has not made the best of its case.

✓ What Johnson & Johnson did right

- The fruit comparison is potent, and needs to be used more widely.

✗ What Johnson & Johnson did wrong

- Responding in public through communications staff rather than have them shape a message for technical staff is a misjudgment.
- Transparency dictates either consistent policies internationally, or a clear explanation as to why the policies differ.

ETHICS BRANDJACK External campaigners make things difficult for a major multinational.

91 Sam Brownback and Emma Sullivan
November 2011

Sam Brownback is a significant, if controversial, politician. He was a US senator who ran a serious campaign for the Republican Party's presidential nomination in 2008. He was the choice of the more intelligent social conservatives, but ultimately lost ground to the more humorous and personable Mike Huckabee, governor of Arkansas. After leaving the Senate, Brownback was elected governor of Kansas, his home state. Governors generally have a better record than senators in running for president, so it is entirely possible that he will have another go at the White House. He needs a better social media team if he does.

Emma Sullivan was a high school student who did not approve of Brownback's politics. Media commentators – perhaps patronizingly – suggest that the only thing she knew about the governor was that he had vetoed a bill providing funding for the arts. What does seem to be true is that her Twitter account is not devoted primarily to politics: the more traditional obsessions of teenagers, including shopping and *Breaking Dawn* seem to be bigger issues for her. In researching this case study – in the midst of a presidential election campaign – I had to delve two months into her Twitter stream to find a political tweet.

Sullivan's controversial tweet arose from her high school visit to the governor's office. She tweeted: "@emmakate988 just made mean comments at gov brownback and told him he sucked, in person #heblowsalot." Apparently, she was joking and had not actually told Brownback that he sucked. The tweet went viral and came to the attention of Brownback's office and the office was in touch with Sullivan's school principal. In a clear example of insensitive overkill, the principal told Sullivan to apologize, which she refused to do. This had the effect of shifting the debate to censorship. Should the governor really be responding to tweets by teenagers and demanding that they apologize? Should the governor not be seeking to earn respect rather than simply demanding it?

Following the controversy, Sullivan had over 11,000 followers, although she was following just 104 others. It is not unreasonable to suspect that quite a few people who followed her expecting reasoned political debate drifted away when they discovered that much of her Twitter stream is devoted to other subjects. Nonetheless, she had twice as many followers as the governor of Kansas, although she follows half as many people, and does not tweet as often.

Learnings

People in positions of power should not be seen to act against ordinary citizens, let alone high school students. Engage, debate, even respond with charm or humor, but never, ever, try to shut people down or demand apologies.

Sullivan claims she was bullied by other high schoolers, who called her a "whore" and various other charming epithets as a result of the controversy. Although the governor was not responsible for this, the fact that his office handled the situation so badly and sought to exert pressure on Sullivan obviously associated him with charges of bullying in the wider sense.

Quite properly, Brownback apologized for the overreaction by his staff.[45]

> **What Brownback and his office could have done better**

- They could have ignored Sullivan entirely. Any engagement was sure to bring attention to a critic who would otherwise have been ignored.
- They could have engaged in a friendly way, such as joking or offering to talk to her.

STAFF BRANDJACK There is no reason to doubt Brownback's claim that the overreaction was by his staff, but he still bears responsibility for this.

92 SapientNitro: embarrassing promotional video
November 2011

SapientNitro describes itself as "an interactive marketing, creative design, and technology services agency." The best that can be said about this particular exercise on the agency's part is that it was a brave experiment. Visually, and even musically, its self-promotional video is more than competent. Where it falls down is with the lyrics. This is made worse by the fact that the musical style chosen makes the lyrics hard to follow, so the video is subtitled. Bad lyrics that are just about tolerable as part of a song look deeply awful when written down.

In politics, people often argue that it is not the scandal that brings you down, it is the cover-up. That can often be the case in social media. In this instance, the video attracted considerable mockery on the company's Facebook page.

Then, as though no one at the company had ever followed past social media controversies, the team began deleting critical comments. Social media denizens greatly prize transparency and open debate. Deleting comments, especially without a clearly stated policy and good reason (such as for profanity), deeply offends people.

Learnings

Remember, even if your lyrics work as lyrics, they may not work as poetry. You probably aren't Paul Simon.

☑ What SapientNitro did right

- It was a brave experiment that showcased the agency's technical capacity.

☒ What SapientNitro did wrong

- The lyrics were weak and looked embarrassing when appearing as subtitles.
- Deleting comments simply because you don't like the content always offends people.

SELF BRANDJACK An embarrassing video potentially undermines the agency's claim of core competence and deleting comments suggests (at best) naiveté about social media conventions.

93 Skyrim for PS3 complaints: fake Twitter account
November 2011

Skyrim is the fifth saga in the Elder Scrolls series of fantasy role-playing games from leading games publisher, Bethesda, so it automatically hit the market with an existing fanbase. But as publishers of other sequels have learned, this is both a strength and a weakness. Existing fans are a ready-made market, but they are hypercritical of any problems they perceive with a product. Also, existing fans of a product are often already organized and aggregated, which is especially likely to be the case with computer games, where the target public is, of necessity, tech friendly. Computer games were a major discussion feature in user-generated Internet content long before social media, with hundreds of discussion groups dedicated to the subject back in the early 1990s on Usenet.

When Skyrim was launched, there were consistent complaints about speed of use, especially on PlayStation. The mass of social media devoted to gaming spilled over into coverage in the MSM, although so much professional media coverage of gaming exists only in the digital format that there is no clear line between the two.

The company annoyed one fan so much that he began a fake Twitter account imitating Pete Hines, VP of PR and marketing at Bethesda. Hines' Twitter account is @dcdeacon and the fake account was @dcdaecon, with two letters transposed. The brandjacker even began responding to messages to the real Hines. The brandjacker was sending messages that would have reflected badly on Bethesda, had they actually come from the company, and it is reasonable to assume that some gamers, at least, did not notice the transposed letters and so assumed that the messages were legitimate. Gamers complaining about the quality of the product would have been surprised and angry to get a message like: "Everyone at Bethesda hates you #die." A genuine fan posting to the fake Hines got the response: "The patch will be developed when we feel like it. Stop crying and be thankful we even made a version for the subpar PS3."

Learnings

Fake Twitter accounts can be shut down by Twitter. This is one example where an approach to Twitter would probably have been justifiable and wise. The account has been suspended by Twitter, although it is not clear whether it was Bethesda, Hines, or one of the disgruntled fans who complained.

An account that is a clear parody – like @bpglobalpr – is best ignored. Genuinely funny copy entertains the Twittersphere and trying to get such accounts shut down irritates people and doesn't work. This situation is different. Although there was humor in the account, and this was recognized by some users, it does also seem to have been something of a stalking incident, with gamers being genuinely deceived by offensive messages, apparently from Hines.

Where Bethesda may have gone wrong is in allowing Hines to become the face of the company in the first place. Gamers want reassuring messages from the geeks, not the marketing guys. The role of PR and marketing in this situation is to manage the process of communication, but let the technical personnel engage directly with the public. That said, although Hines may not be the best face for the company – and perhaps needs a better job title if he is to be that face – he does seem to engage with an active fanbase, essential for a company like Bethesda.

✓ **What Bethesda did right**	

- It engaged with its fanbase.
- It got the fake Twitter account removed on the basis it was deceptive (assuming this was actually Bethesda).

CUSTOMER REVOLT BRANDJACK	Organized fanbase was already aggregated when a fake Twitter account got them even more riled.
IMPERSONATION BRANDJACK	Brandjacker interposed their fake tweets as responses to tweets raised with the real Hines.

94 FedEx employee throws computer monitor over the fence

December 2011

The situation was a difficult one, but left FedEx with little choice. A customer posted a video on YouTube that clearly showed a FedEx deliverer taking a package out of his van and throwing it over a tall fence, higher than his head. The video secured more than 4.5 million hits in a few days. The package apparently contained a computer monitor that was seriously damaged.

Let us imagine, for a moment, that this had happened in the pre-social media world. It would have seemed obvious to the customer what had happened, but proving it would have been difficult. If FedEx had taken the customer's complaint at face value, then it could presumably have identified and disciplined the driver responsible. But it might have been tempting for the company to simply deny responsibility. With video evidence, there was no choice, and the company apologized and made recompense to the customer immediately. But social media have a much greater effect than this. What could have been a simple customer complaint became a major crisis. The video was immensely popular, partly because it is extremely funny, in a slapstick sort of way.

In a substantial blog and vlog, Matthew Thornton III, a senior VP at FedEx, took full responsibility. The blog was titled "Absolutely, Positively Unacceptable."[46] Thornton stated: "I want you to know that I was upset, embarrassed, and very sorry for our customer's poor experience."

Learnings

FedEx did the right – frankly the only – thing in apologizing and compensating the customer immediately. It also handled the wider crisis well, with frequent tweets and @replies to people posting the video, explaining its regret.

✓ What FedEx did right

- It settled immediately with the customer.
- It addressed the issue strongly across social media, including a substantive blog from a senior executive.

| STAFF BRANDJACK | Appalling behavior by rogue employee provides fuel for a social media storm. |

Notes

1   Wikipedia citing *Le Monde*: www.lemonde.fr/afrique/article/2011/01/17/revolution-du-jasmin-une-expression-qui-ne-fait-pas-l-unanimite_1466871_3212.html, accessed 01/20/2014.

2   Wikipedia: en.wikipedia.org/wiki/John_Galliano, accessed 01/20/2014.

3   *NY Times* blogs: runway.blogs.nytimes.com/2011/02/28/natalie-portman-condemns-galliano/?_r=0, accessed 01/20/2014.

4   NPR: www.npr.org/blogs/thetwo-way/2011/03/09/134358398/in-video-npr-exec-slams-tea-party-questions-need-for-federal-funds, accessed 01/20/2014.

5   In 2008, then the most recent presidential election, Barack Obama won among people of all educational levels but his biggest margin was among people who dropped out of high school and smallest among people with some college education, according to the *NY Times* exit poll: elections.nytimes.com/2008/results/president/exit-polls.html, accessed 01/20/2014.

6   Chrysler: blog.chryslerllc.com/blog.do?id=1337&p=entry, accessed 01/20/2014.

7   *Advertising Age*: adage.com/article/digital/chrysler-splits-media-strategies-f-bomb-tweet/149335, accessed 01/20/2014.

8   Field and Stream: www.fieldandstream.com/blogs/field-notes/2011/05/mark-zuckerberg-kills-his-own-meat-wants-hunt, accessed 01/20/2014.

9   Jezebel: jezebel.com/5804750/dove-body-wash-strong-enough-to-turn-a-black-woman-white, accessed 01/20/2014.

10 Huffington Post: www.huffingtonpost.com/2011/05/23/dove-visiblecare-ad-racist_n_865911.html, accessed 01/20/2014.

11 The Root: www.theroot.com/articles/culture/2011/05/is_this_dove_ad_racist.html, accessed 01/20/2014.

12 Weiss, G. (2008) "The price of immortality" *Condé Nast Portfolio*, November.

13 Wikipedia: en.wikipedia.org/wiki/David_H._Koch#Political_views, accessed 01/20/2014.

14 Koch Brothers Exposed: www.kochbrothersexposed.com/thepress/category/uncategorized/page/5, accessed 01/20/2014.

15   *New York* magazine: nymag.com/news/features/67285, accessed 01/20/2014.

16   CNN: edition.cnn.com/2011/US/06/26/florida.tsa.incident, accessed 01/20/2014.

17   ABC News: abcnews.go.com/US/tsa-denies-forcing-elderly-woman-remove-diaper-daughter/story?id=13939865, accessed 01/20/2014.

18   Greenpeace: www.greenpeace.org/international/en/news/Blogs/makingwaves/success-barbie-and-mattel-drop-deforestation/blog/37176/, accessed 01/20/2014.

19   *Daily Mail*: www.dailymail.co.uk/tvshowbiz/article-2007956/U2-upstaged-tax-protest-Glastonbury--campaigners-left-deflated-security-pop-balloon.html, accessed 01/20/2014.

20   Lil family blog: www.lilfamily.com/2011/06/starbucks-update-part-3-inaction-and.html, accessed 01/20/2014.

21   *New York Times*: www.nytimes.com/2011/06/26/us/26gas.html, accessed 01/20/2014.

22   Chesapeake Energy: www.facebook.com/note.php?note_id=10150305143547565, accessed 01/20/2014.

23   *Bay City News*: sfappeal.com/2011/07/community-reaction-to-sfpd shooting-of-man-during-muni-fare-inspection, accessed 01/20/2014.

24   Huffington Post: www.huffingtonpost.com/2012/02/22/james-crowell-charles-hill_n_1294352.html, accessed 01/20/2014.

25   EJ's blog: ejroundtheworld.blogspot.co.uk/2011/06/violated-travelers-lost-faith-difficult.html, accessed 01/20/2014.

26   Mashable: mashable.com/2011/08/01/airbnb-ransackgate, accessed 01/20/2014.

27   *Daily Telegraph*: www.telegraph.co.uk/technology/internet/8674678/Internet-Explorer-users-have-below-average-IQ.html, accessed 01/20/2014.

28   Business Insider: www.businessinsider.com/study-internet-explorer-users-are-dumber-2011-7, accessed 01/20/2014.

29   From *The Independent*: www.independent.co.uk/news/uk/crime/a-death-at-the-hands-of-police-ndash-and-a-vigil-that-turned-to-violence-2333590.html, and *The Telegraph*: www.telegraph.co.uk/news/uknews/crime/8682655/Mark-Duggan-killed-in-shooting-incident-involving-police-officer.html, both accessed 01/20/2014.

30   *The Guardian*: www.theguardian.com/uk/2011/aug/07/tottenham-riots-peaceful-protest, accessed 01/20/2014.

31   BBC: www.bbc.co.uk/news/uk-england-london-25648913, accessed 01/20/2014.

32   *Advertising Week*: www.adweek.com/adfreak/nivea-apologizes-wanting-re-civilize-black-man-134226, accessed 01/20/2014.

33   Ibid.

34   Hawkblocker: www.hawkblocker.com/2011/09/12/anders-breivik-lacoste/#comments, accessed 01/20/2014.

35   CNS News: www.cnsnews.com/news/article/obama-banks-dont-have-inherent-right-certain-amount-profit, accessed 01/20/2014.

36   Moviefone: news.moviefone.com/2011/10/31/hilary-swank-fires-manager-chechen-president, accessed 01/20/2014.

37   *The Examiner*: www.examiner.com/article/seal-to-human-rights-watch-leave-me-out-of-your-politics, accessed 01/20/2014.

38   *San Francisco Chronicle*: blog.sfgate.com/mmagowan/2011/10/24/chapstick-sticks-it-to-women, accessed 01/20/2014.

39   Chapstick's Facebook page: https://www.facebook.com/ChapStick/posts/10150349656219821, accessed 01/20/2014.

40   Guido Fawkes: order-order.com/2011/10/09/huhne-should-be-sacked-for-lying-and-briefing-against-theresa-may, accessed 01/20/2014.

41   *The Telegraph*: www.telegraph.co.uk/news/uknews/law-and-order/9923143/Chris-Huhne-and-Vicky-Pryce-jailed-judges-sentencing-remarks-in-full.html, accessed 01/20/2014.

42   *The Guardian*: www.theguardian.com/stage/theatreblog/2011/oct/11/beyonce-de-keersmaeker-dance-move, accessed 01/20/2014.

43   *The Guardian*: www.theguardian.com/world/2011/nov/01/herman-cain-settlement-sexual-harassment, accessed 01/20/2014.

44   Jezebel: jezebel.com/5855115/johnson--johnson-gently-poisoning-babies-with-its-shampoo, accessed 01/20/2014.

45   *Daily Mail*: www.dailymail.co.uk/news/article-2067341/Emma-Sullivan-wins-apology-Governor-Sam-Brownback-tweet.html, accessed 01/20/2014.

46   FedEx: blog.van.fedex.com/absolutely-positively-unacceptable, accessed 01/20/2014.

The case studies: 2012

95 Apple gets Samsunged
January 2012

For decades, the Super Bowl has been a huge forum for TV advertising. Brands would use the expensive, high-profile slot to premiere new advertising concepts. The conventional wisdom was that these new concepts had to be kept highly confidential. Social media have changed everything. Facebook, Twitter, and other digital fora have become accustomed to debate and speculation about what new ads are about to be launched. Brands have begun tapping into that, using teaser campaigns on YouTube.

In January 2012, Samsung took this to a new level, using its teaser ads to launch the phrase "We just got Samsunged" and to take a not very subtle swipe at Apple fanboys (there are fangirls too, but not as many) – the type of people who will camp outside the iStore to buy the latest Apple product on the first day it is available.

The plot is simple. The fanboys are lying on the sidewalk in their sleeping bags when a Samsung user comes by and talks about his map application, which comes as standard with a Samsung. (Apple's map apps have been notoriously poor.) One of the fanboys declares "Ahh, we just got Samsunged."

Learnings

This was not the first use of teaser videos on YouTube to hype expectations around a new TV campaign. The VW ads themed around *Star Wars* a year earlier – which were then effectively parodied by Greenpeace – had used the same technique, but this does seem to be the first time a company combined a teaser campaign with an ad designed to mock its competitors.

☑ What Samsung did right

- The ad gently teases Apple's dedicated fans who, at one point, are watching the latest "unboxing" video.
- It focuses on a clear weakness of Apples – the map app.

CHEEKY BRANDJACK Samsung cleverly mocks its rival.

96 The beautiful and bald Barbie: let's see if we can get it made

January 2012

Within months of its launch, a Facebook page calling for a "beautiful and bald Barbie" had over 150,000 likes. The page brings together parents of children either suffering from cancer or who are bald. Obviously, not all the children with cancer are bald or, at least, are not bald at all times, since it is a function of their treatment, not their underlying condition. For people with alopecia, on the other hand, abnormal patterns of hair growth arise from the condition itself. Illness is especially tragic when it strikes children, whether the condition is life-threatening or something other children might be inclined to mock. It is perhaps worth recalling that the much-mocked child to whom Danny Kaye's Hans Christian Andersen sang "The ugly duckling" was bald.

Mattel never emerged especially badly from this campaign, which implicitly recognized the power of Mattel's Barbie brand, suggesting that, by creating a bald Barbie, Mattel could provide life-affirming inspiration to children. After just few months – March 2012 – Mattel agreed to create the doll. It isn't clear whether the company expected to make money on the doll or whether the decision was made, at least in part, as a goodwill gesture. The doll – who will actually be a Barbie friend rather than the new version of Barbie herself – will have all sorts of accessories such as wigs and headscarves.

Learnings

The first thing to note is that, by making use of Barbie imagery, the Facebook page probably infringed Mattel's intellectual property rights (IPR). Mattel could probably have taken legal action to close the page down. This would have been a major mistake. People are beginning to learn that the social media community does not take well to anything that can be classified as censorship, including closing down comments on proprietary pages and acting in defense of IPR. Such legal action would have elevated the story and cast Mattel as an active villain rather than as a company that could, and arguably should, have done more for vulnerable children.

Acceding to the campaign for a bald doll was a strong PR move. By agreeing to a potentially expensive new product line, for which demand may be limited (although perhaps sales of accessories will offset this cost), the company seems to have taken a risk on a new product line as part of an investment in goodwill. As part of

implementing the change in policy, Mattel brought the founders of the web page – two mothers of young girls with cancer – into the conversation about product development. The speed with which this campaign was successful demonstrates the growing power of viral campaigns.

✓ What Mattel did right

- It refrained from taking legal action.
- It acceded to the campaigners' demands.

CUSTOMER REVOLT BRANDJACK Customers demand a risky new product line and the company agrees.

AGGREGATION BRANDJACK Digital channels bring together campaigners who would otherwise have no platform or interaction with each other.

97 The *Costa Concordia* disaster
January 2012

On 13 January, 2012, the cruise ship *Costa Concordia* ran aground and then capsized off the coast of Giglio, Italy. With or without social media, this story would have dominated global headlines. It had every element of drama: there were heroes and at least one villain; there were deaths and daring rescues. But no news story breaks these days without a significant social media component. During the evacuation itself, passengers and crew were posting live updates to social media sites.

The precise circumstances under which the ship ran aground remain a matter of controversy and legal dispute. Much of the coverage in social and mainstream media in the immediate aftermath of the disaster focused on the recorded and leaked – by and to whom seems unclear – phone call between the captain and the coastguard. The coastguard repeatedly ordered Captain Schettino to get back on board and organize the evacuation of the passengers. The captain drifts between agreeing and offering feeble protests such as "it's dark," which provokes the response "what do you want to do? Go home?" The captain also denies abandoning ship, claiming that he and his senior officers were "catapulted" off the ship by a sudden movement of the vessel. Media reports afterwards suggested that the coastguard had become something of a hero in Italy, to counter the embarrassment people felt at the behavior of the captain. His instruction to the captain – *vada a bordo, cazzo* (get the f**k back on board) – became a popular T-shirt adornment.[1]

There were other heroes. There was another captain on board – the captain of another cruise ship, owned by Carnival, the same company that owned the *Costa Concordia* – who was traveling as a passenger. Captain Roberto Bosio apparently began organizing an evacuation even before Captain Schettino issued the order to abandon ship.

At one muster station, the passengers were apparently marshalled by Rose Metcalfe, a dancer on the ship's entertainment staff, as there were no senior crew available. She was able to get the passengers onto a lifeboat, but there was no room for her. At this point, she sent a message to her Facebook friends asking them to pray for her. She was rescued from the ship by helicopter. She was not the only person reporting live on the events via social media, but is one of those who emerged with considerable moral credit.

In the aftermath of the disaster, the media coverage continued, online and in mainstream channels. It will continue until the various legal cases are settled. It is also brought up every time any other Carnival cruise ship runs into trouble on more minor scales (as happened twice in the early months of 2013, including one that had backed up plumbing with no relief for several days).

Learnings

Carnival was not in control of the story. Multiple stories were emerging from many sources, internally and externally. This was, in part, inevitable. Someone leaked the recording of Schettino's conversation with the coastguard, and that was always going to dominate coverage. Carnival presumably had a role in placing the story of Bosio's heroic behavior, which at least allowed it to dilute the negative coverage. But there were contradictory accounts as to why and whether the ship was off course.

Carnival has continued to play the situation badly. It needs to take control of the media narrative, and that means using credible spokespeople. Immediately after the incident, it was using Captain Schettino as a spokesperson, even though he was visibly emotional and already being blamed by many people for the incident.

Rose Metcalfe has become a spokesperson on maritime safety – but not for Carnival. She is employed by an insurance company. Indeed, Metcalfe was still, at the time of writing, in legal dispute with Carnival. Since she is a crew member who emerged with some credit from the story and (the media impact of these things should not be discounted) is rather photogenic, Carnival might have been wise to settle with her and use her in its own PR recovery.

> **☑ What Carnival did right**
>
> - Getting the Bosio story out was a good move, presumably by Carnival.
>
> **☒ What Carnival did wrong**
>
> - It made poor choices as to its spokespeople and remains in dispute with several of its staff.

STAFF BRANDJACK While the causes of the accident remain unclear, it is difficult to argue that Schettino emerges from the telephone conversation with any credit or sympathy. This dramatically shifted the narrative against Carnival.

98 McDonald's and the power of storytelling
January 2012

McDonald's devised two innovative campaigns built around the power of storytelling. The first was inspired, but the second created an unfortunate vulnerability. Stories are critical. Stories are how we make sense of random data. They are how we understand the world. As PR professional and author, Jim Holtje, puts it, we are "hardwired" to understand and remember stories.[2]

The McDonald's #MeetTheFarmers Twitter campaign was designed to reinforce the strengths of the brand, while putting a human face on the messages. McDonald's has long had a reputation for delivering its product with consistency. A Big Mac is the same wherever you buy it. The venerable British magazine *The Economist* even uses a Big Mac Index to measure which currencies are over- or undervalued. #MeetTheFarmers explored what that consistency of management means for the chain's suppliers. It promoted beautiful stories such as Steve Foglesong's video, "Raising Cattle and a Family," in which the farmer explains the value of being a McDonald's supplier, but also the demanding standards he needs to meet. The whole campaign is well conceived and effectively implemented. It is an imaginative use of YouTube, with other social media outlets driving the traffic.

With this success behind it, it is easy to see why McDonald's wanted to take the storytelling theme further and hear from its customers at #McDStories. While McDonald's has always been a controversial brand, footfall and sales remain strong. There are far more people eating at McDonald's than demonstrating outside. But the relationship McDonald's has with its customers is not the same as, say, Aston Martin. People may not be ashamed to eat there – as critics suggest they should be – but they are not especially proud of it either. In most cases, they probably have few feelings about it other than requited hunger. It is a transactional relationship, not an aspirational one. You do not eat a Big Mac to make your friends envious. You eat it because you fancy a burger. It is not like Dolce & Gabbana, where people like to be seen wearing the label. The relationship is pay, eat, leave.

This is not to say that no one wanted to tell stories of good experiences at McDonald's, but it was always likely to be a tiny proportion of the customer base that would feel motivated to do so. The critics, on the other hand, are definitely motivated to tell their stories, for example: "Watching a classmate projectile vomit his food all over the restaurant during a 6th grade trip" and "I once worked at McDonalds. I have never eaten there since" (both at #McDStories).

McDonald's defended the campaign, claiming that only 2 percent of the tweets were negative. But this is very much the wrong metric. What was the reach of the negative tweets? Just as it is hard to imagine people feeling motivated to tell the story of an especially satisfying Big Mac, it is even harder to imagine them wanting to share *someone else's* story. The critics, on the other hand, share an agenda, actually several, interlocking agendas – looking at environmental issues, animal welfare, nutrition, and a general rejection of capitalism. Each negative story will resonate with other critics who share the same opinions and emotions. On the whole, the feelings customers have about their hastily scoffed burger are entirely their own. For all sorts of reasons, it was always likely that the negative tweets would be more widely shared.

Learnings

McDonald's came up with an incredibly powerful campaign with #MeetTheFarmers. It could stand as a model for effective use of social media by a controversial brand. But it should have anticipated low levels of positive engagement and high levels of negative engagement with its #McDStories campaign.

☑ What McDonald's did right

- Meet the Farmers – a first-rate campaign, built on the power of storytelling and a good feel for social media.

☒ What McDonald's did wrong

- McDStories – a poor idea that bounced badly.

SELF BRANDJACK	Powerful brand got carried away with its success and embarked on a poor follow-up.
AGGREGATION BRANDJACK	Critics combine to damn Big Mac.

99 *Mad Men* courts controversy with season 5 poster
January 2012

The first poster for season 5 of *Mad Men* was an unbranded teaser. It did not include the name of the show, relying on the typeface to indicate to fans what exactly was being advertised. The poster showed just one image, a man apparently falling from a great height, and the date of the new season in the iconic typeface. Teaser campaigns are designed to promote conversation. Passers-by are prompted to discuss the ad, with some being unsure what the subject is and the cognoscenti explaining it to them. One of the messages of the image was to hint at a darker theme to the upcoming season.

Teaser campaigns are an especially powerful – but also especially risky – approach in the socially mediated world. Controversial themes – deliberate or accidental – will be taken up. Conspiracy theorists will always look for hidden layers of messaging, much deeper than anything the creative team ever imagined. It will usually be impossible to find out exactly what was in the team's mind.

In this case, controversy was predictable. The image has an eerie similarity to the searing 9/11 photograph "The Falling Man." Anything that seems to cash in on the emotions that surround 9/11 is always going to be controversial in the US. Cable channel AMC has defended the poster, saying the reference is to Don Draper's life being out of control, and similar imagery has been used since 2007.

Learnings

It was predictable – and may even have been deliberate – that the poster would be criticized as tasteless. This contributed to the conversation that teaser campaigns are designed to generate. One important message from this is that today teaser campaigns are more powerful, but also harder to control. You can never fully predict where the conversation will go. This is a strength for campaigns designed to raise awareness, but can leave you exposed to anger and hostility.

> ☑ **What AMC did right**
>
> - The teaser campaign has a good fit to a cult series in the socially mediated world.
>
> ☒ **What AMC did wrong**
>
> - The tasteless 9/11 reference was probably too hot to touch.

SELF BRANDJACK   A clever campaign probably took one risk too many.

100 LA Fitness refuses to let pregnant member out of her contract

January 2012

This story actually begins in 2011. A pregnant woman who had been a member of LA Fitness for seven years wanted to get out of her contract after her husband lost his job. The chain wanted £360 to terminate the contract. Let's assume the club was right in law. Gyms often have complicated contracts with notice periods and termination payments to end them. Generally, such clubs have a fairly high attrition rate, with many people signing up with great enthusiasm, but finding they no longer get their money's worth when they stop going. Processes that hang on to these members via inertia can be profitable. But, right in law or not, the club was taking a stand on a bureaucratic point in a quite unnecessary way.

What is especially revealing about this incident is that the first media intervention came from the MSM. *The Guardian* contacted the company and asked about it and the company stuck firmly to its position. It was some weeks later when the matter was taken up on Twitter that the company was forced to back down.

Learnings

The first point is that intervention by a national newspaper now seems to have less impact than a viral campaign on Twitter. As recently as 2010, people still talked of social media as a way to spark a story in the "real" media. Just two years later, we are already seeing newspapers being used as a way of sparking a story on Twitter.

$\boxed{\text{X}}$ What LA Fitness did wrong

- It seemed not to have exercised appropriate discretion. This was a longstanding member who wanted to terminate the agreement due to a genuine change in circumstances.

$\boxed{\checkmark}$ What LA Fitness did right

- It recognized the influence of Twitter and backed down.

SELF BRANDJACK	Taking a stand on a bureaucratic principle damages the club's reputation.

101 Susan G. Komen cuts grant to Planned Parenthood, and then doesn't

February 2012

Susan G. Komen for the Cure (commonly known as Komen) is a charity that raises money to fight breast cancer. In 2012, it made grants of $93 million, $700,000 of which was to Planned Parenthood, an NGO devoted to reproductive health. Planned Parenthood is the much more political of the two, and is deeply involved in the American culture wars, especially over the topic of abortion. Komen wanted to end its relationship with Planned Parenthood, as it saw the potential for huge controversy from its relationship with the more political organization. But Komen mishandled the issue badly.

Instead of announcing that it was disengaging from its relationship with Planned Parenthood and explaining the reasons, Komen allowed Planned Parenthood to make the announcement and define the narrative. Unsurprisingly, Planned Parenthood proved more adept at engaging in a political dispute. In the Planned Parenthood narrative, Komen had been manipulated by anti-abortion groups and was taking an anti-abortion stance and not – as Komen saw it – not taking a stance on abortion at all.

The debate was toxic and led to calls for a boycott of Komen. This was the controversy that Komen had been seeking to avoid. While defining its own narrative might not have succeeded, it seems odd that Komen did not even try this approach. Probably, the Komen team anticipated that the story would not gather much attention. Given the high feelings that Planned Parenthood evokes – on both sides – this was always a vain hope. Given the political campaigning skills of Planned Parenthood, it was also always unlikely that Komen would come off better.

The result was that Komen was forced to back down, but chose to do so in an ambiguous way. It renewed the immediate grants, but left open the prospect that they would not be renewed in the future. In one sense, it had to do this. It needed to keep its options open, but choosing to highlight the fact that it might choose not to make future grants left both sides of a deeply divisive issue extremely unhappy.

In 2013, Komen cancelled 7 out of 14 of its signature three-day fundraising walks following further criticism over the CEO's salary and the proportion of funds that go to research.

Learnings

Komen made a significant error of judgment in thinking the issue would ever quietly go away. This led to the team neglecting to develop its own narrative and explanation. The ultimate result was that Komen highlighted the issue of its relationship with Planned Parenthood and then left the relationship damaged but intact. Up until this point, very few people knew that Komen made any grants to Planned Parenthood. They were not even 1 percent of its total grants. Pro-life people became aware of the grants, and that they had been restored. Pro-choice people were offended by Komen's failed attempt to sever its relationship with Planned Parenthood. Komen's relationships with both communities were deeply damaged.

☒ What Komen did wrong

- It failed to anticipate the story.
- It failed to develop and sell its own narrative – not even making the announcement.
- It backed down in an ambiguous way, leaving both sides dissatisfied.

SELF BRANDJACK Poor handling of an inherently controversial issue left the charity looking politicized and incompetent.

102 Oprah in Nielsen box appeal
February 2012

Sunday 12 February, 2012 was the night of the Grammy Awards and the day after Whitney Houston died. The Grammy show scored a huge audience (it's second highest in three decades). This was the background to a fantastically ill-judged tweet from Oprah Winfrey: "Every 1 who can please turn to OWN especially if u have a Neilsen [sic] box."

The Nielsen box is a device that measures TV audiences. If asked what TV programs or magazines they enjoy, people often report significantly more upmarket tastes than more objective measures suggest. The Nielsen box records and reports in real time what channel TVs are tuned to. People are supposed to report which members of the household are watching at any one time. The box cannot, of course, measure who is paying attention. The 5,000 household sample is designed to be representative of the US as a whole, and the figures from Nielsen are used by TV schedulers and advertisers for planning purposes. Nielsen's rules prohibit people from marketing directly to Nielsen box holders, for the fairly obvious reason that this would bias the sample.

Twitter reacted immediately to Oprah's tweet, sent on behalf of her own Oprah Winfrey Network. The following day, Oprah apologized:[3] "I removed the tweet at the request of Nielsen. I intended no harm and apologize for the reference." She also sent @replies to people who commented on the issue, initially defending her tweet and then apologizing.

Learnings

This was very bad form, and as a network owner, Winfrey must have realized this. Presumably, so would anyone authorized to send tweets in her name. There is something rather desperate about appealing for a spike in ratings, but to target those with Nielsen boxes is an attempt to corrupt the ratings system in order to make her own product appear more valuable than it is. How does this differ from seeking to float a company with fraudulent accounts?

☒ What Oprah did wrong

- She gave the appearance of desperation in propping up her network.
- She sought to inflate her viewing figures in order to charge higher fees to advertisers.

☑ What Oprah did right

- She apologized. Whether or not the initial tweet was personally from Oprah, she was right to take responsibility.

SELF BRANDJACK Very bad behavior by a global star.

103 Claire's jewelry chain accused of plagiarism
February 2012

The story began with a blog on the website of Tatty Devine, a small handmade jewelry company. It showed pictures of some of its own necklaces next to designs being sold by Claire's, an international chain selling affordable jewelry. The blog is headlined "Can you spot the difference?" The blog attracted over 200 comments, before Tatty Devine closed the comment facility and there were 2,500 tweets on the subject.

Claire's was slow and cumbersome in its response. Its statement was over-lawyered:[4]

> Claire's Stores, Inc. is a responsible company that employs designers, product developers and buyers, and works with many suppliers to provide innovative collections that bring customers all the latest fashion trends. As such, we take any allegations of wrong doing seriously. We are looking into the matters raised.

Notice, it doesn't directly address the issue or express any emotion. It starts with a boilerplate description that it hopes – surely in vain – will influence the way journalists describe the company. This is a company that had hitherto been praised for its social media engagement. If the PR or social team had been left in charge to make the response, it would probably have been better.

They could have started with some emotion. They could have expressed some urgency about the investigation. "Looking into" something is not as strong as "investigating," and "organizing a full supply chain audit" is stronger still – although the last of these does veer towards the legalese that lets down the Claire's statement. They could have acknowledged that one part of the investigation was talking to Tatty Devine.

The matter was settled in seven weeks. The terms are confidential to the parties, but Claire's withdrew three of the five designs featured on the Tatty Devine blog. It continued to sell two others, and a sixth design not mentioned on the original blog, but perhaps discussed in subsequent comments and tweets. The statement says nothing about a financial settlement one way or another.

Learnings

Tatty Devine raised the issue in an intelligent and modern way. The blog does not, however, indicate that the company first of all approached Claire's for some comment, which might at least have been polite. It would have been required of a responsible journalist.

Claire's muffed its initial response, but then seems to have quickly reached a settlement.

☑ **What Tatty Devine did right**

- The blog post is well put together, and mostly lets the photographs speak for themselves.

☒ **What Tatty Devine did wrong**

- It may not have approached Claire's first.

☑ **What Claire's did right**

- It settled the underlying issue fairly quickly.

☒ **What Claire's did wrong**

- It seems to have let its lawyers write its response. Bad move.

 SELF BRANDJACK While Claire's has never formally accepted wrongdoing, it has withdrawn items from sale, which suggests lack of due diligence; it also messed up its response.

104 "Kony 2012"
March 2012

"Kony 2012" is a video released online via YouTube, Vimeo, and the website of the sponsoring NGO, Invisible Children. The video encouraged people to share it virally with their networks and received celebrity endorsement from, among others, George Clooney, Angelina Jolie, and Oprah Winfrey. The video secured 50 million views in four days. It provoked a response from the White House, and a resolution in the US Senate. It may have contributed to a decision by the African Union (AU) to send troops to central Africa. It did not, however, succeed in its declared goal of having Joseph Kony, leader of the Lord's Resistance Army (LRA), arrested and sent to trial in The Hague by the end of 2012.

The LRA has a declared objective of overthrowing the government of Uganda and installing a theocratic regime in its place. It has operated not only in Uganda but in Sudan, the Democratic Republic of Congo, and the Central African Republic. UN, US, and AU troops have also been involved at various times. Kony is accused of forcibly recruiting children to his army, among many other human rights atrocities. He was indicted for war crimes at The Hague in 2005.

The response to the video was generally positive. Some criticized it for simplifying the situation – a charge that can be made about almost any effort at education – and its accuracy was disputed by some (not just the LRA). Some critics suggested that Invisible Children had elevated the importance of Kony and the LRA.

The follow-up video was announced a few weeks later, in April, but was delayed by two days due to editing issues.

Learnings

A powerful message and a well-crafted video can quickly reach a huge audience. This effort raised the profile of a decades-old and largely ignored conflict. It followed all the rules of narrative structure, with a clearly identified villain. The story has a clear emotional resonance, with children cast as the victims.

☑ What Invisible Children did right

- A well-crafted video with a good narrative and clearly identified villains.
- A well-prepared kick-start to the viral campaign with celebrity endorsers lined up.

☒ What Invisible Children did wrong

- Never promise a follow-up video on a particular date if you can't deliver.

ETHICS BRANDJACK Invisible Children created an image for Kony, where none had previously existed, based on its well-founded objections to the LRA.

105 Goldman Sachs resignation
March 2012

Greg Smith's resignation from Goldman Sachs was as public as it can get. On his last day, he published an article in *The New York Times* slating the company's culture and charging that the atmosphere was toxic and had declined significantly during his 12 years at Goldman.[5]

His principal allegation was that the company cares more about making money off clients than about making money *for* clients. This is an old debate, and the extent to which it matters has been an active debate since at least 1776, when Adam Smith wrote: "It is not from the benevolence of the butcher, the brewer, or the baker that we expect our dinner, but from their regard to their own interest." Greg Smith might easily respond that Goldman's financial products are sufficiently complex that different considerations may apply. On the day the article was published, Goldman began to trend on Twitter and soon a clever parody of the article called "Why I'm leaving the Empire, by Darth Vader" was published on a blog.[6] Something that was going to be a difficult issue, but prone to rational debate, had been transformed in the social media to a matter of ridicule – an altogether much more difficult issue.

Learnings

Ridicule can be extremely difficult to handle. Addressing the issues seriously can make you seem humorless, while letting them hang there leaves the underlying charges unanswered. Perhaps the best response is to accept that the parody is funny ("we all had a laugh about this at the office"), but then move on to address the underlying issues.

Goldman did respond immediately to Smith's original article saying it did not agree with his criticisms. Having an immediate response is fundamental. It means that subsequent MSM coverage (although not necessarily in social media) will at least include a rebuttal. Goldman probably could have gone further. A company blog would have allowed it to respond at more length than its media statement. It is not clear what the company did in terms of internal communications, but this is also critical to a response. Smith was an insider, and his criticisms probably had resonance with at least some people inside the company. Sending the external statement around inside the company would be insufficient. A blog that allows people to debate the issues and managers holding meetings to discuss the issues with their teams would have been valuable.

Not only is it essential for business continuity to maintain internal morale, but in the social age, staff are increasingly important advocates for your reputation.

☑ What Goldman did right

- It responded immediately.

⮞ What Goldman should have done, but may not have

- It should have developed a blog for internal and external use.
- It should have used the criticisms to spark an internal debate.
- It should have communicated core messages to staff.

- It should have tried to assess how widely the criticisms had internal resonance with a view to healing internal relationships (if damaged) and using staff as social media advocates if and when morale is sufficiently high.

| STAFF BRANDJACK | A powerful critique of the company's culture hits the MSM and then goes wild in the social media. |

106 SXSW: Homeless Hotspots
March 2012

SXSW (South by Southwest) is probably the world's leading conference on digital media and is associated with other conferences and festivals for music and film, all of which take place in Austin, Texas, in the spring. At SXSW 2012, the advertising agency BBH (Bartle Bogle Hegarty) launched a promotion called Homeless Hotspots. Homeless people in Austin were equipped with Wi-Fi, T-shirts saying "I am a 4G hotspot," and the ability to accept donations by PayPal.

This was massively criticized online and in the MSM as being "dehumanizing." Such criticism strikes this author as odd, especially as many of the critics did not bother to find out the opinions of the homeless people involved, which seems a far more dehumanizing approach than BBH's promotion. Jon Mitchell of ReadWrite.com, one of the sharpest critics, followed up his blog post with a report of meeting Mark, one of the homeless hotspots, who was very positive about the experience. In Mitchell's words, Mark "was putting on a great show, selling his wares loudly and proudly."[7]

Foremost among the criticisms was that the T-shirts said "I *am* a 4G hotspot" and not "I *have* a 4G hotspot." The idea was that this reduced the people involved to the level of a piece of equipment. This has to be set against the obvious fact that BBH was giving homeless people something valuable they could sell. This seems a much more positive thing than simply making a donation, as it gives people an opportunity to succeed by their own skills and efforts. An obvious comparison would be with homeless people selling *The Big Issue*, although sales of a dead-tree magazine are inherently limited to the number of copies you have. Access to Wi-Fi can be sold over and over again, giving the homeless people an almost limitless opportunity to earn both money and a feeling of achievement.

Learnings

BBH must have hoped for a great deal of credit for this idea with the SXSW audience – a trendy and somewhat left-leaning group. The result was a torrent of disapproval and not much being said in the advertising company's defense. Some of the criticism centered on the fact that the initiative was being taken by an advertising company, as though sucking homeless people into the evils of the market is a bad thing.

✓ What BBH did right

- It correctly identified an issue that would have resonance with its audience.

✗ What BBH did wrong

- It seems to have misread its audience badly.

| **SELF BRANDJACK** | An error of judgment at BBH earned strong disapproval. |
| **ETHICS BRANDJACK** | The agency has now become associated with negative attitudes towards homeless people, the precise reverse of its intent. |

107 What's in a name? The "pink slime" debate
March 2012

How much does the name of a product matter? Well, if the choices are "lean finely textured beef (LFTB)" or "pink slime," it seems pretty clear which one the public will find most appetizing. Another name sometimes used is "soylent pink," a reference to Harry Harrison's 1966 novel *Make Room! Make Room!* and the 1973 film version *Soylent Green*. Needless to say, the names describe the same product.

The product is processed beef offcuts, mechanically recovered from the carcass. The fat has been removed to render it almost entirely lean and it has been treated with ammonium hydroxide. It sounds scary, but, then, dihydrogen monoxide sounds so scary that Penn and Teller persuaded a whole rally full of environmentalists to sign a petition to have it banned – and dihydrogen monoxide is water. According the website beefisbeef.com, ammonium hydroxide is "found naturally in all proteins we eat – plant or animal – and one of its roles is to prohibit bacteria from forming." One result of injecting "pink slime" into ground beef is to reduce the fat content.

As a result of a large-scale social media campaign and a report on ABC News, it emerged that in the US a product can be labeled as "100% ground beef" and still contain up to 15 percent LFTB. Perhaps this is reasonable, and the additive is still beef and is certainly ground – heavily ground: that's what "finely textured" means. In Canada, the product cannot be sold at all, because of the ammonia content, and a few years ago LFTB was used in pet food and cooking oil, but in 2001 the US Food and Drug Administration (FDA) approved it for limited human consumption.[8]

As a result of the scare, leading US food chains such as Krogers have withdrawn from sale products containing LFTB and Walmart has introduced a labeling policy that will identify whether or not ground beef contains LFTB.

Learnings

Winning the battle for the name was plainly a key success for the critics of the product. In part, they were able to do this as they were the ones who first went public with talking about it. By the time the beef industry started talking about LFTB, the public was already talking about "pink slime." This is not to say that the beef industry was excessively secretive about its processes, but it had no particular reason to talk about them. If the beef industry had got there first, proactively talking about what it was doing to reduce the fat content of ground beef, there might have been a different ending to this story.

☑ What the beef industry did right

- It hit back with science and tried to shift the debate to fat content. This was not enough to undo the damage.
- It has maintained strong relations with regulators. There seems no risk of the product being banned, and there will no doubt remain a market for cheap, lean beef.

☒ What the beef industry did wrong

- It failed to anticipate the way in which this story could be negatively spun and so did not establish its own narrative or nomenclature first.

FAKE BRANDJACK While not a malicious hoax, the scare story here seems to have little foundation and the beef industry has been caught off guard by its own lack of transparency.

108 Heineken "sponsors" dogfighting
April 2012

Images from a dogfight in Mongolia began to circulate virally, which included a prominently displayed Heineken banner. People began to accuse the Dutch brewer of "sponsoring" dogfighting. Heineken responded within hours that it did not know what the event was but was able to confirm that the images did not appear to have been photoshopped. This was not a fake brandjack designed as an attack on the company. It immediately promised a full and transparent investigation and, perhaps more importantly, sounded human, not legalistic:

> Heineken is aware of a shocking photo of what appears to be a dogfighting match in a foreign country with Heineken branding visible in the background. We'd like to thank the community for bringing this issue to our attention.

> We are as appalled by this image as you are and have asked the Heineken Global Office to immediately investigate the circumstances of this event and whether Heineken was involved in any way.

> If you have any further information regarding this picture, such as the source, or the venue where it was taken, please let us know in this thread.[9]

The response is powerful because it is not defensive, it expresses empathy with the feelings that the images have aroused, and it promises to come back with more information. People will understand that you do not have all the information to hand, *provided it is clear that you are actively seeking the information and will report back when you have it*. In this case, the promise is made more powerful by an express appeal for information.

The story turned out to be that Heineken was a supplier of beer to the venue and had sponsored a promotional event at the same venue earlier in the week. The Heineken branding had not been removed. No one at Heineken had been aware that the branding was still on display at the venue, or even that the venue occasionally hosted dogfights. Heineken subsequently decided not only to stop sponsoring any events at that venue but also to stop supplying the venue and conduct an audit of all its outlets to ensure they did not host events that contradicted the firm's brand values.

Learnings

There are other responses Heineken could have made, which would not have worked so well. It could have denied any liability for the events staged at venues it supplies. While true, this would have looked defensive and suspicious. It would not have achieved the same level of empathy with the customers who were horrified by the images. Telling the story of how the images came to exist made Heineken's lack of liability clear, but as a conclusion that customers drew themselves from the facts, not as an assertion by the company.

Heineken could have claimed "cultural sensitivity" on the lines of "it is not for Heineken, as a Western company, to tell Mongolian people what is and isn't acceptable." Dogfighting is so widely reviled in Western cultures that such a stance would not have worked. To compare dogfighting in Mongolia with bullfighting in Spain and Mexico would also have flopped. (Heineken was certainly sponsoring bullfighting as recently as 2008, according to a letter from the company published by the League Against Cruel Sports.[10]) Most people in the US and (most of) Western Europe, including Heineken's home country (The Netherlands) would have reacted in one of two ways, either a cri de coeur of "that's different" or one of "good point. Why *do* you sponsor bullfighting?"

If anything, Heineken was going much further than its publics might expect. Refusing even to supply venues where dogfighting takes place goes beyond the reasonable expectation of most people. After all, individuals can buy Heineken products whether they are dogfighters, terrorists or even (somewhat closer to the bone) drunk drivers.

☑ What Heineken did right

- It responded immediately, promising to investigate and report back.
- It sounded human and empathetic, not lawyerly and defensive.
- It took action to prevent a recurrence.

ETHICS BRANDJACK	Clash of values leaves company with no choice but to declare for Western values.

109 Dole Food Company: product recall
April 2012

In April 2012, the Dole Food Company, one of the largest producers of bagged fresh fruit and vegetables, was forced to recall some of its products because of a salmonella scare. Two days after the recall, PR Daily investigated the state of Dole's social media response. The company had a press release about the issue buried on its website, but very little response in social media and no company blog.[11] (This is a company with 36,000 permanent employees, as well as almost as many seasonal staff.)

There are, of course, risks in responding too quickly and on too large a scale. You might make statements that later turn out to be false or talk up the significance of a relatively minor crisis. But the risks of not responding are generally greater. People who have picked up inaccurate or partial (in either sense of the word) information from media (social or otherwise) will want to check with your owned channels for your side of the story. If it is hard to find, people will conclude you have something to hide. If the risks are restricted to a small product line, tell people this, or they will assume that all your products are contaminated.

Within a few days, Dole was able to identify how many bags of salad were at risk (756), the use-by date, the states they were sold in, and the universal product codes on the bags. With this information, people could rapidly establish if their salads were at risk. This suggests solid procedures for crisis *management*, but still aching gaps in the crisis *communication*. Armed with this information, Dole could have been aggressively taking it to social media. Placing all the data in an easily digestible form on its blog and then driving traffic via social media would have been a laborious, but not especially complex, task. Anyone posting about the crisis on Twitter, for example, could have received an @reply with a hotlink: "@bloggs, check whether your salad is safe here bit.ly/qwertyu."

This would only have dealt with the immediate issue. Rebuilding trust is a longer term investment. Again, use of owned channels, including using social media to drive people to your blog, would be a major part of it. It should involve real stories by real people. Getting staff engaged on social media to talk about the rigorous processes that keep food from getting contaminated can be a powerful way of restoring trust through transparent engagement.

Learnings

☑ What Dole did right

- It managed the actual issue.

☒ What Dole did wrong

- It seems to have tried to bury the story or, at least, failed to engage properly with reassuring messages.

SELF BRANDJACK An internal failure put customers at risk.

110 Aviva accidentally fires all its staff
April 2012

One of the features of email is that it is as easy – and sometimes easier – to email an entire category of people (a whole company, department, or all recipients of a message to which you are responding) than to select the people who actually need to know. Without the need to stuff and stamp envelopes, an email to 1,300 people looks just like an email to one. Pressing the "send" button is no harder.

Probably, everyone has accidentally replied to all when they meant to reply to one person. It is embarrassing, but it is not a disaster. Unless, of course, you accidentally dismiss 1,300 employees by sending an email that was intended for just one of them. Then, you are in a sticky situation indeed. This is what happened at Aviva – a major insurance company based in London, UK. The email did not, precisely, tell staff that they were all dismissed. It was a terse reminder to one person, who already knew he was leaving, that he needed to clear his desk and return all company property. One would like to imagine that when actually firing people, Aviva handles it in a more sensitive way. It is not even clear that the staff member who was leaving had been fired, rather than choosing to leave the company for, say, a better job. The matter was reported on social media in seconds and, given the size of the company, the MSM were not far behind.

The accident happened at a particularly awkward time for Aviva, which was undergoing some restructuring and, no doubt, some people were concerned about their future with the company. In such a context, the email would have been more than usually disconcerting. In practice, many people replied immediately asking if this was a mistake and within five minutes HR had issued a groveling apology.

The company treated the inevitable media enquiries with an appropriate *mea maxima culpa* and a certain amount of good humor. In the circumstances, it was rather well handled.

Learnings

Everyone makes the occasional mistake, and this one was a doozy, but everyone involved, from HR in immediately acknowledging and correcting the mistake to PR in dealing with the media in a friendly and helpful way, acquitted themselves rather well.

☒ **What Aviva did wrong**

- It was a simple, but concerning, mistake. HR handles a great deal of confidential information and needs to do so with discretion.

☑ **What Aviva did right**

- It corrected the mistake and apologized.
- It accepted the inevitable teasing in the media with good grace.

STAFF BRANDJACK An embarrassing error goes around the world in minutes.

---

111 Spirit Airlines ad spoofing Secret Service prostitution scandal
April 2012

In April 2012, while protecting the US president on a trip to Cartagena, Colombia for the Summit of the Americas, several Secret Service agents were exposed as having engaged the services of prostitutes, which is illegal in 49 US states, but not in Colombia. As a result, the Secret Service introduced new rules governing officers working abroad including covering the use of prostitutes, persons who officers may entertain in their hotel rooms, and the consumption of alcohol.

Spirit Airlines – a low-cost carrier with a reputation for controversial advertising, having previously teased Arnold Schwarzenegger, Tiger Woods, and Anthony Weiner over sex scandals – ran an ad that made rather unsubtle reference to the scandal. It showed a man who looks a lot like a Secret Service agent surrounded by bikini-clad models and the slogan "more bangs for your buck" while advertising a price of $19.80 to fly to … Cartagena. The ad does not appear to have run all that widely, but attracted tremendous earned media coverage, as critics from both sides of America's culture wars combined to attack it. The slogan "more bangs for your buck" is critical to the sexual innuendo and the airline's key message of cheap flights. It is just not possible to report on the story without mentioning the fact that the flights are cheap, and most media covering the story included a visual of the ad.

The result is that Spirit generated considerable coverage that broadcast its key message to everyone. It even got, ah, two bangs for its buck, as the story was reported again when the company withdrew the ad. The media, still declaring it tasteless, generally displayed it again.

It's true that this story is a little more controversial than teasing celebrities. Sex tourism is a genuine problem. The age of consent varies from one jurisdiction to another, and is not well enforced in some places. People travel abroad for sex, which even the least puritanical among us would condemn as exploitative. Incidentally, the president himself also joked about the incident during a speech, promising to make the Secret Service observe a curfew in future.[12]

Learnings

It is unlikely that Spirit was disappointed by the result of this campaign. The news reports about the ad probably reached many more people than the ad itself. The first objective of an ad is to garner attention, and this one did. It delivered the key message and, while controversial, was taken in good humor by many people.

If your objective is to grab attention with a controversial campaign, it isn't even necessary to run the ad at all these days. You can display it on your website or Facebook page and wait for the controversy to do the rest. You can even insulate yourself, somewhat, from the opprobrium by asking your community whether they think the ad is offensive. "You see," you can say later, "we are sensitive to this issue, which is why wanted to check whether people thought this was funny or offensive."

✓ What Spirit did right

- It tapped into a major news story to gain attention.
- It chose a good-humored way of delivering a key message.
- It backed down in the face of criticism, garnering a new wave of coverage.

✗ What Spirit did wrong

- It possibly overlooked the difference between this sex scandal and the marital infidelity of celebrities.

 Publicity courting airline courts publicity.

112 Barack Obama: "Polish death camps"
May 2012

On May 29, President Obama, at a ceremony to honor Jan Karski, a hero of the Polish resistance, referred to Karski giving a first-hand account of atrocities at a "Polish" death camp in the Warsaw ghetto.[13] Any such reference infuriates Poles and Polish Americans, who believe that any reference to the death camps in Poland (which included Auschwitz and Treblinka) should make clear that they were Nazi death camps in German-occupied Poland.

Radek Sikorski, Poland's British-educated foreign minister, responded with strongly worded tweet: "The White House will apologize for this outrageous error." That's a translation from the Polish, and the author cannot vouch for the quality of the translation, but note the translator suggests this is not a *request* for an apology, but a *demand*. The tweet goes on to refer to "ignorance and incompetence." It is extremely unusual for a foreign minister to speak in such strong terms about the executive branch of an ally. Within a few days, President Obama communicated his "regret" for the careless wording.

A slip such as this from the leader of the free world is unusual and, frankly, crass. Of course, no one at the White House believed that Poland was responsible for the Holocaust, and a cynic might even suggest that if there had been no collaborators in Nazi-occupied Europe (and there were, in every country), those countries might be less sensitive about such slips of the tongue. But the Polish government has been campaigning on this issue for years. The White House and State Department should most certainly have known that, and been alert to this potential error.

Learnings

The fact is that the president misspoke about a highly sensitive issue. The US government should have been alert to the issue and a State Department official should probably have been slapping his forehead the moment the president said what he did. They should have got ahead of the story and apologized before the Polish government lodged its objection.

X What the White House did wrong

- Either the president's brief was sloppily prepared or he drifted off message. That's a bad error and shouldn't happen.
- It should have spotted the error and issued the apology immediately. "Regret" is not enough, and if it had acted proactively, it could have apologized without seeming weak.

X What the Polish government did wrong

- Sikorski's undiplomatic tweet may have slowed the White House response and made what could have been apology into a mere "regret."

Serious error of judgment in either speech writing or speech
delivery.

113 Best Buy affair leads to slow burn crisis
May 2012

When will people learn that, in the age of social media, information eventually leaks out?

In December 2011, Richard Schulze, Best Buy founder, confronted Brian Dunn, then CEO, about an affair with an employee, but Schulze chose not to report the issue to the board. Respect for Dunn's privacy? Or a breach of good practice? Obviously, a CEO might exercise bias in promotions or awarding of contracts on any number of grounds. Dunn may have had friends to whom he was loyal, despite never engaging with them in anything more physical than a game of golf. The assumption that someone might be biased by a sexual relationship and not by a friendship is certainly open to challenge. But there is a reasonable point that passionate relationships do sometimes lead people to disengage their critical faculties.

How many times do people have to have sexual contact before it becomes necessary to declare things? This will be a matter of judgment, but a CEO should consider questions of liability. Could the partner allege sexual harassment if the affair goes wrong? Could someone passed over for promotion allege unreasonable bias? When does it become appropriate for a CEO to excuse themselves from critical decisions about the career of the other party to the affair?

In the case of Dunn, the news began to leak both internally and externally. An audit committee began an investigation. Dunn then left the company during an investigation described by the *Wall Street Journal* as being into his "personal conduct." It also noted a 55 percent decline in the share price over five years.[14] Then, in May, Schulze resigned from the role of chairman. As the story unfolded over a period of months, the company's share price declined by a third.

Learnings

It is often hard to separate one crisis from another. If financial results had been stronger, perhaps Dunn would have been more confident in declaring his affair and perhaps the board would have been more tolerant. It is even possible that the atmosphere of uncertainty that can surround poor financial performance contributed to leaks concerning the affair. But the clear lesson is that if there is a story to tell, it is best to take control and tell the story yourself.

☒ What Best Buy did wrong

- It failed in transparency, allowing the story to leak out slowly and at embarrassing moments.

SELF BRANDJACK Behavior falls short of best practice and embarrasses the company.

114 Yahoo! CEO pads his résumé
May 2012

Scott Thompson served just four eventful months as CEO of Yahoo! before leaving the company in complicated circumstances. His departure was first reported on the tech blog AllThingsD before *The New York Times* and CNN Money followed up.[15] Thompson's departure followed reports in the *Wall Street Journal* that he had been diagnosed with thyroid cancer, and the company confirmed that his departure had been influenced "in part" by the recent diagnosis, but Yahoo! was involved in several difficult issues at the time.

The allegation that Thompson had lied about his degree came from an activist shareholder group, Third Point, which had been engaged in disputes with the Yahoo! board for some time. The allegation emerged about a week before Thompson left his role as CEO. Thompson had claimed to have a degree in accounting and computer science, but his degree was in accounting only. To make matters worse, the enhancements to his résumé had been included in the company's annual report, a legal document the CEO must personally certify as being accurate. Yahoo! described the inaccuracy as inadvertent. According to CNN, Thompson apologized to Yahoo! staff over the inaccuracies in his résumé, but did not clarify his own role in the error. Although the exaggerated qualification predated Thompson's period at Yahoo! – it had been mentioned on the PayPal website when Thompson was a director of parent company eBay – eBay's filings with the SEC were accurate.

In the board reshuffle that followed Thompson's departure, Yahoo! settled its dispute with Third Point, bringing three of the four directors nominated by Third Point onto its board.

Learnings

The social media age is the age of transparency. Inaccuracies in what you say – even when they are minor and inadvertent – can prove serious problems. The issue was compounded in this case by the inclusion of the inaccurate material in the annual report, a document that is filed with the SEC. There are many groups out there with the motive – and now the means – to dig up information from your past and present it to the world.

☒ What Yahoo! did wrong

- It filed incorrect information with the SEC. This is a no-no under any circumstances and in today's media environment, it was always likely to emerge.

STAFF BRANDJACK Although emanating from the CEO, this counts as a staff brandjack, not a self brandjack, as the matter concerns the CEO himself, not the company.

115 Fiat photobombs VW Sweden

May 2012

As the Google Street View car drove past the HQ of Volkswagen Sweden, it captured what is, presumably, an unusual sight: a Fiat 500 parked directly in front of the VW building's entrance. It is likely that this took precision timing, but the photo will continue to appear on Google Street View for about a year. It was cleverly done, but also relied on a certain amount of luck and some patience. Apparently, a Fiat employee saw the Google Street View car driving around Södertälje, Sweden, and realized it would eventually drive directly in front of VW's HQ, so he simply followed it around for 45 minutes then, at the key moment, nipped ahead of it to park in front of VW's HQ.

Learnings

Luck, patience, and a good sense of humor combine to create a worthwhile stunt. Not only is the photo itself established on Google Street View, but the company earned a good deal of media coverage positioning it as fun-loving.

> ☑ **What Fiat did right**
>
> - It took advantage of an opportunity that presented itself. It was almost certainly an initiative by a single Fiat employee. There is no way a multinational would have approved a stunt like this fast enough to pull it off.

CHEEKY BRANDJACK Clever and fun.

116 Starbucks asks Ireland what makes it proud to be British

June 2012

Have you ever assumed that someone was American when they were in fact Canadian, or Australian when the person was actually from New Zealand? You are nowhere near the level of offense you would cause by labeling an Irish person as "British." Yes, of course, it is more complicated than that. Northern Ireland is part of the UK, and around half of the people there identify as British. This just makes it all the more sensitive to those – from any part of Ireland – who identify as Irish.

On the first weekend of June 2012, the UK had a four-day weekend, with the Monday and Tuesday both public holidays, to mark the Diamond Jubilee (60 years on the throne) of Queen Elizabeth II. This is only Britain's second Diamond Jubilee, the first being for Queen Victoria in 1897. Following the wedding of Prince William the previous year and preceding the London Olympics, which were later in 2012, it was a time of national celebration in Britain and the other Commonwealth realms where she is queen. She is not, of course, queen in Ireland, although her father was king there, and Ireland was part of the UK for Victoria's Jubilee.

It was against this background that StarbucksIE (Starbucks Ireland) sent its unfortunate tweet:

> @StarbucksIE Happy hour is on! Show us what makes you proud to be British for a chance to win. Don't forget to tag #MyFrappuccino

The reaction from the Twitterati was instant, and varied from outrage to amusement, with some cynicism about the lasting damage this would do to Starbucks:

> @JohnMadden 78 Right now someone in Starbucks Ireland is wishing there was a Twitter version of the memory wipe thing from Men in Black.

@LeoIE Someone in @StarbucksIE is in trouble. Actually no, Starbucks don't really care about local culture, just about imposing their own.

@PaulMWatson 4,481,430 – number of Irish complaining about the @StarbucksIE mistake. 0 – number of Irish who will stop buying Starbucks.

Starbucks, of course, apologized.

For all the fuss, only a minority of those voting in a poll on TheJournal.ie were either mildly (24%) or very (20%) annoyed. A plurality (42%) were "actually mildly amused" and 12% were not bothered either way. (The last figure is sure to be an underestimate, since the poll is of people who read the article and could then be bothered to vote in the poll.)

Learnings

Social media are instantaneous, and it is easy to make errors. It helps to acknowledge and apologize quickly. Starbucks actually took four hours to apologize and explain – when the nature of the mistake was blindingly obvious: it sent the tweet from the wrong account. How much internal discussion do you need before responding to this situation? As @LeoIE's tweet above suggests, it exacerbates the problem if your existing image is as a somewhat remote multinational.

☒ What Starbucks did wrong

- It sent the tweet from the wrong account.
- It took far too long to apologize.

SELF BRANDJACK Unfortunate error; slow response.

117 "Gay Pride" Oreo sparks Facebook protest
June 2012

Kraft Foods, owner of the Oreo brand, posted a rainbow Oreo – with six[16] multi-colored layers of cream – on its Facebook page. The image was posted during Gay Pride week and amid an ongoing culture war in the US about, among other things, gay marriage. The slogan "Proudly support love!" left no one in any doubt that the cookie brand was declaring its side in that debate. That's a brave thing for a cookie brand to do. At the time, no state in America had voted in a public ballot in support of gay marriage, and even liberal states such as Washington and California (twice) had voted against. Polling suggested that opinion was moving, but polling had underestimated opposition to gay marriage in the past.

Just a year later, large majorities now regard gay marriage as "inevitable" but the margins actually favoring it are still small. By taking sides in a debate such as this, brands take on needless risks. If we assume that the market for Oreo cookies broadly reflects the balance of opinion in America, then any stance is likely to alienate half your target market, and while the other half may think well of you, it is unlikely to significantly up its purchasing.

Sometimes, there is value in taking a stance – other than the one of standing on principle. Disney, for example, has long provided partnership benefits to its staff. It does this despite the fact that its core market is parents with young children, not gay people. One reason may be that its staff – often recruited from Broadway shows – include a fairly high proportion of gay people. Any business has to balance the views and interests of its various publics.

It is difficult to see any particular benefit to Kraft in taking this stand, despite a history of controversial advertising, including a picture of a baby being breastfed while holding an Oreo in an online-only ad in Korea. The ad was withdrawn and was apparently never meant for public consumption. (The point of the breast ad is that Oreos are supposed to be particularly good with milk, although as people dunk them, it is difficult to see how that could apply in this case.)

Learnings

There were widespread calls for a boycott of Oreos at the time. Naturally, such calls were controversial, heavily criticized by some and backed by others. This is an approach I might have counseled against, even though Kraft's stand on the issue chimes with my own views. That said, evidence for an impactful boycott is slight. Google searches for "boycott Oreos" turn up numerous matches for June 2012, but almost nothing thereafter. This does not seem to have become an ongoing issue for the brand.

☑ What Kraft did right

- It took a stand on principle on an issue where it appears to have almost no business interest.

ETHICS BRANDJACK Oreo heavily criticized for a stance on moral issues.

SELF BRANDJACK Kraft deliberately jumped into this issue when it didn't have to.

118 @Sweden anti-Semitism row
June 2012

Sweden is mostly known as a tolerant, friendly, liberal country. That Sweden was the country that experimented with social media by allowing individual citizens to control the "@Sweden" Twitter account should not be surprising. Under a project called Curators of Sweden, a new Swedish person is given control of the account every week. It is a brave experiment, but it certainly has risks.

So where would one expect a liberal country such as Sweden to stand on the question of anti-Semitism? It may be a complex question. Anti-Semitism was fairly common prior to World War II, but its reputation – along with ideas such as eugenics – took a considerable bashing as a result of the war and subsequent discoveries about the Holocaust. Countries that were occupied by the Nazis all had collaborators and generally prosecuted and executed them after the war. Sweden was not occupied. It remained neutral throughout the war, continuing to supply Nazi Germany with iron ore. It is at least arguable that Sweden had little choice, as Denmark and Norway were occupied by Germany. Finland was, at first, occupied by the USSR and later by Germany. Although Sweden sheltered refugees, including many Jewish people, it also cooperated with the Nazis. Germany moved troops across Sweden to participate in Operation Barbarossa. Some Swedes even volunteered for the SS, but Sweden, unlike occupied countries, did not purge itself of Nazi sympizers afterwards. Eugenic policies, abandoned in other parts of Europe, continued in Sweden into the 1970s.

Does any of this mean Sweden is especially prone to anti-Semitism today? Probably not, but it may be that Sweden lacks the immediate sensitivity on the issue that other European countries have. Neutrality enabled the country to avoid the soul-searching and recriminations that occupied countries went through in 1945. Certainly, for one week in June, the @Sweden Twitter account was run by someone who was heavily criticized for lacking sensitivity about these issues. Sonja Abrahamsson asked numerous questions about Jews and pointed out that the Nazis had made them wear stars in public so that people could tell them from others. She claimed that you can't tell if someone is Jewish without seeing his penis – and even then you can't be sure. At no point does Abrahamsson (an ironically Semitic name) express sympathy for Nazi policies. She is expressing curiosity, and trying to do so in 140 characters. A challenging task, given the inherent sensitivities of the issues.

Learnings

Abrahamsson herself was clear that she realized raising these questions was a mistake. No one has ever claimed that the @Sweden project means people posting tweets are going to be in any way representative of Sweden. It is inherent to the project that they cannot be. Random sampling gets you oddities. It may even be that the storm of protest around this issue – which followed closely on a sympathetic article about the Curators of Sweden project in *The New York Times* – helped draw attention to the project.[17] It may have got the account more followers from curious people who want to know what happens when you let just anyone use your Twitter feed. Abrahamsson was not the first embarrassment. A previous user attracted the nickname "masturbating Swede" after listing his hobbies online.

☒ What Abrahamsson did wrong

- She stepped, rather thoughtlessly, into a controversial area, where 140 characters may not give you enough space for all the caveats you need.

☑ What Curators of Sweden did right

- It remains a fascinating and noble experiment. This will not be the last embarrassment, but the project still deserves support.

SELF BRANDJACK	The project inherently encourages – or is at least wide open to – controversy.

119 Veet gets flashmobbed on Amazon
January–July 2012

The flashmob is a product of mobile technology. It doesn't depend on mobile Internet, just on text messaging, and dates to the 1990s, both for organizing political protests and for fun, staged events.

In the early part of 2012, reviewers on Amazon began voting spoof reviews of Veet hair removal gel to the top of the reviews section on Amazon. Anyone can submit a review and people vote on whether or not they found the review helpful. At the time of writing, the three most popular reviews are all spoofs from people describing what happens if you rub the gel on your genitals. (It hurts. A lot.) A year on, the top three reviews (the only ones visible unless you select "more reviews") are all spoofs, dating from January, July, and April 2012.

Neither Amazon nor Veet seems to have done anything about this. Amazon would probably be reluctant to agree to have the reviews taken down – as it might if they contained racist or otherwise offensive material – and there is no indication that Veet has requested it. Amazon would also probably not participate in efforts to game the system and vote other reviews higher, although Veet could seek to orchestrate this on its own.

It's not clear that either Amazon or Veet is being damaged by this. Amazon is simply allowing its review procedures to continue as normal. The Amazon community chooses the top reviews, not the company itself. Veet benefits from earned media (including blogger) coverage of the issue. While the spoof reviews are somewhat mocking of the product, they don't suggest that the product is in any way defective, just that it can be painful if you use it in a way contrary to the instructions on the packaging.

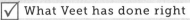

Learnings

Any product can be the subject of mocking, and affecting outrage over this can make the brand owner seem humorless.

☑ What Veet has done right

- It seems to have done nothing, and this is the right call.

CHEEKY BRANDJACK   Humorists successful target a product through reviews.

AGGREGATION BRANDJACK   Cooperation by disparate parties puts these reviews to the top.

120 Argyll & Bute Council and the NeverSeconds blog
June 2012

Martha Payne writes a blog (NeverSeconds.blogspot.com) about her school lunches. Up until June 2012, it was fairly basic, with a photograph of her meal and her review. There was (and still is) a link to the JustGiving page of Mary's Meals, a charity that builds kitchens in Malawi for children who would otherwise have no access to a hot meal. Martha's blog is now internationally famous and there is a biography of her available for sale on Amazon. At the time her blog went global, Martha was nine. A large part of the credit for Martha's fame goes to the unbelievable incompetence of Argyll & Bute Council in western Scotland.

Martha was called out of a math class one day and told she was now banned from taking photographs in the lunch hall. She reluctantly went home and wrote her "last" blog. The next entry was written by her father, explaining that he had phoned the council to ask if the school had the authority to close down her blog. The council responded that the school had done so on its instructions. The following day, the story was written up in the *Daily Telegraph*.[18] The item went live at 08:00 and said that Martha had raised £2,000 (around $3,000) to build kitchens in Malawi. When this author checked three hours later, the total was already almost £9,000.

A tweet this author addressed to @argyllandbute was, within seconds, retweeted by well-followed connections in the UK, the US, and the Philippines. The council remained silent and, indeed, had not tweeted in several days. Since the *Daily Telegraph* item contained no comment from the council, the author tried to contact the PR department. There was no PR landing page on the website and no dedicated phone line. The switchboard connected me to someone who gave no comment other than that a statement would be issued later that day.

The statement, when it came, was all about the quality of the school lunches and did not address the issue of closing down a pupil's blog. It was defensive and implied that staff felt under threat for their jobs. It also claimed that no one other than the Payne family had complained about the quality of the food. Whoever wrote it seemed to be unfamiliar with nine-year-olds. It would be surprising if there is any school in the Western world where only one person has ever complained about the food. If this rather unlikely claim had been true, then it would have directly contradicted the suggestion that staff were concerned about their jobs. If the food had been overwhelmingly popular, a single critic would not have threatened the job security of the cooks.

The PR department was silent largely because the head of department had been suspended over an unrelated issue, and then two other people had been suspended after an investigation into the first issue uncovered an exchange of tactless emails unrelated to the first issue. By the time the NeverSeconds crisis arose, three of the four members of the PR team were under suspension. All have subsequently left the council's employment.

As the morning wore on, #NeverSeconds was trending strongly on Twitter and the fundraising total for Mary's Meals was rising. By the end of the day it reached £64,000 (around $100,000). By noon, UK time, the issue was being reported on the US political blog the Drudge Report – the blog that exposed the Monica Lewinsky scandal. As blogger Willard Foxton put it: "Ok, #never-seconds now on @drudge_report. Congratulations, @argyllandbute, you have just been upgraded to INTERNATIONAL laughing stock!"

In a lunchtime interview on BBC Radio 4's *The World at One*, the leader of the council backed down. The previous statement was removed from the website and replaced by one that began "There is no place for censorship in Argyll and Bute."

A year on, Martha had raised enough money to build 19 kitchens in Malawi. What had you done when you were 10? She has visited Malawi and her endorsement is sought by national and international media for campaigns on the quality of school food.

Learnings

At whatever level these decisions were being made, they were made according to the wrong set of priorities and with little or no consideration given to the PR implications. They don't even seem to have given much consideration to the core business of the council. The first statement was focused on "protecting" staff. But schools and councils do not exist for the benefit of their staff. Schools exist for the sake of the pupils, and this decision was threatening the evolving education of a remarkably erudite pupil.

✓ What Argyll & Bute Council did right

- It backed down in the face of overwhelming global pressure.

✗ What Argyll & Bute Council did wrong

- It lacked the infrastructure to engage. Its PR team was not available and was outside the decision-making loop. It was almost absent from social media.
- It was insensitive to its own priorities, focused on the needs of its staff and not those of its clients and service users.
- Its handling of media enquiries – when people could get a statement at all – was clunky and unresponsive.
- It acted as though its staff should be immune from public criticism when councils are supposed to be accountable.

 Appalling behavior by the council leads to international criticism.

 The council completely lost sight of the reason it runs schools.

121 **Lance Armstrong doping scandal**
June 2012–January 2013

Lance Armstrong was, by turns, a hero and villain to Americans and many others worldwide. He came back from cancer to win the Tour de France seven times in succession, but allegations of illegal doping reached such a cacophony that he was eventually forced to confess, and his name was struck off the roster of winners.

Armstrong was a competitive triathlete and one of the most successful professional cyclists in the history of the sport. He came back from retirement twice – his first retirement being precipitated by testicular cancer. In his second professional career, he won seven Tour de France titles and simultaneously promoted his charity – the Lance Armstrong Foundation, later the Livestrong Foundation – dedicated to fighting cancer. His reputation as a sporting hero, charity fundraiser, and role model for cancer survivors became so strong that there was talk of his running for governor of Texas and, after that, who knows?

He also became a skilled crisis communicator. Rumors of his involvement in doping, including bullying other team members into using performance-enhancing drugs, had been circulating throughout his career. For many years and especially during the second half of 2012, Armstrong maintained a strong defense of his record. The facts seemed to back him up. As Armstrong put it on his website: "I have competed as an endurance athlete for 25 years with no spike in performance, passed more than 500 drug tests and never failed one."[19]

The evidence that was pursued by, first of all, a two-year investigation by the US Department of Justice (eventually dropped) and then by the US Anti-Doping Alliance (USADA) was based on the testimony of Armstrong's teammates. Armstrong's case was that admitted drug cheats were being given immunity in exchange for testimony against Armstrong. Why was he the only person being pursued by USADA for what it alleged was a massive conspiracy involving dozens, maybe even hundreds, of people?

The answer is that USADA was pursuing a PR advantage in its campaign against drug use. Banning a minor athlete, whom most people had never heard of, would achieve little. Banning Armstrong would be a major PR coup. Athletes take performance-enhancing drugs for a reason – to win. If USADA could establish that taking drugs would lead to athletes losing the titles they took the drugs to win, it would establish a major deterrent. Conversely, allowing a high-profile athlete, dogged by rumors of being a drug cheat for years, to hold his titles would give the message that you *can* get away with it.

Even convicting Armstrong after the fact was something of a pyrrhic victory, since he had, after all, passed all those drug tests. Catching him demonstrated conclusively that the net was one with major holes.

The social age, however, made it essential that Armstrong should be convicted, in order that USADA could salvage at least some credibility by arguing that it caught up with him in the end. Rumors that had been controllable in the 1990s were now everywhere. Every time Armstrong insisted his innocence, some people were becoming increasingly convinced that the drug prohibition policy was failing. Cheats could win, and get away with it.

In July 2012, Armstrong brought a case in a Texas court to have the USADA drop its charges, as the Justice Department had already done. On key issues, however, Armstrong's case failed, although the judge did criticize USADA for the timing of its investigation and its single-minded pursuit of Armstrong. On August 24, 2012, USADA stripped Armstrong of all his titles won after 1998, including all his Tour de France victories. Armstrong accused USADA of "outlandish and heinous claims." But he also claimed that its arbitration procedures were so "one-sided" that it was not worth his pursuing the matter; as he put it, "enough is enough," so he abandoned his formal defense, while continuing to assert his innocence.

Throughout his campaign, Armstrong demonstrated the effectiveness of the hard-hitting, terse remark, especially in the social media age. He responded to a 202-page report from USADA with an email to *The New York Times*. In 2011, he famously rebutted a CBS *60 Minutes* investigation with a single tweet: "20+ year career. 500 drug controls worldwide, in and out of competition. Never a failed test. I rest my case."

Learnings

It was a hard-hitting, well-argued campaign by a man with a strong base of public goodwill from his sporting and health triumphs. He was much better adapted to the Twittersphere than the quasi-judicial procedures of USADA. Yet Armstrong was let down by one fatal flaw in his campaign. This was not PR. This was propaganda. The blade in the heart of his campaign was a simple one, as he eventually confessed on *The Oprah Winfrey Show* – he was lying.

☑ What Lance Armstrong did right

- In many ways, it was a valiant defense. The fast, hard-hitting tweet; the strength and consistency of his messaging. These are all things from which any crisis team can learn.

| ☒ What Lance Armstrong did wrong |

- It was the one, unforgivable sin that let down the professionalism of his PR and destroyed his career. *He lied*. That he did it so strongly and consistently is why he got away with it for so long. But he lied, and no amount of spin could undo the facts.

SELF BRANDJACK   Cheat and liar eventually brought down by his own deception.

122 Chick-fil-A takes a stand on gay marriage
July 2012

A month after Oreo took a stand in favor of gay marriage, Chick-fil-A, the US fast-food restaurant chain, decided to jump the other way, with the CEO publicly supporting traditional, biblical marriage. This decision was at least as controversial as the Oreo rainbow cookie.

Aside from the calls for a boycott – which, unlike Oreos, still seem to be current a year later – Chick-fil-A faced two additional challenges. First, the company lost its relationship with the Muppets. The Henson Company is now part of Disney, and the range of Muppet toys associated with Chick-fil-A was withdrawn. Second, politicians in Boston and Chicago argued that the franchise was not welcome in their cities. Consumer boycotts are one thing – and a good reason for avoiding controversial issues – but for city authorities to threaten to deny the franchise permission to operate is different. If the policy had been pursued – and both politicians subsequently argued that such was not their intention – it would have been open to challenge under the First Amendment to the US Constitution. Denying a business the freedom to operate on the grounds of its CEO's controversial views is a potential infringement of freedom of speech.

There are still blogs and Facebook pages calling for a boycott of Chick-fil-A a year after the immediate controversy.

Chick-fil-A positions itself as a Christian, family chain that does not open on Sundays, and has long supported conservative causes.

Learnings

Taking a stance on controversial social issues has clear risks and few benefits. One possible implication of the difference between this situation and that of Oreo is that liberal campaign groups may be more effective at organizing boycotts than conservative groups.

X	What Chick-fil-A did wrong

- It took a controversial stance that was sure to alienate a slice of the public with little upside potential for the business.

SELF BRANDJACK	CEO takes a stance, presumably knowing that it would have major risks for the group.

ETHICS BRANDJACK	CEO position puts him at odds with the morality of a section of his customer base.

123 The peculiar "deserve to die" controversy
July 2012

The "deserve to die" campaign was hosted on a website but the viral teaser campaign was organized offline. In a weird inversion of modern understanding of viral campaigns, the teasers for the website were all posters.

In all cities all over the US, posters began to appear charging that various groups – hipsters, cat lovers, the genetically privileged – "deserve to die." There was nothing on the poster to indicate the cause that was being advertised, but, just so that we were sure this really was the 21st century, it included a web address. The web address included the reassuring message that no one deserves to die and showed a clock counting down. The website was to raise awareness of a deadly disease, killing lots of people who don't deserve to die and, at the end of the countdown, it would be revealed which disease was the subject of the campaign.

It must always have been anticipated that the campaign would be controversial. Indeed, that was the point. By offending people, it stoked conversation and drew attention to the forthcoming great unveiling. The problem was that the countdown was called off and the culprit came out of the closet early. Perhaps this was because the level of controversy turned out to be even greater than anticipated or perhaps because the website gave away that 160,000 Americans a year were dying of the disease, and a few minutes on Google could reveal that this was the approximate figure for the number of lung cancer deaths.

The campaign was run by Lung Cancer Alliance to promote the idea that lung cancer was overlooked for funding compared to other cancers that kill fewer people. The theme of the campaign was that people have less sympathy with sufferers from lung cancer because they associate it with smoking – a voluntary behavior.

Probably the oddest thing about the campaign remains the fact that the key message was held solely online, but the teaser campaign was run offline using posters.

Learnings

There is no doubt that Lung Cancer Alliance stoked considerable and deliberate controversy. You can't get people talking without offending some people.

✓ What Lung Cancer Alliance did right

- It created a major talking point around its campaign, both before and after the unveiling.
- It drew attention to its key messages: that lung cancer research is underfunded and people are less sympathetic to sufferers of this cancer than others.

✗ What Lung Cancer Alliance did wrong

- It miscalculated. Building your whole campaign around a teaser and a countdown is a great idea. Being forced to abandon the countdown makes you look foolish.

SELF BRANDJACK Miscalculation undermines the whole theme of the campaign.

124 Shell and the Greenpeace Arctic Ready parody
July 2012

The Shell parody site, ArcticReady.com, is good. It is very, very good. This author worked in Shell's media relations team for a while but still can't see the flaws in the design, the visuals, or the look and feel. The site looks just like a legitimate Shell site, until you read the copy. The visuals are beautiful, and just the sort of thing that Shell – which the *Financial Times* describes as having an enviable record on the environment – might well use in some of its material. The text, however, tells a different story:

> You can't run your SUV on 'cute'. Let's Go.
>
> Your ignition is my extinction. Let's Go.
>
> End polar bear attacks in our lifetime. Let's Go.
>
> It's about time someone avenged the Titanic. Let's Go.

The main target of the campaign is defending the fragile ecology of the Arctic, although there is also mention of melting icebergs, which is, presumably, mostly a reference to global warming. Global warming poses the same risk to ice cover whether the fossil fuels are extracted from the Arctic or elsewhere. (Although a spill might impact the rate of ice depletion too, since oil is black and would absorb more heat than ice would.) Over a period of two days, July 16–18, 2012, Greenpeace ramped up its impressive social media resources to draw traffic to the site.

Almost a year on, a search for "Shell let's go" (Shell's slogan) puts the Greenpeace parody site top in organic matches, although Shell.co.uk (for this UK-based user) and Shell.com are second and third. Shell had to buy a sponsored link to appear higher up the page than Greenpeace on a search for the company's own name and advertising slogan.

Knowing that the social media space reacts strongly against any attempts to restrict debate, even in the name of asserting intellectual property rights or actions for defamation, Greenpeace also launched a Twitter feed – @ShellIsPrepared – which threatens action against the spoof Arctic Ready website. It is beautiful. Greenpeace used a spoof Twitter account to threaten legal action against its own spoof website. There's no evidence that Shell took any action against Arctic Ready, although the fake Twitter feed has been suspended.

The following month, a video did the rounds of social media that purported to show an "Epic. PR. Fail." by Shell.[20] The video was picked up by Gawker and Ben Smith of BuzzFeed, who forwarded it in good faith to his 80,000 Twitter followers. The video seemed to show an event at the Space Needle in Seattle at which an elderly guest of honor is shown a model of an oil rig, but when she holds up her glass to catch the oil, she is sprayed all over. The person filming on a phone is forced to stop by an event organizer. The whole event was staged, probably by corporate pranksters The Yes Men. Smith followed up his tweet with another stating that the video was a prank. A fake press release was also issued, threatening to sue the makers of the fake video. This was also seriously reported.

Learnings

Huge controversy can be generated in social media by a debate, especially if an apparently large and powerful organization is trying to "silence" pranksters or NGOs. Smart companies generally don't engage with this. (Although there are plenty of others that will.) Seemingly, it is no longer necessary for companies to argue

with NGOs to create a debate in social media. The NGOs can debate with themselves, while creating the impression they are being picked on by big bad corporates.

☑ What Shell did right

- It ignored the campaign and continued to make its own case for energy exploration and its own environmental record.

☑ What Greenpeace did right

- It effectively parodied a Shell website.
- When Shell refused to threaten legal action, it invented its own Twitter feed to threaten on Shell's behalf.

ETHICS BRANDJACK   Another outstanding campaign from Greenpeace.

IMPERSONATION BRANDJACK   Now at the meta-level, Greenpeace impersonates Shell being angry at Greenpeace for impersonating Shell.

125 BMW Olympic sexism row
August 2012

Twitter and Facebook were alive with rumors that BMW was giving away cars to male Olympians but not to the women. Anna Watkins, a gold medalist in rowing, was asked about the rumors on *Newsnight*, BBC Two's flagship news program. She said:

> It did work out that way, yes. It's a bit of a coincidence because it's the individual dealers that chose who to give the cars to, so it wasn't any grand strategy but it did just happen that there were a dozen or so (cars) for the men and none for the girls.[21]

So, from very early on, it was clear that there was no strategy at work but that individual decisions may have been influenced by sexism. The figures didn't really seem to back that up, as Watkins herself later clarified on Twitter: "To be fair to BMW plenty of female athletes got cars, it was just within the rowing team that it ended up wonky." There's a fair point there, that none of the British men in the rowing team won gold medals, whereas Watkins was one of a pair who won gold.

It seems as though the decision as to which athletes would get the two-year lease on a BMW was unconnected with the Olympics. Retired athletes and others not competing in the London Olympic Games were included. According to *The Telegraph*, of the 150 or so athletes who received cars under the sponsorship deal, 51 men and 38 women were competing in either the Olympics or Paralympics. This disparity is probably no greater than the difference in profile between men's and women's sport.

Learnings

The sponsorship deal seems to have been unconnected to the Olympics, although choosing high-profile British athletes was going to have an overlap with the Olympic selections. The first question to ask is why was it unconnected to the Games? With London hosting the Olympics for the first time in more than 60 years, this was clearly going to be the major sporting story of the year.

Allowing individual dealerships to choose athletes to sponsor was an interesting choice. Creating these individual links seems to have strengths. Dealerships could choose athletes connected with their franchise area and promote the connection themselves. One drawback is that it meant there was no central strategy with anyone able to monitor issues such as the balance between men and women or ensuring that the most high-profile athletes were being sponsored by someone.

✓ What BMW did right

- It allowed its dealerships to develop local links.

✗ What BMW did wrong

- It seemed slow – at least in social media terms – to respond to charges of misogyny.
- It lost any central direction of the program.

FAKE BRANDJACK The charge of misogyny or sexism does not seem to have been justified, but BMW could have been quicker to counter it.

126 Progressive accused of impropriety
August 2012

The US Progressive Corporation hit a major crisis in August 2012 following a blog by Brooklyn comedian Matt Fisher, titled "My Sister Paid Progressive Insurance to Defend Her Killer In Court."[22]

The details are hard to reconstruct, as even Matt Fisher concedes. His blog states he does not rule out the possibility that his sister was at fault in the car accident, although he cites two indicative pieces of evidence that suggest otherwise. First, the other driver's insurance company paid up immediately. Second, an independent witness stated that the other driver ran a red light.

Here is where we hit the fact that the MSM still has a theoretical commitment to impartiality, whereas blogs and social media do not. Bloggers and social commentators generally took Fisher's side uncritically. *The New York Times* took a different approach and it was only from the paper's coverage that the author learned there was another side to the case. Three other people formed the view that Fisher's sister was at fault: the other driver claimed that Fisher ran the red light; this was endorsed by the passenger in Fisher's car and believed by the police officer who took statements at the scene, but did not witness the accident.[23] The other driver's insurance company may have paid up immediately, but he was only insured for $25,000, so it seems possible that this decision simply reflected the low level of the payout compared with the cost of defending a claim.

It was the other driver's underinsurance that became the issue of dispute between Fisher's estate and Progressive. She carried insurance against being involved in accident that was the fault of an underinsured driver. Progressive refused to pay up, claiming it had not been established that the other driver was at fault. Fisher's estate therefore had to sue the other driver to establish his and, therefore, Progressive's liability. Progressive chose to be represented at the trial and made several interventions on the other driver's part – hence the hard-hitting headline of Matt Fisher's blog. The Fisher family ultimately won their case.

As social media and the MSM began to pick up on the story, Progressive fell back on legalisms, stating: "we properly handled the claim within our contractual obligations." No doubt that is technically true, or at least was true in the opinion of Progressive's lawyers. It also said it did not serve as counsel to the defendant in the Fisher family's case. Also, no doubt, technically true. But it seems the company did have a lawyer there who was cooperating with the defendant's formal counsel, and working against the interests of the Fisher family.

Matt Fisher is a writer and a comedian. He has a way with words. He can spin a narrative. Progressive's attempts to play in the space were much weaker, and may have been guided by paying too much attention to lawyers.

Progressive was slow to respond, and its attempts to hide behind technicalities were labeled "the worst kind of PR nonsense," although they strike this author as having the tone of a lawyer, not a PR professional. As the crisis continued, Progressive began to make better use of its blog to spell out its position in more detail, but its responses on Twitter were labeled "spam" by Gil Rudawsky writing in PR Daily.[24] Again, this may reflect a slowly and carefully crafted message that went through several stages of approval, including legal counsel, which was then used over and again when more personal responses may have been more appropriate.

To make matters worse, Progressive's Twitter avatar is Flo, its beaming, big-haired, red-lipsticked spokesmodel. Given the sensitivity of the subject – a young woman had died, after all – the smiling model may not have been appropriate for the tweets.

Learnings

According to Cleveland's *The Plain Dealer*, over 1,100 people posted on Twitter that they had shifted their insurance from Progressive as a result of the crisis.[25]

When there is a question of legal liability, organizations are understandably inclined to listen to their legal counsel. Unfortunately, the instinct of lawyers is for silence or, when forced to respond, craftily worded phrases that hide more than they reveal. Such a response is not only ineffective but actively counterproductive in the social world. Even the best PR response would not have greatly helped in the circumstances. The pathos was clearly on the side of the bereaved Fisher family, and it is difficult to read Progressive's actions as anything other than a series of extreme measures to avoid paying a claim for which it ultimately proved liable.

☒ What Progressive did wrong

- It waited too long to respond.
- It repeated the same message ad nauseam.
- It stated that it "did not serve as the attorney for the defendant" without clarifying its full role. According to Fisher, Progressive's attorney delivered the closing address on the defendant's behalf. (Technically, this would probably have been on Progressive's behalf, as it was a co-defendant.)

➡ What Progressive could have done better

- It could have had a varied set of responses to Twitterati, so as not to appear like spam.
- It could have considered using a different avatar for its responses to this and other tragic issues.

SELF BRANDJACK	This does seem like poor behavior by the company.
ETHICS BRANDJACK	Progressive was being attacked for the morality of its behavior.
AGGREGATION BRANDJACK	Fisher was able to assemble a considerable body of critics to lambast the company.

127 Bic "For Her" pens attract spoof reviews at Amazon
August 2012

Bic's "For Her" brand of pens attracted so many spoof reviews that any real reviews got buried, and reviewers competed to post the wittiest and most popular contribution.

Bic's own description of its product is:

> BIC Cristal For Her has an elegant design – just for Her! It features a thin barrel designed to fit a women's hand. It has a diamond engraved barrel for an elegant and unique feminine style.[26]

The Amazon community was not so flattering. The algorithm at Amazon is very sophisticated. Not only do popular reviews get voted to the top, but extracts from popular reviews are posted above them. These are divided between positive and negative reviews in an A vs. B format – but in the case of Bic For Her, the positive and the negative were both ironic. The top two reviews (both positive and negative) were from August 2012 but, almost a year later, spoof reviews continue to come in. All the most popular reviews are ironic, and the first two pages of reviews when listed by "most recent" contain not a single serious review.

Reviewers praise the product, including one woman who remarked that for years she had struggled to use "cumbersome man's pens" and another who claimed she had wanted to buy one but had been forbidden by her husband. Men complain that their hands are far too big and strong to find such a delicate product useable. Other points made are that the pens are extremely effective for drawing ponies, kittens, and unicorns, but do not function for math. One woman commented that the product appeared not to be battery powered, and was not the "For Her" product she had expected.

A user called Shamil Khan submitted:

> AS a Muslim I find this pen very provocative with its look at me colouring and curvy contours. I believe Bic should be more sensitive to Muslim

men like me who may wish to take this pen out in public by providing a Black covering and also a disclaimer stating that this pen is unsuitable for driving or having an opinion of its own.

Learnings

This differs somewhat from the flashmob reviews of Veet in that, in this case, the reviewers are mocking the entire premise that there is a market gap to be filled. In the Veet case, the amusing reviews are an abuse of the process. In this case, it seems to reflect the actual views of the Amazon community. In fairness, we should acknowledge that the product may be selling extremely well. This would not be apparent from the review process. It is not likely that people who are happy with the product would post reviews. Who reviews a pen?

Given the apparent absence of serious reviews, there is a case for saying Amazon is simply the wrong forum for selling this product – although the author suggests this tentatively, without knowing the level of sales. The product is consistently ridiculed by the Amazon community, and the claims made by the manufacturer are mocked. There doesn't seem to be an obvious way of combating this, since it is not likely that happy customers can be persuaded to write positive reviews for an inexpensive and transactional product. The community would be unlikely to vote such a review to the top of the pile, even if any were submitted.

☒ What Bic did wrong

- It portrayed the value of the product in a risibly patronizing way.
- It failed to anticipate the level of mockery that the Amazon community would inflict on the product.

SELF BRANDJACK	This product was always open to ridicule, and the Amazon space is obviously open to that use.
AGGREGATION BRANDJACK	People gather to make a point about a product.
UNANTICIPATED RESPONSE BRANDJACK	Community mocks patronizing product.

128 Barack Obama: International Talk Like A Pirate Day
September 2012

Brands are often happy to jump on fake "holidays" to demonstrate how fun they are. The US president is no different. And why should he be? He is one of the most followed brands in social media. So when it came to International

Talk Like A Pirate Day, it seemed like a fun idea to issue a photo of the president apparently engaged in a conversation with a pirate, complete with eyepatch, hook and fake beard (the pirate, that is). Unfortunately, there is also a serious side to being president of the US. People – starting with the Drudge Report – were happy to contrast the president's issuing of the photograph with his unavailability to meet with Benjamin Netanyahu, the Israeli prime minister. The picture, along with sarcastic remarks about the important demands on the president's time, was shared throughout the social space.

The dichotomy – at least as regards the Netanyahu non-meeting – was not as great as it seemed. The picture had actually been taken three years earlier, and the "pirate" was a White House speech writer. Although, of course, Obama had been president at that time too. And the White House could hardly blame blogs and the Twitterati for sharing a photo the White House itself had issued from the @barackobama account.

Learnings

Fun pictures can be fun, but it is probably worth considering how something amusing might be contrasted with the serious issues you also deal with. This is especially the case for a controversial brand with (almost) as many detractors as supporters, which is the normal situation in politics.

✓ What the White House did right

- It tried to join in the fun.

✗ What the White House did wrong

- It failed to consider the serious issues and how the picture might backfire.

SELF BRANDJACK It is always important to remember, not everyone in social media wishes you well.

129 Mitt Romney: 47%
September 2012

In what may have been the most important and defining story of the 2012 election, Mitt Romney was exposed as saying in a private meeting that some 47% of American voters are "dependent on government" and would "vote for the president no matter what."

This is going to be a pattern at elections from now on: stories filmed on camera phones and uploaded to YouTube will provide turning points in elections around the world. The biggest embarrassment to hit Gordon Brown in the UK 2010 general election was from the MSM – he forgot he was still wearing a microphone from Sky News. It is not new for politicians to be caught unawares in semi-public environments: in the 2001 general election, Tony Blair was harangued by the partner of a cancer patient, and in 2006 Senator George Allen was filmed by a camera-operator working for his opponent and used an apparently racist nickname for the cameraman. But the 47% remark was different. Romney was in a private meeting and was speaking to fundraisers at a private home. It is not known who recorded the remarks, but they were apparently recorded in May, some four months before the story was leaked to the Huffington Post.[27]

Romney said:

> There are 47% of the people who will vote for the president no matter what. All right, there are 47% who are with him, who are dependent upon government, who believe that they are victims, who believe the government has a responsibility to care for them, who believe that they are entitled to health care, to food, to housing, to you-name-it – that that's an entitlement. And the government should give it to them. And they will vote for this president no matter what. And I mean the president starts off with 48, 49 … he starts off with a huge number. These are people who pay no income tax. Forty-seven per cent of Americans pay no income tax. So our message of low taxes doesn't connect. So he'll be out there talking about tax cuts for the rich … My job is not to worry about those people. I'll never convince them they should take personal responsibility and care for their lives. What I have to do is convince the 5–10% in the center that are independents, that are thoughtful, that look at voting one way or the other depending upon in some cases emotion, whether they like the guy or not.

It is worth noting that Romney's political analysis here is open to an obvious challenge. If people only ever cast their votes according to whether or not they are net payers or receivers of tax money, the Republican Party has a much bigger problem than Romney suggests. The number of voters who would be with the Democrats "no matter what" would *start* with the 47% who pay no federal income tax at all, but there are others, especially seniors, who pay some income tax but, at the same time, receive social security (pensions) and Medicare (free healthcare) from the government worth far more than the tax they pay. A great deal of the federal government is financed by taxes levied on a small proportion of the population.

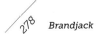

Learnings

This is politics, and Mitt Romney himself, despite keeping somewhat out of public life since losing the election, has been pressed to comment on the issue several times. Contrasting things with "twenty five or thirty years ago," Romney commented "everything you say is being recorded. That's just the nature of politics today, and you have to get over it and live with it."[28]

During the campaign itself, he tried to explain that the point he was trying to make was that a message of tax cuts, inevitably, has limited appeal to people who don't pay taxes, but since the campaign, he has conceded that his comment was "just completely wrong."

It left him open to jibes that the president needs to be president of all the people, contrasting with Romney's remark *"my job is not to worry about those people."* Of course, the "job" he was talking about was candidate, not president, but that is a subtle distinction to communicate, and his message reinforced the Democrats' position that he was the candidate of and for the super-rich.

It is fruitless to speculate about what might have been. Fruitless, but fun. Half a percent more in the polls would have given him Florida – a state with a great many net recipients of federal benefits. He would have needed an extra two points to get both Ohio and Virginia, and he would still have come up short in the Electoral College without New Hampshire, where he would have needed almost three points, although two points would have been enough to give him a lead in the popular vote.

☒ What Romney did wrong

- He inelegantly expressed his view, if you believe his later clarification, or perhaps just said what he really thought.
- He forgot that there is no such thing as a private meeting when you are seeking the most public office in the world.

SELF BRANDJACK Badly judged remark, leaked with great precision.

130 **Berman and Sherman nearly come to blows**
October 2012

At the 2012 elections, California was using new district boundaries drawn on a nonpartisan basis for the first time. Previously, the district boundaries had been drawn mostly to preserve incumbents. The result was several elections in which two members of Congress faced off against each other using a new electoral system of a nonpartisan primary, with the top two contesting the general election. The most closely fought was between Brad Sherman and Howard Berman – both Democratic members of the House of Representatives – who very nearly came to blows. The event was filmed on a phone and uploaded to YouTube, where it rapidly went viral.

The video seems to show the taller, 56-year-old Sherman pulling the 71-year-old Berman toward him and yelling "you want to get into this?" Berman appears visibly shocked, and a uniformed security officer moves on to the stage to separate them.

This confrontation did not prevent Sherman from going on to win the election by a 60:40 margin. Sherman had been the favorite all along, as about 60 percent of the new district had previously been in his district. Berman had previously represented about 20 percent of the voters. Berman had been backed by around two-thirds of the other California Democratic representatives, while Sherman had secured the valuable endorsement of former President Bill Clinton.

Learnings

If you are in public, there is no such thing as private any more. Politicians – and others who depend on the support of the public – need to assume they are always on camera. In a crowded room, especially a political debate, the chance that someone is recording on their phone is extremely high and the footage can be on YouTube in seconds. Sherman should certainly have realized that his behavior – which was rude on any reading – could easily have been taken as threatening by the older and smaller man.

X What Sherman did wrong

- He apparently forgot that anything he does and says in the heat of the moment is probably being filmed and can be broadcast instantly around the world.

SELF BRANDJACK Sherman – much the younger and larger man – behaved boorishly at best.

131 The BlackBerry as black sheep
October 2012

The New York Times ran an article on the declining popularity of the Black-Berry and the phone's maker, RIM, which has since changed its name to BlackBerry.[29] This provoked an immediate response from RIM, which claimed the paper did not contact the company before producing the article. If true, it is a possible breach of journalistic ethics or good practice. BlackBerry users also responded, with a number of celebrities, including Piers Morgan, posting their support for the embattled company and its products. Like Morgan, social media guru Donny Halliwell was using the #TeamBlackBerry hashtag.

But there is no fightback in social media that will be ignored. This is especially true in the smartphone market, where product lines have dedicated bands of fans, often hostile to users of other products.

#TeamBlackBerry was pretty successful. There is a Facebook page with 28 million likes, which compares favorably with 21 million for iPhone, although there is a separate Apple page with 10 million likes: not necessarily different people from the iPhone likers.

Despite allegations of technical problems (this author can confirm them. His Bold was twice caught in a recursive loop, which meant wiping all data on the first occasion and a repair, in reality a replacement, on the second), BlackBerry has retained a loyal fanbase, which it has been able to deploy during a difficult time.

The arrival of the BlackBerry 10 was "announced" in a cleverly staged stunt. The CEO and a vice-president were seen using their new models at an NBA game. Nearer the launch, 20 members of the #TeamBlackBerry blogging community were given advance models to review.

Learnings

BlackBerry, like its competitors, has an engaged group of users and fans. If the product is seen to fail, people will be critical and in a loud way. BlackBerry created the smartphone market, and its users are often early adopters. They are connected.

But the company has proved adept at using its fans to counter its critics. People see their choice of smartphone as saying something about them: BlackBerry is the business or professional user; Android is the uber-geek; iPhone is stylish and trendy. People have also invested in familiarity with systems and in the purchase of apps. They don't shift platforms without a good reason. (At the most trivial level, upgrading to the latest model in the same line often gives you a spare charger, whereas shifting lines does not.) This both deepens the base of support that a smartphone operator can tap into, but also heightens the emotional reaction of fans who feel "betrayed" by an upgrade that goes wrong.

☒ What BlackBerry did wrong

- It left some in its fanbase feeling neglected and let down by technical failures.

☑ What BlackBerry did right

- It recruited its high-profile, connected fans to lead the fightback.

CUSTOMER REVOLT BRANDJACK Smartphone operator neglects its fanbase, then fights back.

132 Mitt Romney: binders full of women
October 2012

How can you take a generally positive record on appointing women to senior positions and make it seem ridiculous, while bringing to the fore of a campaign issues that you would rather not have debated? Answer, come up with a nerdy phrase that reminds people of your awkwardness, which will be mocked within minutes of your uttering it.

In the second presidential debate, Mitt Romney pointed out that he had a good record of appointing women to his cabinet when he was governor of Massachusetts. He claimed that the first group of names put to him were all men, so he approached women's groups and asked for résumés of qualified women and they responded with "binders full of women." The phrase was awkward, and was likely to remind people of Romney's gilded life as the son of a state governor and a hugely successful businessman. This is the man who had said of his relationship with suppliers "I like being able to fire people," often misquoted as "I like firing people." In the 2008 primary season, Mike Huckabee contrasted himself with Romney, saying that people wanted to vote for someone who reminds them of the guy they work with, not the guy who laid them off.

While the debate was still being broadcast, the phrase "binders full of women" was already trending on Twitter. A parody account on Twitter, purporting to be a binder owned by Mitt Romney, had 30,000 followers *before the debate was even over.* The following day, there was a parody Facebook page with 274,000 likes. Social media move very, very fast. It is worth noting that the Twitter account might well have existed (and had followers) before the debate. The reference to Romney's "binders" could have been a name change for an existing account.

Romney's critics also took to Amazon, where they posted reviews of binders being offered for sale saying either that they were suitable or unsuitable for women. Others voted these reviews to the top.

Supporters of Romney tried to return to the issue he was seeking to raise, and pointed out that his record in office of appointing women to positions could be compared favorably with other governors and President Obama. Opponents preferred either to mock him for his awkwardness, or widen the debate to women's issues generally, including the Republican Party's position on abortion, and some embarrassing Senate candidates making fatuous statements about rape.

Learnings

Romney was widely agreed to have won the first presidential debate, and to have acquitted himself well in the other two. Even the president joked that he was well rested for the second debate "after the nice long nap I took during the first."[30]

This experience shows, more than anything, that the social media age puts a premium on consistency. Even a small stumble, especially one that leaves you open to ridicule, can damage a campaign. Social media are especially suitable for satire and mockery. The sheer speed with which this Internet meme took off demonstrates the versatility of social media, especially when there is an entrenched group of people in the camp of your opponents.

✓ What Mitt Romney did right

- He was consistent and clear in his debates – commanding, even, in the first.

✗ What Mitt Romney did wrong

- It was an embarrassing slip, and it played to issues that didn't work for him.

SELF BRANDJACK A verbal slip, which might just have revealed something about Romney's psychology and view of employment.

133 Jack Welch queries US unemployment numbers
October 2012

Jack Welch, the legendary former CEO of GE, queried US unemployment figures in the month before the presidential election, suggesting dishonesty by "these Chicago guys." The main "Chicago guy" was, presumably, the president of the US, as his chief of staff of the day was Jack Lew, born in New York and spending most of his professional career in Washington DC. Obama's first two chiefs of staff were both "Chicago guys;" in fact, Rahm Emanuel left the White House to become mayor of Chicago and was replaced by the brother of his mayoral predecessor.

The full Welch tweet said: "Unbelievable jobs numbers … these Chicago guys will do anything … can't debate so change numbers." He later suggested that he should have ended it with a question mark instead of a full stop, to indicate that he was raising questions. Welch was inundated with criticism for his tweet, varying from people disagreeing with his interpretation to people attacking his business record. GE grew in value by 4,000 percent during his 20-year tenure, but lost jobs and his policy was to dismiss the weakest 10 percent of managers each year.

People also suggested, wrongly, that Welch was affiliated with the Romney campaign and that his wife once worked with Romney. (She worked at Bain Consulting. Mitt Romney was a founder of Bain Capital.)

Welch responded with an article in the *Wall Street Journal* setting out his views in more detail.[31] Although he made a good case that the figures were not particularly reliable, he cited no evidence that they had been deliberately changed to suit the political agenda of the president, or any other "Chicago guy." Welch challenged the reliability of the way the data is collected and pointed out that the headline fall in unemployment from 8.1 to 7.8 percent was mostly due to people dropping out of the job market altogether, not to people finding jobs. Depressing news appeared to be good news through what the liberal *New York Times* called a statistical fluke. But a fluke is not the "Chicago guys" changing the figures.

Learnings

The limit of 140 characters is not much space to get across your message, so be prepared to defend what you meant, and what you appeared to be saying, which may not always be the same. Welch should have anticipated that he would attract a storm of criticism.

This is politics, not business. Brands have devoted followers who will attack anyone who appears to be "dissing" their side. It is not surprising it got personal, especially as Welch's original tweet also seemed personal.

☑ What Welch did right

- He queried some surprising numbers that were out of line with general economic trends.

☒ What Welch did wrong

- He suggested a deliberate dishonesty in the figures, which he failed to back up.
- He made it a personal slight on the president's integrity.

SELF BRANDJACK An error of judgment rather bigger than missing out the question mark.

134 Lord McAlpine: false allegations of child abuse
November 2012

The BBC ran a documentary about a long-running child abuse investigation into care homes in North Wales, in which the corporation implicated a "senior Conservative" politician. Rumors were soon circulating on social media, fanned, in part, by a number of high-profile figures such as Sally Bercow, Alan Davies, and George Monbiot. It soon emerged that the rumors linking the abuse to Lord McAlpine were wholly false, as has now been accepted by all parties.

Newsnight, BBC Two's flagship news program, was already embroiled in scandal before this story broke. Ironically, it was under fire for not following through on a story about sexual abuse in which longstanding BBC star, Jimmy Savile, was implicated. Having failed to make true allegations against Savile, it went on to make untrue allegations against McAlpine. The program was promoted in advance by tweeting the suggestion that it would make significant revelations.

The program did not name McAlpine, but it was always likely, given the number of people who knew it was he the program had in mind, that the name would leak. Given that the BBC was positively promoting discussion around the program on Twitter, this likelihood was greatly enhanced. The allegation was made by one of the victims of child abuse, but normal journalistic checks were not carried out.

It is necessary to understand that McAlpine, while fairly prominent in politics in the 1980s, was not a household name. He was treasurer of the Conservative Party – an appointed position responsible for fundraising. This author, although a political columnist, could not, offhand, name the current holder of that position, let alone recognize that person on the street. It is beyond belief that a child in a care home could reliably make the identification. While it does seem possible that an abuser would claim to be someone powerful and influential, in order to intimidate a victim into silence, it should cross a journalist's mind that a child abuser just might lie about his identity. Despite this, the victim was never shown a picture of McAlpine and asked if he was, indeed, the abuser, and the BBC did not contact McAlpine for a comment. An ITV presenter brandished a piece of paper containing McAlpine's name, which, when examined by freeze frame, was legible.

After the broadcast, and after McAlpine's name had been trending on Twitter, someone did show the victim a picture of McAlpine, and he immediately confirmed that this was *not* the person who had abused him. He also publicly apologized to McAlpine, whose name, by this point, had been fairly widely reported. The BBC and ITV both apologized profusely and made substantial payments in settlement of the libel which, at McAlpine's direction, went to the BBC charity, Children in Need. McAlpine also pursued damages against several prominent social media personalities. Monbiot and Davies apologized immediately, and Monbiot agreed to work for charities to the value of £25,000. Sally Bercow, however, denied that her tweet had been libelous.

The text of Bercow's tweet was: "Why is Lord McAlpine trending? *innocent face*." In court, the phrase "innocent face" became the subject of dispute. McAlpine claimed it was meant insincerely, and was meant to suggest that Bercow knew exactly why, and, given the simultaneous speculation about the identity of the "senior Conservative," would lead people to the conclusion that McAlpine was the person. Bercow claimed that the phrase was meant to be taken sincerely, which the judge rejected. At that point, Bercow reached a settlement with McAlpine. As several Twitterati commented: "Why is Sally Bercow trending? *libel face*."

George Entwistle, director general (DG) of the BBC and a former editor of *Newsnight,* was interviewed by John Humphrys on BBC Radio 4's *Today* program. In a genuinely astonishing (and Sony award-winning) piece of journalism, Humphrys went some way to restoring the BBC's reputation, while utterly destroying that of his boss. The 15-minute evisceration of Entwistle was so comprehensive that the DG resigned later that day, after just 54 days in post.

Learnings

We are in the age of transparency. It is no longer enough to keep someone's name, officially, quiet. Journalists need to assume that names will leak. The nod and the wink of "we know who we mean, but we won't tell you" does not work anymore. And if you allude to allegations this serious on Twitter, you had better be prepared to defend yourself in court.

☒ What the BBC did wrong

- It failed to check its story sufficiently.
- It thought it could defend itself from a libel suit by not publicly revealing the name.
- It thought it could provoke conversation on Twitter without taking the consequences.

☑ What the BBC did right

- It allowed John Humphrys the freedom to interview his boss aggressively.
- It apologized and settled.
- It took responsibility, right at the top of the corporation.

| SELF BRANDJACK | Shoddy journalism, somewhat redeemed by outstanding journalism after the event. |

135 Oprah endorses Microsoft Surface – in a tweet from an iPad

November 2012

Oprah Winfrey's media power is unmatched and her endorsement of products is immensely powerful. For relatively unknown brands, getting onto Oprah's show can be hugely significant. That makes it all the more important that her endorsement is seen to be an honest reflection of her opinion. Indications that it is not need to be managed carefully.

Although Twitter no longer displays the client or device used to send a tweet, some Twitter clients do, and users were able to get a screen grab of the tweet that clearly showed "via Twitter for iPad." The full tweet read: "Gotta say love that SURFACE! Have bought 12 already for Christmas gifts. #FavoriteThings."

Defenders of Oprah point out that there was no indication whether or not Oprah personally sent the tweet. It may have been sent by a member of her social media team, meaning it might have reflected her personal view, even if some of her staff use iPads. Other explanations offered were that she might genuinely love Surface but still use iPad for some purposes. There was no Twitter app for Surface at the time, although it is still possible to use Twitter.com. It has also been pointed out that "Favorite Things" is a specialized Oprah term. To qualify, companies must be willing to give away a copy of the product to every person in her studio audience. Apple is notoriously stingy about such things. Still, the wording of the tweet clearly implies that Oprah personally prefers the Surface tablet to its competitors. The fact that the tweet was sent via an iPad casts some doubt on that.

The story raced all over social media, and was picked up in the MSM, including *Time* and Business Insider.[32] Yet, still, there was no comment from Oprah herself. Several plausible and reasonable explanations were doing the rounds, but none of them came from Oprah. Was she hoping that if she ignored the story it would go away? Once it was in *Time* that seems rather unlikely. Or was she just not willing to put her name to any of the plausible explanations being offered?

Months later, the praise of Surface is still on her website – she describes it as being like a Mercedes-Benz – but no explanation of the rogue tweet is supplied.

Learnings

For a star to endorse a product simply for the money and without explaining that and to do so while actually preferring a major a competitor would be an outrageous breach of trust. In the UK, the Advertising Standards Authority requires celebrities to use the hashtag #ad when endorsing a product for money. If any one of the several reasonable explanations for the misstep is true, why did Oprah remain silent through a social media and MSM storm? Months later, these questions are still unanswered.

☒ What Oprah did wrong

- She may have breached her fans' trust.
- She certainly sat quietly through a media crisis, refusing to explain the apparent discrepancy.

SELF BRANDJACK This was, at best, a careless misstep that was badly handled and never explained.

136 Cheerios memories app hijacked by GMO activists
November 2012

Cheerios – the General Mills cereal brand – invited its community to share their childhood memories of the brand on its Facebook page and via a smartphone app. It was an interesting experiment in brand co-creation, but was immediately hijacked by critics of the brand opposed to genetic modification. Brand co-creation, in which communities are invited to develop concepts they associate with the brand, is one of the great themes of social media marketing. But, as with the McDonald's campaign, #McDStories (CS 98), it leaves the company open to brandjacking.

In this case, the Cheerios brand – often associated with childhood and babies' transition to solid food – had a great many memories to tap into. Cheerios is a fairly healthy cereal, not loaded with fat or sugar, which even led to a dispute with the American FDA over whether the health claims the company made about the foodstuff made it an "unapproved drug."

The dispute with GMO activists arose when General Mills made a donation to the campaign against California's Proposition 37, an initiative that would have required labeling of all food products containing GMOs (genetically modified organisms) and would have banned foods containing any genetically engineered products from using the word "natural" in labeling or advertising. This led to a widespread suspicion that some General Mills products – although not necessarily Cheerios – contain GMOs. General Mills maintains that, in common with most of the food industry, it has a policy of opposing state-by-state labeling laws, which would add to industry costs.

As in many brandjacking cases, the brand was being targeted for the perceived failings at a corporate level rather than any associated with the brand itself. Greenpeace targeted Kit Kat because Nestlé used palm oil purchased from Sinar Mas, not necessarily because it used palm oil in Kit Kats. This makes a lot of sense to activists, as sometimes the overarching corporation is relatively anonymous compared with the strength of the individual brands.

The activists' campaign was successful, in that it overwhelmed the Cheerios Facebook page, and the brand even stopped posting on its own page for a while. It did not achieve success in the way that the Greenpeace campaigns against Nestlé, Burger King, Mattel, and Unilever all did, probably because the campaign didn't have a simple and achievable goal. Greenpeace wanted the target companies to boycott Sinar Mas and APP – relatively small parts of the supply chain. This was an instance of a retaliatory strike at General Mills over its opposition to Proposition 37, a measure that had already (narrowly) been defeated before the campaign began.

Learnings

It is arguable that General Mills should have anticipated this. Proposition 37 was controversial, and was defeated in a vote on the same day as the presidential election, in November 2012. Launching a brand co-creation initiative in the immediate aftermath of that vote was always going to be risky.

The relatively limited statement that the group put out – explaining that it opposes state-by-state labeling laws, but not really elaborating on its position vis-à-vis GMOs – was probably wise. Arguing the merits of genetic modification was not likely to win many converts. If the company does not use GMOs, it could, of course, say so, and even adopt voluntary labeling, which it could apply across the board, without the need for different labels in different states. That it has not done so raises suspicions that it does, in fact, use GMOs.

But a voluntary labeling policy would be a big step. A company that labeled some of its products and not others would, rightly, attract charges of hypocrisy. Why make the claim for product X if you don't think GMOs are dangerous, and, if you do, stop using them in product Y. And a labeling policy is more than a temporary statement regarding your supply chain. Effectively, it would become a commitment not to use GMOs in the future, as abandoning the labels later would be a big deal. A company that doesn't happen to use GMOs, but has no particular policy of avoiding them, would be unwise to adopt the labeling approach.

☑ What Cheerios did right

- This was an imaginative and potentially effective campaign.
- Once the Facebook page was hijacked, it refrained from closing down the debate.

☒ What Cheerios did wrong

- It failed to anticipate that launching a campaign against the immediate background of Proposition 37 was going to be problematic.

SELF BRANDJACK Imaginative campaign, launched at an unfortunate time.

ETHICS BRANDJACK Many activists feel strongly about GMOs, and this issue is not going to disappear.

137 American Apparel ad withdrawn after ASA ruling
December 2012

American Apparel has long had a history of controversy. The company uses advertising that has been accused of bordering on the pornographic and has taken a stance in favor of legalizing illegal immigrants to the US and in favor of gay marriage. In December 2012, one of its ads was criticized by the UK Advertising Standards Authority (ASA) for sexualizing youth. American Apparel criticized the ruling, but also agreed to abide by it, and withdrew the ad in the UK.

American Apparel likes to take stands. One of the most fundamental is its pledge that its clothing is made in the US and "sweatshop-free." Alongside that is the commitment to "Legalize LA," a campaign in favor of undocumented (that is, illegal) immigrants in Los Angeles, and its support of "Legalize Gay," a campaign against Proposition 8, the measure that banned gay marriage in California.

The company's controversial advertising has made use of former porn actors and has been widely criticized for its overt sexuality. The ad the ASA admonished featured a model who was apparently 23 at the time of the photoshoot, but looks much younger, and is described by the ASA as "having sexual undertones and a voyeuristic quality." The ASA ruling was that the ad "inappropriately sexualized a model who appeared to be a child and was therefore irresponsible."[33]

As part of its defense of the ad, American Apparel cited the fact that it had been featured in the adult magazine, *Vice*. To those who believe that the ad promotes pedophilia or, at best, hebephilia (attraction to early adolescents, likely to be underage, but post-pubescent), the chosen medium would probably have exacerbated the bad taste of the ad.

The company commented:

> We'll abide by this ruling as we have in the past with similar ASA decisions, but American Apparel will not be altering our classic advertising aesthetic which is internationally recognized for its artistic and social values.[34]

Learnings

Controversy has always been a way of raising a brand's profile, and one American Apparel has deliberately courted. Taking a political stance, especially on divisive issues, drives conversation. Ads that are considered by many to be in bad taste – especially those that are banned – drive conversation. The social media age is all about conversation. American Apparel is well plugged in, with a well-liked Facebook page. At the time of writing, some months after the ASA banned the ad, the Facebook page still features the same model, although in a different pose. Comments have not been disabled, as several commentators criticize the picture for using such a young looking girl. Such comments are the overwhelming tone of reaction to that particular picture. The page as a whole has almost 1.5 million likes. American Apparel is fully engaged with Twitter, with several corporate accounts and others for particular countries.

 What American Apparel did right

- It has engaged strongly with its audience and encourages debate on controversial issues.

✗ What American Apparel did wrong

- For all the talk about "artistic and social values," this ad crosses a line.

SELF BRANDJACK Deliberately courting controversy can go too far.

138 CB2 apologizes for wallet mocking the homeless
December 2012

The blogger Jezebel slated CB2 for selling the "Lucky Beggar Wallet," a product designed to look like the iconic white and blue coffee cups of New York City, which are often used by panhandlers to hold their donations.[35]

CB2 is the younger, trendier arm of home furnishings retailer Crate & Barrel, itself established when its founders were only 23 (albeit in the 1960s). The company has a strong presence in social media. While this means that the company would have been well placed to fight back, if it had wanted to, it also suggests its target market is heavily engaged in social media, making the company vulnerable to brandjacking.

Certainly, CB2 did not make a stand on this, issuing an immediate statement to Yahoo!'s Shine blog:[36]

> We made a bad decision when we purchased this product. We apologize for the product and the insensitive language used in its description. We

have pulled the product from our stores and our website. Please accept our apologies for this lapse in judgment.

The group then used its Twitter and Facebook presence to tackle the issue strongly, reiterating the apology.

The product is still available from other outlets, and has both positive and negative reviews on Amazon. The top-rated reviews are positive. The negative comments all focus on the argument that the product mocks the homeless, including one reference to the fact that the product was pulled by CB2.

Learnings

It is interesting that campaigners did not make much of the victory over CB2 by redirecting the campaign elsewhere. There seems to be no concerted campaign against Amazon, for example, a company that would certainly keep the negative reviews posted on its page. Although Amazon has a record of taking a stand for freedom of speech, it is not likely that it would regard retailing a third-party product that takes no particular stand on any issue, but is seen by some as being offensive, as being comparable to its duty to promote free speech as a publisher.

CB2 reacted immediately to the campaign, which seems to have then fizzled.

☑ What CB2 did right

- It apologized immediately and withdrew the product from sale.
- It followed up in social media to allay ongoing concerns.

ETHICS BRANDJACK   Retailer criticized for insensitivity to the plight of the homeless.

139 NASA publishes "Why the World Didn't End" video early
December 2012

NASA (National Aeronautics and Space Administration) produced an interesting educational video discussing the end of the Mayan calendar, and discussing astronomical risks that could bring an end to the world (at least as we know it), such as a near Earth object colliding with the planet. It began by announcing the date as December 22, 2012 and reporting that the world didn't end yesterday. Unfortunately, it published it on December 14. This would presumably have been embarrassing if the world actually had ended a week later, although – depending on the suddenness of the cataclysm – no one might have noticed.

The connection between astronomy and calendars is fundamental. In Heinlein's story *Universe,* set in a civilization that has spent generations in the interior of a spacecraft and become disconnected from its past, the characters have no notion of astronomy or any way of measuring time. The fundamental units for measuring time – year, month, day – are all astronomical phenomena, so Heinlein's characters do not even understand the concept of measuring time. This makes NASA the ultimate authority for measuring time, and explains why all time zones are measured with respect to the time of day at the Royal Observatory in Greenwich, London.

The Mayan civilization was remarkable for its attitude to measuring time. Its long count calendar goes back a billion billion times further than the big bang. But, while estimating the universe to be very much older than it really is, Mayans thought the Earth was much younger, believing that it was created on August 11, 3114 BC. That was not the beginning of the Mayan calendar, though, it was already on 13 baktuns. On 21 December 2012, the calendar rolled round to 13 baktuns again. But, according to NASA, that was never meant to indicate the end of the world. The author, writing in 2013, can certainly confirm that the world did not end, but NASA, publishing the film a week early, had no similar absolute assurance.

Learnings

One of the great features of digital technologies is that they enable precisely controlled release of material. In crisis communications, financial PR, and many other fields, this is a powerful weapon. But it is a little embarrassing when the ultimate authority on the passing of time gets its calendar wrong.

✓ What NASA did right

- It engaged with a popular media story to meet its objective of communicating science in a popular and understandable way.

✗ What NASA did wrong

- It forgot to check its calendar, Mayan or otherwise.

SELF BRANDJACK A silly mistake, but one that probably attracted more attention to the video than it would otherwise have received.

140 NRA opts for social media silence after Newtown school massacre

December 2012

On Friday December 14, Adam Lanza killed 27 people (including himself), 20 of whom were children, mostly at Sandy Hook Elementary School in Newtown, Connecticut. Immediately, advocates of gun control began using this event to press their cause. President Obama referred to his support for gun control at his press conference on the issue. By contrast, gun-rights group the National Rifle Association (NRA) stayed silent throughout the weekend, commenting for the first time the following Tuesday.

The NRA issued no comments to the media during this time, stopped tweeting, and closed comments on its Facebook page. In its statement on December 18, the group said its silence had been out of respect for the victims. The NRA was heavily criticized for its silence, although there seems little doubt that it would have been criticized if it had responded. If the NRA had pointed out that the killing took place in a legally enforced gun-free zone, as spree killings nearly always do, where no one other than the killer was armed, the group would most certainly have been accused of politicizing the tragedy. This charge was not widely made against the president or other gun-control advocates.

Was there a response that the NRA could have made? Many people – passionately and sincerely – believe that gun control would have reduced the probability of a tragedy like the Sandy Hook shooting. Others, with equal passion and sincerity, believe that gun control – or "victim disarmament", as gun-rights advocates call it – greatly exacerbates such tragedies. If one side in this debate is willing, and able, to use mass killings as examples for its case, should the other side not also participate? No debate is better for the silence of one side.

As in many political debates, there is not enough willingness on any side to concede the sincerity and goodwill of opponents. Critics of the NRA come close to arguing that it favors mass killings and its supporters fear that the government needs to confiscate weapons from private citizens to advance some other nefarious ends.

Learnings

Closing comments on its Facebook page – where the group had 1.7 million likes at the time – was probably a wise move. Not only was the page likely to be a magnet for people criticizing the group, but

The case studies: 2012

NRA supporters would certainly have argued back. Independent supporters of the group could have used an NRA-branded page to put arguments the group would not have approved of, and those arguments would then have been taken out of context and attributed to the group. Imagine, for example, if one person had posted that the killings "served Connecticut right" for introducing gun-free zones. Even the argument that the gun-free zone policy may have contributed to the problem would have enraged people with a different view.

But, the total silence was almost certainly a mistake. Why wait until Tuesday to say that your policy of not commenting is out of respect for those killed? The group could have said that immediately. It could also have argued that it would be wrong to politicize the tragedy by engaging in the legitimate debate about policy before funerals – both explaining its own position and, by implication, condemning those of the other persuasion for doing what the NRA refrained from doing.

✓ What the NRA did right

- It refrained from politicizing the tragedy.
- It closed its Facebook page to comments at a time of high passions on both sides.

✗ What the NRA did wrong

- It opted for complete silence, without even explaining its policy.

 By not commenting, the NRA left itself open to the charge that it was hiding from the issue.

Notes

1   *The Telegraph*: www.telegraph.co.uk/news/worldnews/europe/italy/9022477/Costa-Concordia-Italians-buy-t-shirts-with-Get-back-on-board-for-s-sake-logo.html, accessed 01/20/2014.

2   Holtje, J. (2011) *The Power of Storytelling*. New York: Penguin.

3   *NY Daily News*: www.nydailynews.com/entertainment/tv-movies/oprah-winfrey-apologizes-tweet-improperly-asked-nielsen-subscribers-tune-article-1.1021906, accessed 01/20/2014.

4   Claire's Facebook page: https://www.facebook.com/claires/posts/10150686855570342, accessed 01/20/2014.

5   *New York Times*: www.nytimes.com/2012/03/14/opinion/why-i-am-leaving-goldman-sachs.html?pagewanted=all&_r=0, accessed 01/20/2014.

6   Daily Mash: www.thedailymash.co.uk/news/society/why-i-am-leaving-the-empire-by-darth-vader-201203145007, accessed 01/20/2014.

7   Jon Mitchell: readwrite.com/2012/03/11/sxsw_in_a_nutshell_homeless_people_as_hotspots#awesm=~otta139ThMGaLS, accessed 01/20/2014.

8   As a vegetarian, the author makes a declaration of disinterest in the debate about this product's safety.

9   PR Daily: www.prdaily.com/Main/Articles/3_PR_lessons_from_Heinekens_bizarre_dogfighting_cr_11435.aspx#, accessed 01/20/2014.

10   League Against Cruel Sports: www.league.org.uk/news/689/Heineken-sponsors-bullfighting, accessed 01/20/2014.

11   PR Daily: prdaily.com/Main/Articles/9_social_media_crisis_questions_Dole_failed_to_ans_11436.aspx, accessed 01/20/2014.

12   *Sydney Morning Herald*: www.smh.com.au/world/secret-service-gets-cinderella-curfew-at-obamas-ball-20120429-1xsm2.html, accessed 01/20/2014.

13   *New York Times*: www.nytimes.com/2012/05/31/world/europe/poland-bristles-as-obama-says-polish-death-camps.html?_r=0, accessed 01/20/2014.

14   *Wall Street Journal*: http://online.wsj.com/news/articles/SB10001424052702303815404577335551794808074.

15   CNN: money.cnn.com/2012/05/13/technology/yahoo-ceo-out.

16   The tradition of seven colors is somewhat arbitrary. The Oreo version merged indigo and violet.

17   *New York Times*: www.nytimes.com/2012/06/11/world/europe/many-voices-of-sweden-via-twitter.html, accessed 01/20/2014.

18   *The Telegraph*: www.telegraph.co.uk/education/educationnews/9333163/Martha-Payne-girls-hit-school-dinner-blog-NeverSeconds-banned-by-council.html, accessed 01/20/2014.

19   Reuters: in.reuters.com/article/2012/06/13/usa-lance-armstrong-doping-idINDEE85C0GE20120613, accessed 01/20/2014.

20   PR Daily: www.prdaily.com/Main/Articles/Pranksters_target_Shell_with_fake_news_release_and_11862.aspx, accessed 01/20/2014.

21   *The Telegraph*: www.telegraph.co.uk/sport/olympics/9469478/London-2012-Olympics-Sexism-row-over-BMWs-for-the-boys.html, accessed 01/20/2014.

22   Matt Fisher: mattfisher.tumblr.com/post/29338478278/my-sister-paid-progressive-insurance-to-defend-her, accessed 01/20/2014.

23   *New York Times*: www.nytimes.com/2012/08/18/your-money/progressives-side-of-the-insurance-case-that-blew-up-on-the-internet.html, accessed 01/20/2014.

24   PR Daily: www.prdaily.com/Main/Articles/Worst_kind_of_PR_nonsense_How_Progressive_botched_12433.aspx, accessed 01/20/2014.

25   *The Plain Dealer*: www.cleveland.com/business/index.ssf/2012/08/progressive_corp_stung_by_bad.html, accessed 01/20/2014.

26   Amazon: www.amazon.co.uk/BIC-For-Her-Medium-Ballpoint/dp/B004FTGJUW, accessed 01/20/2014.

27   Mother Jones: www.motherjones.com/politics/2012/09/secret-video-romney-private-fundraiser, accessed 01/20/2014.

28   Huffington Post: www.huffingtonpost.com/2013/06/06/mitt-romney-upset-47-percent_n_3397283.html, accessed 01/20/2014.

29   *New York Times*: www.nytimes.com/2012/10/16/technology/blackberry-becomes-a-source-of-shame-for-users.html, accessed 01/20/2014.

30   *NY Daily News*: www.nydailynews.com/news/election-2012/obama-romeny-share-laughs-al-smith-gala-article-1.1187248, accessed 01/20/2014.

31   *Wall Street Journal*: online.wsj.com/news/articles/SB10000872396390444897304578046 260406091012, accessed 01/20/2014.

32   Business Insider: www.businessinsider.com/oprah-surface-tweets-ipad-2012-11, accessed 01/20/2014.

33   Advertising Standards Authority: www.asa.org.uk/News-resources/Hot-Topics/~/ media/Files/ASA/Hot%20Topics/Children%20Hot%20Topic%202013.ashx, accessed 01/20/2014.

34   *NY Daily News*: www.nydailynews.com/life-style/fashion/american-apparel-ad-banned-uk-article-1.1220428, accessed 01/20/2014.

35   Jezebel: jezebel.com/5965607/cb2-sells-wallet-inspired-by-new-yorks-iconic-homeless-people, accessed 01/20/2014.

36   Shine: shine.yahoo.com/work-money/cb2-pulls-lucky-beggar-wallet-apologizes-making-fun-170100018.html, accessed 01/20/2014.

5

chapter

Engagement and transparency: turning your company inside out

Brandjacking turns every previous notion of power in the economy upside down. Everyone is a celebrity. Everyone is a VIP. It is not surprising that an organization like Greenpeace can damage your brand, but when an ordinary customer like Dave Carroll or a lone satirist like Josh Simpson can come to dominate the discussion around huge brands like United Airlines or BP, the world is clearly changing. Imagine, for a moment, if it had not been Dave Carroll, obscure Canadian folk singer, but Sir Paul McCartney, global superstar, whose guitar had been damaged: "I am terribly sorry, Sir Paul. Allow us to replace your guitar immediately, Sir Paul. And please fly with us, first class, forever, at absolutely no cost, Sir Paul. Please don't tell anyone we broke your guitar, Sir Paul." What businesses are only starting to realize is that they are going to have to treat us all like that from now on.

But once you find yourself on the wrong end of a brandjack, how can you engage with your publics and rescue the situation? Let's take one of the toughest: BP. BP faced at least three crises: the Greenpeace campaign to redesign its logo, Josh Simpson's (Leroy Stick's) Twitter brandjack, and the serious failure in its core business that was the Deepwater Horizon disaster. Let's play a thought experiment here. Let us imagine that BP had asked all its 100,000 staff to log on to Twitter and repeat the same key messages:

1 BP took every reasonable precaution against disaster, but was unlucky.
2 It was just an accident, and could have happened to any responsible business.
3 BP is doing everything it can to mitigate the disaster, and the long-term damage to the ocean will be minimal.

Unfortunately, it is hard to measure the success of PR. The most sophisticated methods are complex and expensive. The simplest methods are not very useful. Volume measurements – the equivalent of the old column inches method, or advertising value equivalent – would tell you that BP did very well in the summer of 2010. The company's volume of media coverage was enormous. The opportunities for people to see these messages were sky high. Their volume on social media, which was already huge, would have gone through the roof if this strategy had been adopted. All the engineers, who love metrics, would have looked at this volume of social media traffic and been delighted. Even sentiment measures would have been good. If 100,000 people had tweeted the company's key messages, that would have been a big success in sentiment terms. Of course, there would have been responses, pushing the volume measures even higher, although somewhat balancing the sentiment measures.

The trouble is that, much as such a strategy might have had the BP bods nodding with satisfaction at the sentiment and cheering the volume to the rafters, it would have been a disaster. It would have been worse than hiding behind the sofa, which is, let's face it, pretty much what BP did. Even sticking your fingers in your ears and chanting "I can't hear you" is better than spamming Twitter with inauthentic corporate speak. Apart from trying to shut your critics down, there is nothing the Twittersphere likes less than trying to drown your critics out. Spamming social media with corporate key messages would have irritated people beyond measure.

Let us try a different experiment, then. What if BP had told its 100,000 staff to log on to Twitter, Facebook, and all the rest, and tell the truth? What if BP had said to its staff: "Go and tell everyone what you really think about working at BP. Tell them how *you* think we have handled the Deepwater Horizon issue." Well, I don't know how that would have turned out. With a diverse group of 100,000 people, you can guarantee some diverse opinions. We can all imagine some of them. Some might well have said something rather like the imagined key messages I included above. Some might have said: "Bloody Tony Hayward – earns £2 million a year, and can't even get the basics right." The diversity of opinion would have given the words credibility. People would have believed in the engagement. People would have found the messages authentic.

How would BP have fared if it had adopted such a policy? It is impossible to say. I don't know the company from the inside. I don't know how opinions would have balanced out between the people denouncing management and those expressing support. Maybe some deeply damaging revelations would have come to light. What is much clearer is this: if you have a good organization, if your strategy is sound, if your staff are motivated, engaged, and loyal, mobilizing them in this way would be effective. Would it have worked for BP? How would I know? But a strategy like this would work for a well-run organization and fail with a poorly run organization. I can't tell from the outside which of these would apply to BP.

Before any organization embarks on a strategy like this, a great deal of groundwork has to be put in place. Remember the rule from Terence Fane-Saunders? Seventy-five percent of crisis management work is done before the crisis begins.[1] To make a transparency strategy work, you need to engage with your staff first. If you just want your staff to parrot your key messages, you can arrange that with a single email. If you want your staff to understand and engage with those messages, you need to do a lot more.

For one thing, if you are to free your staff to talk openly in a permanently recorded medium, you need to be sure they understand what they *can't* say. Obviously, it would be unacceptable to reveal confidential or proprietary information. You can't reveal anything that is market sensitive, except through proper channels. That is the law. You can't reveal information about patents or copyrights. You can't reveal, should you be one of the trusted people who knows this, the home addresses of staff members. Training people to this effect should not be hard. After all, a business trusts its staff – or at least a well-run business does. The existence of Twitter does not make it unacceptable to betray valuable confidences. Such behavior has always been unacceptable. Staff can't reveal price-sensitive information over dinner, and they can't reveal it on Twitter either. But if you want authentic engagement, then people ought to be able to express their *opinions* about anything. People with insider *knowledge* have to be restrained in how they use it, but opinions are free.

There is no doubt that I am advocating a radical strategy here. For years, organizations have sought to maintain the idea that their reputation can be manipulated by strict control of who is allowed to speak and the messages they deliver. If that ever worked, it doesn't work now. This really is the idea of advertising, and not PR. Advertising is based on the idea of broadcasting your message *at* the audience, not engagement *with* your publics. Note the different terms: an audience is a passive group of people you talk at, whereas publics are people with whom you have relationships. Such relationships – like your interpersonal relationships – involve something other than you talking and the other person listening. Relationships involve judging you by your actions, and your ability to listen as well as what you say about your own all-round wonderfulness.

Jeff Jarvis, skilled brandjacker (see CS 4) as well as author and academic, set out the rule that there is an inverse relationship between control and trust.[2] This is nothing new to PR practitioners. Your advertising agency has always been able to guarantee you a page in the *Wall Street Journal*. It has always been able to guarantee to get your messages in. It is simply a matter of writing a check. But PR professionals have always offered something different. It is precisely because we *can't* guarantee to get your message in, that it is of value when we do. There is credibility in the third-party endorsement. If your messages are on the editorial pages of the *Wall Street Journal,* it is because the journalist and the editor were persuaded of their credibility. That is what builds trust.

Social media, being built on credibility, authenticity, and engagement, are the natural home of the PR practitioner, and not the advertising agency. Just look at the trouble Habitat made for itself when engaging in advertising behavior on Twitter (CS 29). That is not to say that PR professionals will not have to change their behavior too. The rules are changing. But the skills that are required for this new world are PR skills, not advertising skills. It is not just a matter of getting your message broadcast. It is a matter of developing credible messages, and getting them believed.

It is not just PR that is changing. It is the whole nature of organizations. It is about building glass walls, and letting people see inside. That is what I mean when I say that the solution to a technology that turns your structure upside down is to turn your whole organization inside out. But that's just a phrase; what this book gives you is the steps you need to take to achieve that goal.

Most people give you 10 rules. This book is much better value, and gives you 11 steps for managing brandjacking.

Before:

1 *Listen:* Find out where the conversation is taking place. Who are the influential people discussing your issues? Listen to your critics. Are there ways you can engage with them and share the burden of big decisions?
2 *Research:* Talk to your staff and other key publics – suppliers, customers, shareholders, and so on. Find out who is engaging in social media. Do they know your story? Do they follow you?
3 *Share:* Share rules and share responsibilities. Develop a reasonable policy about what your staff can discuss in public. People treat a policy as permission to engage, not a restriction on engagement. Train your staff.

Discuss scenarios. What is it appropriate for staff to talk about in public? Develop a culture of transparency.

4 *Plan:* Think about the most obvious issues that could impact your business. You will not think of them all, but try to anticipate. Find out who is discussing those issues, even if they have never discussed your organization.

5 *Speed kills:* You have procedures for approving official communications from the organization. Are they suitable to the social world? Are they suitable for crisis situations? You will probably need an abbreviated command-and-control procedure to implement if a crisis arises. Who decides that a crisis has arisen?

6 *Train:* Are your senior people appropriate spokespeople? Can they be trained? Identify people who combine a broad understanding of the organization with the ability to communicate. Then find people with a deeper understanding of the departments within your organization who can communicate.

During:

7 *Turn your organization inside out:* Involve people at all levels in sharing message development and communicating to their networks.

8 *Cultivate humor:* An *appropriate* light-hearted approach can be effective in dissipating hostility. But a light-hearted approach is not always appropriate. In some crises, people have died, or suffered a terrible wrong.

9 *Tell a story:* Be the source of your own story. We are hard-wired to understand and remember stories.

10 *Engage:* Be transparent and reach out to conversation participants. Feed your friends; persuade the neutrals; engage with your critics.

11 *Review:* Measure how your messages are being received and repeated.

Notes

1   In conversation with the author.
2   Jarvis, J. (2009) *What Would Google Do?* New York: Collins Business.

Index

Printed and bound by CPI Group (UK) Ltd, Croydon, CR0 4YY